Soldiers of Peace

The Road to Peace Series

Will War Ever End?
A Soldier's Vision of Peace for the 21st Century

The End of War:
How Waging Peace Can Save Humanity, Our Planet, and Our Future

Peaceful Revolution:
How We Can Create the Future Needed for Humanity's Survival

The Art of Waging Peace:
A Strategic Approach to Improving Our Lives and the World

The Cosmic Ocean:
New Answers to Big Questions

Soldiers of Peace

How to Wield the Weapon of Nonviolence with Maximum Force

by Paul K. Chappell

Westport and New York

Manufactured in the United States of America

Third Printing

Prospecta Press
An imprint of Easton Studio Press
P. O. Box 3131
Westport, CT 06880
(203) 571-0781

www.prospectapress.com

Book and cover design by Barbara Aronica-Buck
Cover image, iStockphoto/delectus
The statue of Lady Justice adorns the Fountain of Justice in Frankfort, Germany. Historically the sword of Lady Justice has represented moral force. Martin Luther King Jr. has called nonviolence a powerful and just weapon: "It is a sword that heals."

Paperback ISBN: 978-1-63226-083-3
eBook ISBN: 978-1-63226-084-0

Manufactured in the United States of America

For all those working to create
a more peace literate world.

Contents

I regard myself as a soldier, though a soldier of peace. I know the value of discipline and truth.

—Mahatma Gandhi

Nonviolence is a powerful and just weapon. It is a weapon unique in history, which cuts without wounding and ennobles the man who wields it. It is a sword that heals.

—Martin Luther King Jr.

Author's Note

Soldiers of Peace is the sixth book in the seven-book Road to Peace series. This book series, which can be read in any order, is about waging peace, ending war, the art of living, and what it means to be human. *Soldiers of Peace* focuses on five* new forms of literacy we must achieve to solve our most serious problems and survive as a global family.

- Literacy in our shared humanity
- Literacy in the art of living
- Literacy in the art of waging peace
- Literacy in the art of listening
- Literacy in the nature of reality

These new forms of literacy empower us to become soldiers of peace who can wield the weapon of nonviolence with maximum force. Rather than merely addressing surface symptoms, the weapon of nonviolence confronts the underlying problems that threaten peace, justice, happiness, and human survival. To heal the root causes of our personal, national, and global problems we must also journey toward the constellation of peace. This book discusses how the four stars in the constellation of peace emit a light that can guide us toward survival, prosperity, gentleness, and greatness.

* These five are among the seven forms of peace literacy. I introduce the last two forms later in the preface.

Preface

The Constellation of Peace

Reasons for Realistic Hope

I am not a pessimist or an optimist, but a realist. Today the word "realism" is rarely used to describe reality, but has instead become a disguise for cynicism. As I show in my other books, I am a realist because extreme trauma, a lifetime of studying the human condition, and my experiences in the military have allowed me to understand the many causes of violence and rage, along with their potential cures. As I will show in this book, I am a realist because I perceive the nature of time realistically, which has given me an abundance of realistic hope.

My existence has also given me realistic hope. In 1958 only 4 percent of Americans supported interracial marriage between blacks and whites. By 2013 the amount of support had grown to 87 percent.[1] I am living proof of the change in attitude toward interracial marriage, because my mother is Korean, my father was half black and half white, and I grew up in Alabama.

My father, Paul B. Chappell, was born in 1925 and grew up in Virginia during the Great Depression. Half black and half white, he lived under segregation. My father was a career soldier who served in the army for thirty years and retired as a command sergeant major—the highest enlisted rank. He met my Korean mother while he was stationed in Korea. They married in 1975, and I was born in Maryland in 1980 when he was fifty-four years old. My parents moved to Alabama when I was a year old. I was their only child.

Since my childhood, my father told me that the only place in America where a black man had a fair chance was in the army. Because he grew up before the civil rights movement, and the army had desegregated prior to the major civil rights victories, he believed that black men were treated better in the army than in civilian society. In fact, one of the influences that led Rosa Parks to oppose segregation was her job as a seamstress on a desegregated military base. Historian Jeanne Theoharis, in her book *The Rebellious Life of Mrs. Rosa Parks*, tells us:

> One further insult in Montgomery [Alabama] came from the disconnect between the treatment blacks encountered on the integrated trolley on Maxwell Air Force Base and the city's segregated buses and other public spaces. Indeed, blacks and whites worked together at the Maxwell base, which had an integrated cafeteria, bachelor hall, and swimming pool. Rosa had worked at Maxwell for a time, and [her husband] Raymond's barber chair was on the base. "You might just say Maxwell opened my eyes up," Parks noted. "It was an alternative reality to the ugly policies of Jim Crow." Parks sometimes rode the bus [on the military base] with a white woman and her child, sitting across from them and chatting. When they reached the edge of the base and boarded the city bus, she had to go to the back. Thus, Rosa Parks had direct personal contact with desegregated transportation in her own hometown. This visceral experience highlighted the sheer arbitrariness of segregated public transportation and made riding the city bus even more galling.[2]

My parents pressured me to go to West Point, not only because they thought I would have limited opportunity as a result of being part black, but also because they had seen how white people, African Americans, and Koreans rejected me as a racially mixed outcast. After all, white people were not the only ones who opposed interracial marriage, which was illegal in nearly all southern states prior to the 1967 Supreme Court decision *Loving v. Virginia*. Marrying when interracial marriage was still controversial in many parts of the country, my parents did not feel welcome in African

American or Korean communities. Many Koreans did not like that my mother had married a black man, and many African Americans did not like that my father had married an Asian woman.

When I told my mother in 2009 that I was leaving the military, she shouted, "Are you out of your mind? Nobody is going to hire you. It's bad enough you look Asian, but you're also part black. Nobody is going to give a job to a black man who looks Asian."

My parents did not tell me lies. On the contrary, they told me their truth. They were describing life as they had experienced it and trying to protect me from the suffering they endured.

I left the army in 2009 as a captain and began working as the Peace Leadership director for the Nuclear Age Peace Foundation, a nonprofit organization cofounded by its current president, David Krieger. When I told my mother about this new job, she asked me, "When David Krieger hired you, did he know you're part black?"

"Yes," I replied.

She said, "Well you need to thank him, because he is a white man and he hired you, even though he knew you were part black." I have thanked David Krieger in words many times for giving me the opportunity to work full-time for peace, and I thank him with my actions by doing my best to serve the mission of peace.

The United States of America is far from perfect today and has a long way to journey on the road to peace, but I'd much rather be part Asian and part African American in 2015 (the year I am writing this book) rather than before the civil rights movement in 1915 or during slavery in 1815. Today I often meet people who respond in a positive way to my mixed racial background, which is something I could not imagine as a child in the 1980s. This is also something my father, who died in 2004, could not imagine. Again, our country has a long way to journey on the road to peace, but if we have made progress, why can't we make more progress?

I am treated much better than my ancestor Wyatt Chappell, a slave born in Alabama in 1835. Today I have the freedom to read books filled with life-changing wisdom and I can also express my ideas through writing, but he was born into a world where it was illegal for slaves to learn to read and write. Wyatt Chappell lived during an era when an ordinary white person could murder a black person, admit to the murder without claiming self-defense, not even accuse the black person of committing a crime, and not be put on trial. Slaves were treated as pieces of property with no rights, and both enslaved and free black people were deemed too incompetent to testify in court against white people.

Under the system of state-sanctioned slavery, slaves had no legal protection against their owners. A slave owner could murder disobedient slaves, rape his female slaves, and punish his male slaves by castrating them. William Lloyd Garrison, a white man who dedicated his life to abolishing state-sanctioned slavery, said, "There is no legal protection in fact, whatever there may be in form, for the slave population; and any amount of cruelty may be inflicted on them with impunity. Is it possible for the human mind to conceive of a more horrible state of society?"[3]

Racism is still a problem in America today. I have experienced this problem firsthand, but African Americans are no longer subjected to the full horror of state-sanctioned slavery, which denied literacy to slaves and gave them no legal protection against being beaten, murdered, raped, worked relentlessly without pay, bought and sold as property, and stolen as infants from their mothers. As I explain in *The Cosmic Ocean*, if someone during the era of American state-sanctioned slavery looked white but had inherited a small amount of African American blood from an ancestor, that person could also inherit the status of a slave and be denied basic education and any legal protection against being raped and murdered.

Due to the sacrifices of countless people, I grew up with far more freedom than my ancestor Wyatt Chappell, but how else has our country and the world changed for the better? Although injustice still exists in many places, what other examples of progress give me realistic hope that more progress is possible?

Today I often hear people say that our world has always been kind to white people. But this is not true. Many white people have been slaves throughout history. It is a myth that Europeans have never suffered from racism, when racism for most of human history was not based on skin color, but where a person was from. To offer just one example of racism based on location, for hundreds of years the English saw the Irish as a separate, subhuman race. The English also treated the Irish like slaves. English writer Charles Kingsley, who lived during the nineteenth century, called the Irish "white chimpanzees." He said, "To see white chimpanzees is dreadful; if they were black, one would not feel it so much, but their skins, except where tanned by exposure, are as white as ours."[4]

Under Anglo-Norman law, an English person could murder or rape an Irish person, and because the victim was Irish the English person would not be punished. In his book *The Invention of the White Race*, historian Theodore Allen explains how the Irish under English rule were treated in a way similar to how the U.S. government treated African Americans and Native Americans during the nineteenth century:

> If under Anglo-American slavery "the rape of a female slave was not a crime, but a mere trespass on the master's property," so in 1278 two Anglo-Normans brought into court and charged with raping Margaret O'Rorke were found not guilty because "the said Margaret is an Irishwoman." If a law enacted in Virginia in 1723 provided that "manslaughter of a slave is not punishable," so under Anglo-Norman law it sufficed for acquittal to show that the victim in a killing was Irish. Anglo-Norman priests granted absolution on the grounds that it was "no more sin to kill an Irishman than a dog or any other brute."
>
> If the Georgia Supreme Court ruled in 1851 that "the killing of a negro" was not a felony, but upheld an award of damages to the owner of an African-American bond-laborer murdered by another "white" man, so an English court freed Robert Walsh, an Anglo-Norman charged with killing John Mac Gilmore, because the victim was "a mere Irishman and not of free blood," it being stipulated that "when the master of the said John shall ask damages for the slaying, he [Walsh] will be ready to answer him as the law may require."

> If in 1884 the United States Supreme Court, citing much precedent authority, including the Dred Scott decision, declared that [American] Indians were legally like immigrants, and therefore not citizens except by process of individual naturalization, so for more than four centuries, until 1613, the Irish were regarded by English law as foreigners in their own land. If the testimony of even free African-Americans was inadmissible [in court], so in Anglo-Norman Ireland native Irish of the free classes were deprived of legal defense against English abuse because they were not "admitted to English law," and hence had no rights that an Englishman was bound to respect.[5]

The Irish were hated not only because of where they were from, but also because so many of them were Catholic. Racism toward Irish Catholics was common in the United States, especially in the nineteenth century. The Irish have far more rights today than they did in the past, and if an English or American politician living in the twenty-first century said Irish people were subhuman, many would call that politician insane. During my lectures I rarely meet people who know the full history of how badly the Irish were treated. Most people today think of the Irish simply as "white people."

Italian Americans are another group considered "white" today, yet in the past they were viewed as a subhuman race. The largest mass lynching in U.S. history did not involve African Americans, but Italian Americans. Although many people assume that lynching is synonymous with hanging, the term *lynching* actually refers to mob violence that targets and executes a specific person (who is accused of committing a crime or offense) without approval of the legal system. Hanging is only one way a person can be executed by a mob—only one form of lynching.

Encyclopædia Britannica defines lynching as "a form of mob violence in which a mob executes a presumed offender."[6] A lynching is different from a massacre, because lynchings target specific individuals who are accused of committing a crime or offense, and as Richard Gambino clarifies in his book *Vendetta*, massacres target groups of people "without regard to their individual identities and in which no specific offense on their part is alleged."[7]

Today Italian Americans are widely regarded as white people, but for many years Italian immigrants (particularly Sicilians) were treated as subhuman. This is a part of American history that many of us living today did not learn about in school. Author Ed Falco explains:

> The largest mass lynching in U.S. history took place in New Orleans in 1891—and it wasn't African-Americans who were lynched, as many of us might assume. It was Italian-Americans. After nine Italians were tried and found not guilty of murdering New Orleans Police Chief David Hennessy, a mob dragged them from the jail, along with two other Italians being held on unrelated charges, and lynched them all. The lynchings were followed by mass arrests of Italian immigrants throughout New Orleans, and waves of attacks against Italians nationwide.
>
> What was the reaction of our country's leaders to the lynchings? Teddy Roosevelt, not yet president, famously said they were "a rather good thing." The response in *The New York Times* was worse. A March 16, 1891, editorial referred to the victims of the lynchings as ". . . sneaking and cowardly Sicilians, the descendants of bandits and assassins." An editorial the next day argued that: "Lynch law was the only course open to the people of New Orleans . . ."
>
> John Parker, who helped organize the lynch mob, later went on to be governor of Louisiana. In 1911, he said of Italians that they were "just a little worse than the Negro, being if anything filthier in [their] habits, lawless, and treacherous . . ."
>
> The decades go by, they turn into centuries, and we forget. We've forgotten the depth of prejudice and outright hatred faced by Italian immigrants in America.

> We've forgotten the degree to which we once feared and distrusted Catholics. If we remembered, I wonder how much it might change the way we think about today's immigrant populations, or our attitudes toward Muslims?[8]

Although prejudice is still a problem in the United States, never have so many people from various ethnic backgrounds and religions fallen under the label "American." If that seems hard to believe, it is because so much history has been forgotten that we do not realize how bad things used to be, and also because people so often *romanticize the past* (a topic I will discuss later in this book). America certainly has problems with race today, but if we have made progress, why can't we make more progress? By learning to wield the weapon of nonviolence with maximum force, we can create this much needed progress within our communities and throughout the world.

History shows us that progress is possible. The question we must ask now is, how much more progress is possible? The only way to truly answer this question is not with words but with actions—by waging peace and becoming literate in new ways. To create more progress we must become literate in our shared humanity. If we do not spread this new form of literacy, humanity will not be able to cooperate to solve its most serious problems, because racism is very effective at surviving, adapting, and growing. Racism is an idea, and violence cannot kill an idea. Only education, in the form of literacy in our shared humanity, can bind racism with the chains of love and truth. Progress is never invincible and is easily lost if we do not protect it, which is why we must not be complacent in the struggle against racism or any injustice.

Spreading literacy in our shared humanity is a challenging mission, but our ancestors also embarked on challenging missions against seemingly impossible odds. For example, in 1800 American women could not vote, own property, or go to college, but the women's rights movement changed this. Imagine what would happen today if an American politician running for president said on national television that women should not be allowed to vote, own property, or go to college. How would the American public react? How would the many women politicians in both the Republican and Democratic parties respond? Many Americans would call this person insane. Most men in the Republican and Democratic parties, such as former presidents George W. Bush and Bill Clinton, would fiercely oppose the argument that their daughters should have been denied entry to college and no woman should be allowed to vote or own property.

Although an American politician who says women should not have the right to vote would sound insane to most Americans today, probably less than one percent of Americans supported women's right to vote in 1800, because it was not yet a publicly debated issue and many women did not yet believe they should have the right to vote. In 1800 many women did not even believe they should have the right to own a bank account, sign contracts, or own property. Women's rights activist Ernestine Rose, who was born in 1810, had difficulty in the 1830s getting her fellow women to support women's right to own property. In historian Judith Wellman's book *The Road to Seneca Falls* (which is about the first women's rights convention that took place in Seneca Falls, New York, in 1848), she describes the struggles of women's rights activists in the early nineteenth century:

> In the course of [Ernestine] Rose's travels, she circulated a petition among women to support Herttell's bill for married woman's property rights. It was with "a good deal of trouble," she remembered, that she convinced five women to sign this petition. "Women at that time had not learned to know that she had any rights except those that man in his generosity allowed her," Rose explained.[9]

The rights that women have today would have seemed impossible to most people living centuries ago. In 1800 women did not have the universal right to vote in any country, but by the late 1960s women could vote in over a hundred countries.[10] Women's rights don't exist in every country today, but wherever you find a lack of women's rights, you will also see a women's rights movement. Today there are women's rights movements in Pakistan, Afghanistan, and Saudi Arabia. But three hundred years ago, there was not a single women's rights movement anywhere in the world asking for full political, social, and economic equality.

When people suffer from injustice today, I certainly do not tell them, "Well, at least you don't have it as bad as an African American living under state-sanctioned slavery, an Irish person living with no rights under English rule, or an American woman living before the women's rights movement," because I despise all injustice, no matter how small it is. Just as a tiny amount of cancer cells can threaten our body, a tiny amount of injustice can threaten a community. Like cancer, injustice can also spread if we do not resist it. As Martin Luther King Jr. said, "Injustice anywhere is a threat to justice everywhere."[11]

However, it is important to have a broad historical perspective that reveals how progress can occur. The broader our perspective is and the better we understand how to walk the challenging path to progress, the more realistic hope we can have. Recognizing how much progress has happened in history can also protect us from becoming bitter, hopeless, and cynical as we strive to overcome the unjust systems that still exist in our world.

Attitudes in the United States and around the world have changed in many other ways. Imagine what would happen if an American politician running for president in the next election said on national television that the sun revolved around the Earth, and people who don't believe that should be put on trial. How would the American public react? Again, many Americans would call this person insane. Nicolaus Copernicus, who lived during a time when people believed the sun revolved around the Earth,* realized the Earth actually revolved around the sun, but he was afraid to express his realization because it might cause him to be put on trial, imprisoned, and executed.

According to Erik Gregersen, senior editor of astronomy and space exploration for *Encyclopaedia Britannica*:

* Copernicus was not the first person to theorize that the Earth revolves around the sun. An ancient Greek named Aristarchus (along with others) pondered this long before Copernicus was born. But Copernicus offered a degree of mathematical detail that provided more support for this theory than anyone we know of who came before him. Because of his methods, Copernicus is often credited with helping to start the scientific revolution.

> Aristotle's view of the universe [with the Earth at its center] became doctrine in the Catholic Church and stayed so through the Middle Ages. But during the Renaissance, many people began to question old ideas. Polish astronomer Nicolaus Copernicus (1473–1543) deduced that Earth revolved around the Sun, which meant that Earth wasn't the center [of the universe]. Copernicus was so afraid of the Catholic Church's reaction that he was reluctant to put his theory in writing. His book, *De revolutionibus orbium coelestium*, was not published until he was on his death bed in 1543 . . .
>
> In 1632, Galileo published a book called *Dialogue Concerning the Two Chief World Systems*, which confirmed Copernicus's idea that Earth moved around the Sun, not the other way around. For his views, he was summoned from his sickbed at age 70 and put on trial by the Catholic Church [and forced to publically recant his ideas], which resulted in his being put under house arrest for the remainder of his life.[12]

To offer another example of how viewpoints in the United States and around the world have changed, imagine what would happen if an American politician running for president in the next election said on national television that earthquakes, hurricanes, and droughts were caused by angry gods, and we had to sacrifice human beings to please these gods. How would the American public react? Yet again, many Americans would call this person insane.

I am not exaggerating when I say Americans would call this person insane. People in our society are called insane for having views far less extreme than this. If a person running for president suddenly advocated human sacrifice as a way to stop natural disasters, people would think this person was suffering from a serious psychological disorder and would want medical professionals to get involved. If an American president currently in office suddenly advocated human sacrifice as a way to bring rain and end drought, there would be a massive public outcry for this president to be medically suspended from office and deemed unfit to serve. *Insanity* is also a legal term, and if an American president today advocated human sacrifice as a way to end drought and intended to act accordingly, many people would use this legal term to describe the president's psychological state and would want some form of legal intervention to take place before innocent people were killed.

Although sacrificing human beings to prevent natural disasters and influence the weather would sound insane and extremely unjust today, virtually every major agricultural civilization practiced some form of human sacrifice during at least one point in their history. This included the ancient Greeks, Romans, Aztecs, Maya, Hebrews, Chinese, and Carthaginians, just to mention a few. As I explain in *The Cosmic Ocean*, these people were not insane at all, but were reacting logically to inaccurate assumptions they had about their world. These inaccurate assumptions also caused them to practice animal sacrifice as a matter of government policy.

Animal sacrifice was an official government policy frequently used by countless ancient governments, including the ancient Athenians, who invented Western democracy. Although animal sacrifice is still practiced by a few religious groups in some parts of the world today, no government in the modern world takes animal sacrifice as seriously as the ancient Athenians did.

Describing the Persian invasion of Greece in 490 BC, the Athenian general Xenophon (born in 430 BC) discussed how the Athenian government used animal sacrifice during national emergencies: "The Persians and their friends came with an enormous army, thinking that they would wipe Athens off the face of the earth; but the Athenians had the courage to stand up to them by themselves, and they defeated them. On that occasion they had made a vow to [the goddess] Artemis that they would sacrifice to her a goat for every one of their enemies whom they killed, but, since they could not get hold of enough goats, they decided to sacrifice five hundred every year, and they are still sacrificing them today."[13]

As a testament to how much progress has happened, many ideas that people believed in the past sound insane today, and many ideas we know to be true today would have sounded insane in the past. Also, what if there are ideas that people in the future will know to be true, but these ideas sound insane to most people living today?

The reason I am discussing how attitudes have changed toward race, women's rights, the structure of our solar system, human sacrifice, and animal sacrifice is because there are two possibilities we must consider. The first possibility is that our society today is right about every single issue, which has never before happened in human history. The second possibility is that our society is so wrong about certain issues that people in the future will look at us the way we look at those who treated the Irish as subhuman, or those who supported state-sanctioned slavery, or even those who practiced human and animal sacrifice as official government policy.

What seems more likely? Our society is right about every issue? Or there are issues our society is very wrong about? Certainly, there is much debate about many issues in our society, but those are not the issues we are most wrong about.

How do we know if our society is very wrong about an issue? The issues we are most wrong about are the ones that aren't considered issues yet, because they haven't even reached the point of being publicly debated. For example, universal women's right to vote was a publicly debated issue in 1870, but it was not an issue a thousand years earlier in 870. Ending state-sanctioned slavery was a publicly debated issue in 1850, but it was not an issue in the fifth century BC. We don't know of anyone in the fifth century BC who even conceived of the idea that humanity could end state-sanctioned slavery.

In ancient Greece, democracy was a publicly debated issue in the fifth century BC. Back then Athenians were debating the strengths and weaknesses of democracy, but it was not an issue in the twelfth century BC. Greeks born long before the fifth century BC, such as Homer and Hesiod (who were born around the eighth century BC), did not seem aware of the concept of democracy. Homer and Hesiod probably knew what voting was, because there are stories from the Trojan War (which took place hundreds of years before they were born) about Greek soldiers voting on some decisions. But the idea of democracy as a form of government where monarchies should be abolished, or given so little power that they function more as figureheads, is not an idea that Greeks from Homer's and Hesiod's time period seemed to be aware of.

There might have been some people thinking about these issues back then whose ideas were not written down—we will probably never know—but we do know that ideas such as universal women's right to vote, ending state-sanctioned slavery, and democracy were once so obscure that they had not yet become publicly debated issues. Homer and Hesiod seem to have never heard of democracy as a form of government that could serve as an alternative to monarchy and oligarchy, yet it would be difficult to find any person living in a modern society today who has never heard of democracy.

Before it became a democracy, ancient Athens was ruled by kings for hundreds of years, but democracy became a new idea in ancient Greece around the fifth century BC. Rome had also been ruled by kings for hundreds of years, but representative democracy (rather than direct democracy) emerged in Rome when the Roman Republic formed in 509 BC. Then democracy seemed to withdraw from our world. After democracy ceased to exist in Rome, it did not gain dominance in any country ruled by a monarchy until centuries later.

Democracy is the most fragile form of government, requiring a significant amount of stewardship to sustain. Democracy is like a vulnerable garden, which cannot survive unless people protect and nurture it. Otherwise it will wilt and die. To reap the many fruits of democracy, we must nourish it with the water of waging peace, despite living in a society that doesn't teach us how to wage peace. History offers abundant evidence that democracy is fragile and easily lost if enough citizens do not serve as good stewards of democracy.

Democracy is not only a vulnerable garden, but it is also a garden that is still growing, because humanity's understanding of democracy continues to evolve in new ways. For example, neither America's Founding Fathers nor the ancient Greeks and Romans saw democracy as a form of government that should include all women. In the nineteenth and twentieth centuries, full women's equality became a new plant in the garden of democracy. In the fifth century BC in ancient Athens, the idea of democracy included free men's right to vote, but as the trial of Socrates shows, the Athenian garden of democracy did not include plants such as freedom of speech, freedom of religion, freedom of the press (journalists and newspapers did not yet exist), and universal human rights.

We must also remember that democracy is not all or nothing, but can exist across a broad spectrum in varying degrees, just as gardens can possess varying degrees of vigor, diversity, and health. Many of the plants in the garden of democracy flourished in ancient Athens, and some of these plants also grew in other parts of the world. Although the Aztecs were not democratic as we understand democracy today (they did not have democratic ideals such as freedom of speech, freedom of the press, freedom of religion, the right to vote, universal human rights, or believe that monarchs should have little to no power), a few of the plants in the garden of democracy flourished in Aztec civilization. Archeologist Michael E. Smith explains:

> There is a stereotypical model of ancient government in which all-powerful, autocratic god-kings ruled with an iron fist over a powerless and cowering mass of commoners. In the Aztec case, however, the institutions of government gave commoners and nonroyal nobles some level of say and participation in civic affairs . . . The actions of kings were limited by the royal council—nobles who selected kings and on occasion may have deposed bad kings . . .
>
> These observations pertain to a body of thought, originating in political science, known as collective action theory. Richard Blanton and Lane Fargher were the first to apply this approach systematically to ancient states and kingdoms, where they find wide variation in the extent to which rulers were responsive to the needs of commoners. The Classical Greek poleis, for example, lies at the more "collective" end of the spectrum, whereas various indigenous African kingdoms are among the more "despotic" or autocratic of states. In Blanton and Fargher's analysis, the

> Aztecs are closer to the Greek city-states than to the African kingdoms.[14]

Today the idea of democracy, especially democratic ideals such as the plant of human rights, has become so popular around the world that many despotic governments try to create the illusion that they are somewhat democratic, whether through rigged elections, a constitution that pays lip service to human rights, or some other means. In the twenty-first century, humanity is still experimenting with the garden of democracy. We are still figuring out what democracy truly means and what new plants are missing from our current understanding. As a result, we have to consider the likely possibility that our understanding of democracy is still in its early stages, and that most people hundreds of years from now will have a much more evolved understanding of democracy than most people today.

By evolving our understanding of how to nourish the many plants in the garden of democracy, we can reap the fruits of democracy that will nourish humanity. In order for human understanding to evolve, not everyone has to be convinced. As I explain in *The Art of Waging Peace*, we can never convince every single person about a particular issue, but we don't have to. We only have to convince *enough* people, which creates the critical mass necessary for progress to happen. Because we cannot convince everyone, we need laws. For example, was every single man in America convinced women should have the right to vote? No, and there are still men in America who don't think women should have the right to vote.

During my lectures around the country I often talk to diverse groups. When I speak with a group of fifty people and mention how the women's rights movement greatly inspires me, I realize there might be one or two people in the audience who wish women never gained the right to vote. Two out of fifty is only 4 percent of the audience. That might seem like a tiny percentage, but what if 4 percent of the American population believed women should not have the right to vote? How many would that be? As I write this the American population is around 300 million, and 4 percent of that is a whopping 12 million. That is why we need laws to protect people's rights.

Just as the need for universal women's rights was not a publicly discussed issue for most of human history, what if humanity is facing serious problems today that have not yet become issues? For example, racism and sexism have been two of the biggest problems in human history. But did you know there was no word for racism in the English language until around the 1930s, and there was no word for sexism in the English language until the 1960s? Prior to 1900, racism and sexism certainly existed, but these problems had not yet become words or concepts for most people around the world. To solve any problem we must first give it a name so that it can no longer hide.

If you were to travel back in time to the 1830s and tell Ralph Waldo Emerson (who was considered racially progressive for his time period) that he had racist views, he would probably say, "What does that mean?" If you said, "You think the Irish are subhuman," he would likely say something such as, "But of course they're subhuman! They're Irish!"

Although Emerson opposed slavery, he believed that a small group of people, which included the English, were racially superior to all other people including most Europeans. During the nineteenth century when there was overt racism toward people from Ireland, Italy, and even Germany, it was rare to find white people who weren't racist against other white people, let alone against Africans and Asians. Emerson said, "I think it cannot be maintained by any candid person that the African race have ever occupied or do promise ever to occupy any very high place in the human family. Their present condition is the strongest proof that they cannot. The Irish cannot; the American Indian cannot; the Chinese cannot. Before the energy of the Caucasian race all the other races have quailed and done obeisance."[15]

What if all of us in the twenty-first century are facing problems just as big as racism and sexism, but these problems have not yet become words or concepts for most people living today? I will discuss one problem even bigger than racism and sexism that does not yet have a name, a problem that most people living today are not aware of. Before I can describe this problem, however, I must first emphasize that the people who lived before us were not insane, even though their views might seem insane at first glance when compared to our modern understanding.

To offer an example of knowledge that seems obvious to people living today, but did not seem obvious in the distant past, imagine trying to convince people in 1400 that the Earth revolves around the sun. Would that be an easy or difficult thing to do? In fact, it would be extremely difficult.

To revolve around the sun, the Earth is moving at about sixty-seven thousand miles per hour. But if the Earth is moving through space so quickly, then why don't we feel a sense of motion? Why aren't buildings falling over? If we gaze up at the sky, it looks like the sun is revolving around us. Even in the twenty-first century, we still say "sunrise" and "sunset," even though the sun is not actually moving. It is merely an illusion. Also, if you are on a merry-go-round that is spinning very rapidly, what happens if you let go? You will be propelled off the merry-go-round. Yet in addition to moving through space at about sixty-seven thousand miles per hour, the Earth is also rotating at about a thousand miles per hour, so why aren't people propelled off the surface of the Earth?

If you told people in 1400 that the Earth was not only moving quickly around the sun but also spinning like a top,* they would probably think *you* were insane. Back then an extremely intelligent person might respond, "Are you crazy? I have physical proof the Earth is not moving. The proof is all around us, because nothing is moving! And look up at the sky! I can see the sun moving around me!"

When I mention this during my lectures, people often say, "Just explain gravity to them, and then they will understand." But do you realize how difficult it would be to explain gravity to people living in 1400? Galileo Galilei (born in 1564) thought he had figured out the mystery of why the tides happen. He thought the tides were caused by the motion of the Earth, like a cup of water that moves around, causing the water to slosh back and forth. But scientist Johannes Kepler said the tides were caused not by the motion of the Earth, but by the moon exerting an invisible force that pulled on the Earth's water. Kepler was describing gravity, yet Galileo thought Kepler's idea

* Even though the Earth is rotating at about a thousand miles per hour, this is relatively slow compared to the Earth's size. Nevertheless, the idea that the Earth is constantly spinning still sounded strange to many people raised with an Earth-centric view of the universe.

was one of the most ridiculous things he had ever heard. To Galileo, Kepler's theory sounded like magic.*

However, Kepler was correct and Galileo was wrong. Kepler was trying to explain gravity, yet Galileo, one of the greatest scientific geniuses who ever lived, did not grasp the concept of gravity. So explaining gravity to people living in 1400 would not be easy at all. You might have a difficult time explaining gravity to Galileo since he lacked so much of the commonsense knowledge that we take for granted today.

After Galileo died, Isaac Newton's revolutionary discoveries about gravity revealed that the same fundamental force that causes the apple to fall to the ground also causes the Earth to revolve around the sun. The same fundamental force that causes rain to fall from the sky also causes the moon to revolve around the Earth. Gravity is a fundamental force of nature that moves tiny objects and entire worlds. But again, if you told that to people living in 1400, an extremely intelligent person might respond, "But if that's true, then why doesn't the moon fall into and collide with the Earth, just like every other object that is affected by Earth's gravity? Why doesn't the Earth fall into and collide with the sun?" Isaac Newton had to invent calculus to help explain this. Calculus did not exist when Galileo was alive.

We must remember that our earliest human ancestors were not given an instruction manual that explained how our world works. A thousand years ago, people did not even know what viruses and bacteria were. In a world without microscopes, how could they have known? Our ancestors had to discover all of this knowledge, which so many people today take for granted, and I am amazed that humanity has been able to discover so much.

* Science historian Stillman Drake provides further clarity regarding Kepler's and Galileo's disagreement about the cause of the tides: "Modern readers are prone to overlook the fact that the moon's dominion over the waters was an ancient superstition rather than a scientific anticipation of Newton's general gravitational law. Thus it had for Galileo all the defects of the 'occult qualities' invoked by philosophers as causes. Both Kepler's theory and Galileo's had the defect of implying a single daily tide, and both men appealed to local and accidental phenomena to explain the double period of ebb and flow . . . Kepler was much closer to a correct view of gravitation than others who ascribed the tides to attraction of the waters by the moon, and Galileo was remiss in failing to pursue that idea." (from Stillman Drake's translation of Galileo Galilei's *Dialogue Concerning the Two Chief World Systems* (1632). Berkeley: University of California Press, 1953.)

Each chapter in this book will reveal new truths that are essential for solving our most serious problems, while also shedding light on one of the greatest paradoxes in human history. This paradox is that we know so many truths that people living in the ancient world did not know, yet some of these ancient people knew vital truths that most of us living today don't know. This book will discuss timeless truths that were expressed in the ancient world, which have largely been forgotten in the modern world, and that are necessary for human survival in the twenty-first century and beyond.

In *The Cosmic Ocean*, I explain how intelligent people could believe the reasoning that supports human sacrifice and even state-sanctioned slavery, based on the limited knowledge they had about the world and how that knowledge was filtered through their worldview. If viewpoints have changed so much, does this mean human understanding is completely arbitrary? Not at all, because there is such a thing as truth, and humanity is journeying toward truth.

Some people who believe in moral relativism have told me there is no such thing as truth, *but there is such a thing as truth*. For example, the myth that women are intellectually inferior to men has been used to justify the oppression of women, and the myth that African Americans are subhuman was used to justify state-sanctioned slavery. However, it is a scientific fact that women are not intellectually inferior to men, and it is also a scientific fact that African Americans are not subhuman. These statements express as much scientific truth as Copernicus and Galileo did when they claimed the Earth revolved around the sun. The underlying purpose of the women's rights movement was to expose the truth about women's equality, and the underlying purpose of the civil rights movement was to expose the truth that African Americans are human beings.

Furthermore, it is a scientific fact that Irish people are not subhuman. It is also a scientific fact that no ethnic group is subhuman, and that we are all members of the same human race. Humanity is journeying toward the truth of our shared humanity, and today we must also reveal many more truths. Humanity is facing serious problems that threaten our survival, yet we do not have names for these problems,* just as people for thousands of years did not have words such as "racism" and "sexism" to describe these harmful attitudes. One of the serious problems that threatens human survival, which has not been given a name until now, is what I call being "preliterate in peace."

Preliterate in Peace

Imagine if there were a high school in America today with a zero percent literacy rate, a high school where none of the students or teachers knew how to read. Would this high school get national media attention? Actually, it would probably get international media attention, because today we recognize that literacy is the foundation of education, and we have constructed our society around literacy.

Now imagine going back in time to 1200 BC in ancient Greece. This was around the time period of the Trojan War between the Greeks and Trojans. In 1200 BC the Greek and Trojan societies were almost completely illiterate. This is why none of the characters in the *Iliad*, which takes place during the Trojan War, know how to read. Not even the kings and princes know how to read. Achilles, Odysseus, Hector, and Priam are very intelligent, but they are illiterate.**

Imagine trying to convince the Greeks and Trojans in 1200 BC that they should have universal literacy. Would this be an easy or difficult thing to do? It would be very difficult, because how do you explain the concept of

* In *The Cosmic Ocean* I describe two other serious problems, which I call "brutality" and "spiritual hunger," that have lacked words to describe them.

** There is one possible reference to writing in the *Iliad*. In his introduction to the Robert Fagles translation of the *Iliad*, Bernard Knox says, "In Book 6 Glaucus tells the story of his grandfather Bellerophon. Proetus, king of Argos, sent him off with a message to the king of Lycia, Proetus' father-in-law; it instructed the king to kill the bearer. '[He] gave him tokens, / murderous signs, scratched in a folded tablet . . .'" This reference is so vague that it is unclear whether these "murderous signs" were part of a written alphabet. Also, the written language Linear B was known by a tiny amount of people and used primarily for inventory. As many classics scholars note, Linear B was not used in the ways that other more developed writing systems in the ancient world were used.

universal literacy to people who have never heard of reading and writing?

If you told them, "Writing is a process where you make marks on something, and the marks symbolize sounds," they might respond, "What is the point of that? Why go through all that trouble? Why not just use your voice to communicate, or send a messenger to relay your message?"

If you said, "Literacy allows you to read books and letters," they would respond, "What is a book? What is a letter?" Explaining what books and letters are to people who have no concept of literacy would be difficult, but explaining what we use literacy for in the twenty-first century would probably be impossible. Literacy is more important now than it has ever been, because today we have expanded our use of literacy to include e-mail, text messages, the Internet, Facebook, ordering from menus, buying subway tickets, using street signs to navigate, and much more. How could you possibly explain the concept of the Internet to people living in 1200 BC? How could they even begin to comprehend what the Internet is, if they don't even know what literacy is?

If you are living in a small nomadic hunter-gatherer tribe, then you don't need literacy. But if you are living in a large agricultural civilization consisting of several hundred thousand or several million people, then literacy becomes essential. That is why large agricultural civilizations all over the world eventually reach a point where they try to develop a written language, whether in ancient China, India, Sumer, Egypt, Carthage, Rome, or on the other side of the globe in the land of the Aztecs and the Maya.*

Literacy is something we often take for granted today, but why is literacy so important? When I ask audiences this question, they often say that literacy is important because it allows us to distribute information. But there are two larger reasons why literacy is important. The first larger reason is that, as Francis Bacon said, "Knowledge is power."[16] There is a reason why American slave owners made it illegal for slaves to learn how to read. There is a reason why the Nazis burned books and why throughout history

*The Incas recorded information through a system of knotted strings known as khipu. Also, written languages seem to start out being used for inventory before being used to tell stories. A society can have a written language for many centuries before using it for history, science, and complex math.

dictators have banned books. There is a reason why Malala Yousafzai was shot in the head for trying to promote literacy and education for women, and there is a reason why the Taliban doesn't want women to become educated. When you deny people literacy, you also deny them power.

The second larger reason why literacy is important is that literacy not only allows us to distribute information, but literacy also gives us access to entirely new kinds of information. One of the new forms of information that literacy gives us access to is history. History cannot exist without literacy.[17] This might sound odd, but the reason history requires literacy is because without literacy, you cannot separate history from mythology. If you were to ask an ancient Greek man in 1200 BC who his ancestors were, he might say, "On my father's side my distant ancestor was Zeus, and on my mother's side my distant ancestor was Aphrodite." That would sound normal back then, but that would sound very strange today. Because they lacked a written history, the ancient Greeks and Trojans also did not seem to have any historical memory that they once lived as nomadic hunter-gatherers for countless generations. Instead, they seemed to believe that their ancestors, after being created by Greek deities, had always lived in an agricultural civilization.

Another new form of information that literacy gives us access to is science. Literacy makes every scientific field possible, because literacy allows us to organize and analyze information in new ways. So if you like electricity, then thank literacy. If you have ever benefitted from antibiotics, then thank literacy. In addition, complex math cannot exist without literacy. Algebra, trigonometry, and calculus require a written language.

Because literacy allows the human mind to expand and explore in so many ways, literacy is perhaps humanity's greatest invention. Humanity discovered how to use fire, but we invented literacy. Some people might argue that the wheel is humanity's greatest invention, but history, science, and complex math can exist without the wheel. They cannot exist without a written language. Unlike spoken language, walking, and other natural human abilities that are as old as our species, reading and writing are not natural human abilities, but relatively recent inventions.

A better term for the ancient Greeks and Trojans living in 1200 BC is not illiterate, but *preliterate*, because they did not yet understand why literacy was an essential step in their society's evolution. They lacked awareness of what literacy even meant, because when you live in a preliterate society, you don't realize you are preliterate.

Now the point I want to make is, what if all of us in the twenty-first century are living in a preliterate society and we don't even realize it? We are not preliterate in reading, but in something else. What if we are living in a society that is preliterate in peace, and a major reason why we have so many national problems, global problems, and even personal and family problems is that our society is preliterate in peace. Just as literacy in reading gives us access to new kinds of information such as history, science, and complex math, literacy in peace also gives us access to new kinds of information such as solutions to our national and global problems, along with solutions to many of our personal and family problems.

As I discussed earlier, humanity's understanding of democracy has been evolving, and we have to consider the likely possibility that our understanding of democracy in the twenty-first century is still very limited. Just as the ancient Greeks did not have plants such as universal human rights and women's rights in their garden of democracy—plants that people today realize are essential to democracy—our society is missing another plant that is just as essential. That plant is peace literacy.

Furthermore, just as the ancient Greeks *were not even aware* that universal human rights and women's rights were needed in a healthy democracy, most people living today *are not even aware* that peace literacy is needed in a healthy democracy. Most people living in 500 BC had never even heard of ideas such as universal human rights and a woman's right to full political, social, and economic equality. In a similar way, most people living today have never even heard of the idea of peace literacy.

A democracy that lacks peace literacy will eventually destroy itself in one way or another, because peace literacy gives people the kind of education that inoculates them against manipulation and the seductive lies that spread hatred, dehumanization, and irrational fear. A democracy is only as wise as its citizens, and as I will discuss later in this book, peace literacy is necessary to generate the wisdom that can protect our society from one of humanity's most dangerous powers: the muscle of language.

If humanity remains preliterate in peace, the future of American democracy, along with all democracies around the world, will be a dangerous one. A future where humanity is preliterate in peace will also be dangerous in many other ways. As I discuss later in this book, I grew up in a violent household and had a traumatic upbringing, and peace literacy has helped me transcend my childhood trauma, control the homicidal rage that resulted from that trauma, heal my psychological wounds, and find purpose, meaning, and happiness in life. Peace literacy empowers us to heal the underlying causes of trauma and rage in our society while increasing our purpose, meaning, and happiness in life.

If humanity survives its current global challenges by becoming peace literate, then people in the future will think, "Why didn't people back then realize they were preliterate in peace and that they needed peace literacy? It seems so obvious! No wonder the world back then was so violent and unjust." Although the need for peace literacy seems obvious, the mission of spreading peace literacy is very challenging right now, because so many people today are fond of easy answers and quick fixes that merely address the shallow surface and do not confront the root causes of our problems. Peace literacy is not offering easy answers and quick fixes, but is instead a deep and complex solution to deep and complex problems.

The garden of democracy is filled with a wide variety of plants, but peace literacy is a tree that we need to cultivate in this garden. The tree of peace literacy has seven branches that are capable of bearing fruit that nourishes progress, peace, and the unfolding of our full human potential. These seven branches are metaphors for the seven forms of peace literacy. During an era when humanity has the technological capacity to bring death to our species and most life on Earth, the tree of peace literacy is a tree of life that can protect, serve, and elevate life.

The Seven Forms of Peace Literacy

There are seven forms of peace literacy. All of the books in the seven-book Road to Peace series discuss various aspects of peace literacy. In *Soldiers of Peace*, the sixth book of this series, I focus on the first five forms of peace literacy: literacy in our shared humanity, literacy in the art of living, literacy in the art of waging peace, literacy in the art of listening, and literacy in the nature of reality. In the last book of this series, I will focus on the last two forms of peace literacy, which are literacy in our responsibility to animals and literacy in our responsibility to creation. Here is a brief description of each form of peace literacy.

Literacy in Our Shared Humanity

Literacy in our shared humanity gives us practical and realistic answers to the following critical questions. What does it mean to be human? What is the human condition? What do all people have in common regardless of what culture or time period they live in? When we understand our shared humanity we can see through the illusions of dehumanization, realize when people are trying to manipulate our human vulnerabilities in order to take advantage of us, and achieve our full potential as human beings. An oak tree knows how to be an oak tree. It doesn't need a mentor or role model to guide it. A caterpillar knows how to turn into a butterfly and thrive in the world. It doesn't have to attend school or be instructed by its parents. But human beings, more than any other creature on the planet, must learn to be what we are. We must learn to be human.

Literacy in the Art of Living

Living is the most difficult art form, and most of us are not taught how to live. Many children do not learn the essential life skills that are part of the art of living. Some children learn these skills from their parents, but many parents do not know these skills, and many children learn harmful habits from their parents. Examples of healthy human functioning are also largely absent in the media. How often do you see people on television resolve conflict in a peaceful and loving way? All of us want purpose, meaning, and happiness in life, but our society is not literate in the healthiest ways to achieve this.

Literacy in the Art of Waging Peace

People in the military have excellent training in how to wage war, but most of us have no training in how to wage peace. If people were as literate in the art of waging peace as soldiers are in the art of waging war, how much different would our world be?

Literacy in the Art of Listening

All human beings like to be listened to. In all of human history, nobody has ever seriously said, "I hate it when people listen to me! I can't stand it when people listen to me!" Nobody ever says, "My spouse and I have to go to marriage counseling, because my spouse listens to me all the time and I can't take it anymore!" All of us know that many people in our society do not know how to listen well. To truly listen we must develop empathy. If we do not empathize with people we cannot really hear what they are saying. When we do not listen with empathy we hear only their words. But when we listen with empathy we also hear their emotions, hopes, and fears. We hear their humanity.

Literacy in the Nature of Reality

So many of our misconceptions about peace result from our misconceptions about reality. Only by understanding reality can we fully know why peace is so practical, powerful, and necessary. Only by understanding reality can we develop realistic hope.

Literacy in Our Responsibility to Animals

At the center of ethics is the following question: how should we treat the least powerful among us? How should we treat children, the mentally disabled, prisoners, and marginalized groups? Since animals have so little power—they cannot organize a violent or nonviolent rebellion against us and they are unable to defend themselves with speech—what ethical responsibility do we have to them? How can a greater understanding of ethics improve our treatment of our fellow human beings? Genocide, slavery, and rape are just a few among the many injustices that result from harming those who have less power.

Literacy in Our Responsibility to Creation

As human beings we have the power to protect our planet or drive ourselves and most life on Earth into extinction. We have become our own greatest threat to our survival, which is an alarming yet incredible fact. If we do not become literate in peace, our species will not survive.

Peace Literacy Means Survival Literacy

Peace literacy is the next step in the development of our global civilization, because peace literacy is necessary in an interconnected world where the fate of every nation is tied to the fate of our planet. Because of the dangers posed by nuclear weapons, war, and environmental destruction, being preliterate in peace puts humanity and our planet at great risk. During an era when humanity has the technological capacity to destroy itself, peace literacy means survival literacy.

As a child in school I spent many years learning to read and write, but I did not learn peace literacy skills. If humanity is going to survive during our fragile future, we must create a world where a high school with a zero percent peace literacy rate would get national and international media attention, just as a high school today where none of the teachers or students knew how to read would get national and international media attention. Peace literacy educates us on solving the root causes of our problems rather than merely dealing with symptoms, which is another reason why the survival and well-being of our country and planet depend on peace literacy.

Where peace literacy is concerned, every bit helps us improve our personal lives, the lives of those around us, and our planet as a whole. What is better, a society where 3 percent of people are peace literate, or a society where 10 percent of people are peace literate? What is better, 10 percent or 30 percent? It is estimated that around 83 percent of people in the world today are literate in reading.[18] Imagine how different our world would be if 83 percent of people were peace literate, or if over 50 percent of people were peace literate. Today I would contend that less than 1 percent of the global human population is literate in all seven forms of peace literacy. We must work together to change that. Human survival, along with the survival of most life on our planet, depends on peace literacy.

Humanity Sailing through Time

Many people have described our planet as a ship sailing through space. This well-intentioned metaphor tries to encourage us to live together peacefully by reminding us that we all share the same planetary home. But as a child I found this metaphor disempowering, because we cannot control where the Earth is going; we have no control over our planet's course through our solar system and the universe. This is a good thing, since life flourishes on our planet because its course basically stays the same, revolving around the sun at a distance not too close, not too far.

However, there is a metaphor for the Earth where human beings are not passive passengers on a ship moving through space, but active participants responsible for the direction and destination of our world, a metaphor that can empower us to achieve our highest human potential and solve our global problems. This metaphor involves seeing the Earth as a ship sailing not through space, but time.

The Earth is a ship surging through the waters of time, constantly moving forward into the future, unable to reverse course and return to a previous time period. Humanity today has a lot of power to control the path our planet takes through the wide horizon of the future. And if we make a mistake by wandering down a destructive path, there is no going backward on the sea of time.

Humanity is a crew sailing through time, able to direct where our ship the Earth goes, with two primary destinations on the horizon of the future. Because problems such as environmental destruction, war, and nuclear weapons threaten human survival, we can choose to solve these problems and sail toward survival and prosperity. Or we can choose to sail toward the extinction of humanity and most life on Earth. If our planet metaphorically sinks, due to our delicate biosphere becoming so badly damaged that complex life on Earth becomes unsustainable, we will sink with it.

I have heard people say that humanity should start colonizing Mars as a backup plan, in case we destroy Earth's delicate biosphere. But Mars makes the harshest desert on Earth look like paradise. As I will discuss in the next chapter, I do not romanticize nature, but instead recognize how extremely difficult survival on Earth can be. In fact, scientists estimate that over 99 percent of the species that ever existed on our planet have gone extinct. But compared to the hellish landscape of Mars where there is no running water on its surface (running water quickly evaporates), a person cannot breathe the air, plants cannot flourish, and the magnetic field that deflects solar radiation is fragmented and weak, our planet is a utopia, a Shangri-la, a Garden of Eden.

If we as human beings cannot get our act together and survive long term on Earth, even though this planet gives our species every advantage needed to prosper, what makes us think we will be able to survive long term on the hell that is Mars? As Carl Sagan said, "Like it or not, for the moment the Earth is where we make our stand."[19] If we seriously damage or destroy the Earth's delicate biosphere, there is nowhere else for us to go. There is no other planet anywhere near us that could sustain humanity long term, especially if the abundant Earth could not sustain our current behavior and way of thinking.* Our fate is tied to the Earth, and because we have the power

* I think exploring Mars, especially to discover if there is microbial life and possibly underground water, would be a revolutionary challenge that would give humanity a broader perspective on itself. But the notion that human beings could take our current behavior and way of thinking to Mars and successfully colonize the planet long term (without assistance from Earth) is wishful

to direct its path on the sea of time, its fate is now tied to us.

Human thinking changed enough on issues such as human sacrifice, animal sacrifice, scientific inquiry, women's rights (in most parts of the world), and state-sanctioned slavery to reach a critical mass and create new social norms and laws. Today, human thinking must change in other ways. Unlike many of the issues in humanity's past, which did not threaten human survival, issues such as environmental destruction, nuclear weapons, and war can drive humanity to extinction. When we are dealing with problems that threaten human survival, time is not our friend. If we do not deal with these problems urgently and proactively, our species can drown and go extinct in the sea of time.

This book is about peace literacy, the understanding humanity requires to safely guide our ship the Earth through the dangerous sea of time. All of us can work together to lead humanity away from extinction and toward survival, prosperity, and a sustainable biosphere. In fact, putting our Earth on a safe course is such a difficult underdog struggle that every person who can help is greatly needed. In a world filled with misinformation, myths, and illusions that deny our shared humanity and responsibility to our planet, every soldier of peace matters in the struggle for a brighter future.

A unique constellation of stars can guide us toward a brighter future. Every culture in history has been fascinated by the stars. This is part of our shared humanity. Ancient cultures created stories about constellations in the night sky, and people on both land and sea used the stars to navigate. When African Americans escaped from slavery in the nineteenth century, they often went north by journeying toward the North Star. Sailors around the world used the stars to guide their ships across the dark and unforgiving ocean. Stars helped our ancestors survive and not lose their way, and in the twenty-first century humanity also needs stars to help us survive and not lose our way. The stars humanity needs today can be found in the constellation of peace.

What is the constellation of peace? During this dangerous time in history when humanity has the technological capacity to destroy itself, we can-

thinking. A lot would be required to maintain large indoor habitable environments to provide constant oxygen and heat, and terraforming Mars might not even be possible. Of course, if we became peace literate and our current behavior and thinking became much more sustainable, we could probably survive on Mars or almost anywhere.

not survive in reality unless we understand reality. The four stars in the constellation of peace, which I explore in this book, are metaphors symbolizing four features of reality that are largely misunderstood today. In a world where there is so much confusion, humanity must understand these four features of reality to survive and prosper during our fragile future.

By exploring the four stars in the constellation of peace, we will uncover essential truths about reality, continuing our journey on the road to peace. Since many of our misunderstandings about peace result from our misunderstandings about reality, to become literate in peace we must also become literate in the nature of reality. By gaining literacy in the nature of reality, we can also gain realistic hope, radical empathy, and revelatory understanding.

Soldiers of Peace is the sixth book in the seven-book Road to Peace series. This book series can be read in any order, and *Soldiers of Peace* should be understood as part of a series. If I do not address a subject related to peace in this book, it is probably because I address it in another book. *Soldiers of Peace* focuses on four features of reality symbolized by the four stars in the constellation of peace, because they are so critical to creating peace that they demand their own book. Just as our ancestors used stars in the night sky to guide their ships across unforgiving seas, we must use the four stars in the constellation of peace to guide our ship the Earth across the unforgiving sea of time. As we sail forward on the sea of time, the light from the constellation of peace can help us navigate toward survival, prosperity, and a sustainable biosphere.

In my book *The Cosmic Ocean*, the fifth book in the Road to Peace series, I explain humanity's tendency to neglect the root causes of our problems by looking for easy answers. This book goes deeper than easy answers by working to change our current paradigm of understanding. The first chapter explores the star of struggle, a commonly misunderstood aspect of reality, while the second chapter (the star of training) offers specific guidance and practical steps focused on the process of creating internal peace. The third chapter explores the star of truth, another commonly misunderstood aspect of reality, while the fourth chapter (the star of strategy) offers specific guidance and practical steps focused on the process of creating external peace.

What is peace? Peace is not just the absence of war, but the presence of the light from the four stars discussed in this book. Peace is also the presence of empathy, justice, understanding, and other ingredients explored in the following chapters. In the third chapter I explain that peace is even a weapon that attacks hatred, ignorance, and misunderstanding, rather than people. Martin Luther King Jr. said, "Nonviolence is a powerful and just weapon. It is a weapon unique in history, which cuts without wounding and ennobles the man who wields it. It is a sword that heals."[20]

The constellation of peace empowers us to wield the weapon of nonviolence with maximum force. To successfully sail the dangerous sea of time, we must become skilled at wielding the weapon of nonviolence, just as sailors in history and mythology needed various skills to sail dangerous seas. In Greek mythology, Jason and the Argonauts sailed to retrieve the Golden Fleece. Their ship, the *Argo*, contained soldiers skilled in waging war, including a woman, the archer Atalanta who had deadly aim and exceptional wrestling ability. In a famous incident, she defeated Achilles's father Peleus in a wrestling match. In this book I will discuss four other characters involved in the journey of Jason and the Argonauts (Heracles, Nestor, Medea, and Athena) and, surprisingly, I will reveal what they can teach us about waging peace.

To journey on the sea of time toward survival, prosperity, and a sustainable biosphere, our ship the planet Earth will need soldiers skilled in waging peace. Realizing that the well-being of our world requires people who possess the discipline and courage of soldiers, Gandhi called himself a soldier of peace. He said, "I regard myself as a soldier, though a soldier of peace. I know the value of discipline and truth."[21]

In this book we will discuss what it means to be a soldier of peace, dispelling stereotypes about warriors and peace activists. A soldier of peace has peace literacy skills. These skills are necessary not only for an effective movement, but they also help us create peace with our family members, friends, coworkers, strangers, and even our opponents. These skills are available to everyone, allowing us to achieve purpose, meaning, understanding, human survival, and a more prosperous future.

Some people assume that humanity cannot severely damage or destroy our delicate biosphere, even if we continue to ravage our planet for several more centuries with increasingly destructive technology, but this assumption greatly underestimates our human power to destroy. Some people also assume that humanity cannot be threatened with extinction, even if we ruin our delicate biosphere. But this attitude resembles what the ancient Greeks called *hybris* (the root word of "hubris"), which meant wanton violence resulting from excessive arrogance.[22] The reality is that we are a species, and even a species as brilliant as we are, with so much power to shape our environment, can go extinct. Reality contains laws of thermodynamics and the law of gravity, but there is no law of nature that says humanity must survive forever.

To put all of this in perspective, I want you to consider everything we have discussed so far about the significant changes in attitude toward race, women's rights, the structure of our solar system, human sacrifice, animal sacrifice, and the importance of reading. Although our world is far from perfect and we still have a long way to journey on the road to peace, so much progress has happened that I have met many people who say, "Can you believe that so many people used to support slavery? What were they thinking back then?"

Now I want you to imagine two possible futures. The first possible future is that five hundred years from now, people will look back at us and say, "Can you believe that people used to possess nuclear weapons, wage war, dehumanize each other, and cause so much damage to their environment? What were they thinking back then?" Although this behavior would seem bizarre to our descendants living five hundred years from now, they would also be proud of us, because we created the change that allowed them to exist.

The second possible future is that five hundred years from now, there will be no humans to look back, because our species has gone extinct, most of the life on our planet has gone extinct, and the world is in ruin. Every example of progress I have discussed can be taken away if we are not vigilant. As soldiers of peace, we must learn to wield the weapon of nonviolence with maximum force so that we can protect progress, create more progress, and transform this first possible future into a reality.

CHAPTER 1
The Star of Struggle

Time's Ruthless Flow

Humanity, more than any other species on the planet, has a strange relationship with time. In fact, humanity's relationship with time often seems dysfunctional. By exploring this relationship, we can unlock solutions to our human problems and gain essential insights about what it means to be human. To be effective soldiers of peace and to become peace literate, we must have a realistic understanding of time.

My journey to understand time began when I was a child living in a violent household. In *The Cosmic Ocean* I describe my childhood trauma in detail, discussing how a violent upbringing gave me an immense capacity for rage, and how I transformed my rage into radical empathy.

Because of the trauma I experienced during my childhood, I began to feel that time was my enemy. When I made small mistakes, my father could become so enraged that he would beat me to the point where I feared for my life. Sometimes these vicious attacks occurred for no apparent reason at all. Time felt like my enemy because when I made a small mistake that triggered my father's rage, time never allowed me to take back the mistake. Time refused to go backward, to give me a second chance, even if I felt my life was at risk. Time simply did not care whether I lived or died.

But as a small boy I gained new insights about time from an unlikely source of wisdom: video games. When I played video games as a child, time was my friend. Time was kind. Compared to the way time functioned in the violent and terrifying reality I lived in, time in video games was forgiving and merciful. In video games I had the ability to pause time. Video games also allowed me to replay moments in time, over and over again, as often as

I wanted. If I made a mistake in a video game, I could start over, get back to where I was, replay the moment, and avoid the mistake. In real life, time did not give me second chances, no matter how much agony I was experiencing. In video games, time gave me as many chances as I wanted.

To gain literacy in our shared humanity, we must understand how time affects the human condition. Time, more than any other force of nature, shapes and torments us as human beings. Time does not torment us because it exists, but because it flows in only one direction. If we make a mistake and desperately beg time to turn backward so that we can change the past, time cannot feel compassion for us, no matter how much we beg. If we pray for time to bring back our loved ones or let us relive earlier years of our life, time cannot hear our prayers. Time does not listen to the cries of humanity. Time feels no remorse. Time never relents, always flowing forward, not caring about those it tramples along the way. These characteristics resemble the very definition of ruthlessness.

Time is a thief that steals everything it touches, keeps everything it steals, and destroys everything it keeps. Because of our large brains, human beings have a heightened awareness that allows us to perceive time in this way, which no other species on the planet seems to have. Our heightened awareness of time is part of our shared humanity. As far as we know, no other species on the planet fears growing old as much as we can, desires plastic surgery or dyes its hair to look younger, searches for the fountain of youth and scientific breakthroughs that some say will make us immortal, debates whether there is life after death, fantasizes about time travel, and has an obsession with prophecy.*

Earlier in this book I mentioned that every culture in history has been fascinated with the stars and created stories about the night sky. In a similar way, every culture in history has also been fascinated with prophecy and created predictions about the future. Prophecy has played a central role in every

* Other animals have heightened senses that might help them detect some natural disasters before they happen. Is this the same thing as prophecy? For human beings, prophecy refers to our desire to predict future events beyond what our senses can immediately perceive. Prophecy involves trying to gain knowledge about future events through a religious or scientific method, whereas animals rely on their heightened senses for early warning.

culture we know of, as people look for good and bad omens, hoping these omens will reveal how the future will unfold. To mention a few of the countless examples of humanity's fascination with prophecy, the ancient Greeks sacrificed animals to Apollo the god of prophecy, numerous indigenous cultures have looked for good and bad omens in nature, and many Christians have been interested in the prophecies from the book of Revelation.

Today prophecy can take the form of palm readers, tarot cards, and even science. Science serves many of the same psychological needs that prophecy did thousands of years ago, by helping us predict the weather, natural disasters, and various crises before they happen. Furthermore, modern medical tests that predict illnesses early are a form of prophecy that allow us to take proactive steps to treat those illnesses before it is too late. Economic forecasts that try to predict changes in markets, along with polls that try to predict how people will vote on an issue or political candidate, also feed people's fascination with prophecy. Although these diverse methods of prophecy are not equal in reliability (science has proven to be a far more accurate way than animal sacrifice to predict future events), they all serve our shared human urge to predict the future, which emerges from our shared human awareness that time is ruthless.

When I deployed to Iraq in 2006, I worked with a system called C-RAM (counter rocket, artillery, and mortar). C-RAM included a network of radars that could detect incoming mortars and rockets, then sound an alarm that would warn the people on the base when a deadly impact was imminent, allowing them to take cover. These radars could also be linked with an automatic machine gun capable of intercepting mortars and rockets. C-RAM offered modern scientific prophecy, rather than ancient supernatural prophecy such as animal sacrifice, to combat time's ruthlessness. In war, being warned just a few seconds before an explosion occurs can allow people to better protect themselves, meaning the difference between life and death.

In addition to our inability to control natural disasters and other forces of nature, two aspects of reality make prophecy appealing to all cultures. The first is that human beings are not perfect, but prone to making all kinds of mistakes. The second is that time cannot flow backward. This is a painful combination for humanity. All cultures have a fascination with predicting future events because we all recognize, either consciously or unconsciously, that time is ruthless and does not travel in reverse, no matter how much we beg or pray.* Imagine how much suffering we could avoid if we had the ability to rewind time just thirty seconds. Time's ruthlessness is especially apparent in war, where people are often maimed and killed for making the smallest mistakes.

How do I respond to time's ruthlessness? By being fully aware of time's ruthlessness and not repressing this reality, I am able to recognize and feel deeply connected to the vulnerability and fragility of life. This motivates me to be kind and gentle in all the ways time cannot. As human beings, our survival depends on our ability to give each other the kindness, gentleness, empathy, and mercy that time cannot give us. This is one of our greatest powers as human beings. Because time is so ruthless, the last thing our world needs is ruthless human beings. Every human community, including our global community, benefits from people who are kind, gentle, empathetic, and merciful.** In *The Art of Waging Peace* I discuss how martial arts philosophy teaches us to have a respectful and gentle attitude toward life, and I also share some truths and myths about using violence to protect life as a last resort.

I have heard people say that time is not ruthless, but is in fact kind and merciful because "time heals all wounds." But our wounds, whether physical or psychological, do not heal unless we create the conditions for healing. Time by itself does not heal, because time can further recovery or infection. What we do with time allows us to heal.

I have also heard people say that time is kind and merciful because it gives us wisdom. But again, the growth of wisdom depends on what we do

* People also have a fascination with predicting future events so that they can capitalize on opportunities, because we know that once time passes, those opportunities can quickly become lost. Many people wish they could predict the future when gambling not only to capitalize, but also because gambling is a prime example of time's ruthlessness. If you bet your house and lose, time will not rewind itself for you, nor feel any compassion for you.

** Being "merciful" does not mean neglecting to hold people accountable for their actions. Promoting a society where people are not held accountable for their actions is not merciful because it creates a far more dangerous society. Mercy is concerned with rehabilitating people as much as possible and protecting the well-being of the entire society, rather than acting out of revenge or hatred.

with time. The aging process gives us life experiences, but not necessarily wisdom. What we learn from those life experiences gives us wisdom. Time can make us wise or bitter, because people can become more loving or more hateful as they age. Nearly twenty-five hundred years ago, Buddha said, "Gray hairs do not make a master. A man may grow old in vain."[1]

This book discusses how to make the best use of time by waging peace in our personal lives, communities, and throughout the world. By using time to wage peace, we can heal the root causes of violence, trauma, and injustice on a personal, national, and global level. We should never apathetically leave our problems in the hands of time, trusting that time alone will heal wounds and provide wisdom. This form of apathy is dangerous to our personal well-being and the health of our planet. Time is not a trustworthy custodian of human problems. We must make good use of time by waging peace to proactively solve these problems.

During my four years at West Point and seven years in the army, I gradually realized that despite time's ruthlessness, it is a mistake to perceive time as an enemy. Time may seem ruthless, but it enables everything we admire about human beings. Time allows us to be courageous, selfless, and heroic. Time allows human greatness to unfold, because time is the blank canvas where the masterpieces of human existence can be painted.

These masterpieces are possible because time makes us mortal, and mortality gives us the potential for greatness. So many people around the world despise being mortal, wishing they were immortal instead. But classics professor Elizabeth Vandiver explains how the *Iliad*, written nearly three thousand years ago by the Greek poet Homer, reveals that human mortality is the source of our human greatness. Ironically, the mortality we so often despise is the very thing that makes us capable of what we admire most in human beings: courage, self-sacrifice, and heroism. Vandiver explains how in the *Iliad*, the portrayal of immortal Greek gods such as Zeus reveals truths about the human condition:

> Humans, by definition in the *Iliad*, are the ones who die . . . One aspect of the importance of the gods [in the *Iliad*] is that they are there to provide a contrast [with]

human beings, precisely in this question of mortality and immortality. The gods in the *Iliad* are defined as, are often referred to by the term the *athanatoi*—the deathless ones, the undying ones, the ones who cannot die . . . Mortals, humans, in contrast, are called the *thnêtoi*—the dying ones, but really it almost means the dead ones, as though our lives are so short and so unimportant against the backdrop of eternity that we're dead as soon as we come into existence. The gods are the deathless ones, the humans are almost the already dead ones . . . This contrast between the athanatoi gods and the thnêtoi humans makes for the crucial, defining distinction between gods and humans, the crucial, defining aspect of what it means to be human in the *Iliad*.

The gods of Homer, the gods in both the *Iliad* and the *Odyssey*, are extremely anthropomorphic in many ways. They are conceived of as being humanlike in shape, in appearance, in emotions, in activities, in just about every imaginable way. This is not the only way to conceive of gods. There have been cultures whose gods have not been anthropomorphic, have not been human-form, human-like in character, in appearance, in any other way. But the gods of Homer are extraordinarily anthropomorphic . . . They sleep. They fight. They have sex. They grow angry. They feel love. They feel hatred. They are in many ways very much like human beings projected on a larger scale, and yet they are humanlike creatures who cannot grow old and cannot die, whereas humans by definition must grow old and must die. And this distinction is harped on over and over and over again in the *Iliad*, far more than it is for instance in the *Odyssey* [the other epic attributed to Homer] . . . the *Iliad* has been called a poem of death and this is part of why . . .

So this focus on death as the defining characteristic

of human existence, and this distinction between mortals and immortals, between humans and gods, between the deathless ones and the dying ones . . . highlights the human condition constantly throughout the *Iliad* by contrasting human existence with the gods' state of easy living. The gods are often referred to as the *rheia zoontes*, the ones who live easily, the ones who have no cares, no troubles, no problems, no difficulties, as compared to us humans, who have all the problems, difficulties, troubles in the world, and have to die on top of it . . .

The role of the gods in the *Iliad* varies between grandeur and pettiness. There are times when these gods seem awe-inspiring, magnificent, numinous, grand . . . There are other times, however, when they seem remarkably shallow and petty. And this double nature of the gods, this tension between grandeur and pettiness, has seemed odd to a great many readers of the *Iliad*. There's no question as to why the gods are shown as awe-inspiring and grand, but why are they sometimes shown as petty and trivial? To understand what's going on there, why Homer treats the gods this way in the *Iliad*, I think we need to realize that there are two distinct viewpoints at play here.

When we the audience in effect step into the *Iliad* and look at the gods from the point of view of the human characters, when we stand shoulder to shoulder with Agamemnon or Hector or Paris or Achilles, and look at the gods from that point of view, [the gods] are without question awe-inspiring, magnificent, numinous, glorious, dangerous beings whom it is very wise not to offend. But when we stand side-by-side with Homer the narrator and look at the gods from the point of view of the narrator of the epic, or putting it another way look at the gods on their own terms in the *Iliad*, they sometimes seem shallow, petty, trivial, almost as though they are comic relief. This is to some extent shocking and surprising, the idea of the gods as shallow, petty, and trivial, and yet it is undeniably there in the *Iliad.*

These gods complain loudly about minor injuries . . . When Aphrodite is wounded by [the Greek soldier] Diomedes, he scratches her hand when she is trying to carry her son Aeneas off the battlefield, she drops Aeneas, flies up to Mount Olympus and cries in her mother's lap because her hand hurts. The gods are easily distracted from the troubles even of their human favorites. They brawl with one other. They call each other names. They box each other's ears. They behave in many very undignified ways . . .

So the obvious question is why does the *Iliad* present this double-view of the gods. What does the epic gain from this apparent pettiness of its divinities? It wasn't by any means necessary for [the] epic to portray the gods this way. The gods in the *Odyssey* are much less shallow, much less petty, much less trivial than the gods in the *Iliad.* I think the key point for understanding what's going on here with these gods in the *Iliad* is once again to look at them as a means of comparison for humans. The gods lack human vulnerability. They cannot be seriously wounded. They cannot be killed. And along with lacking human vulnerability, or the possibility of death, they lack human seriousness and any capacity for nobility . . . A being that cannot risk anything serious, an entity that cannot be seriously harmed, let alone killed, is incapable, is almost by definition incapable, of showing courage, altruism, nobility, self-sacrifice, any of those virtues that we admire most in humans, any of those virtues that perhaps come into fullest detail in a war: courage, self-sacrifice, and so forth. An immortal being that cannot even be seriously wounded cannot exhibit any of those traits.

> And so in a very real sense, Homer's gods are more trivial than Homer's humans. Homer's humans can display courage, nobility, and self-sacrifice. His gods can't. And I think the treatment of the gods as trivial highlights that difference [between godlike immortality and human mortality]. This contrast between the humans in the *Iliad*, who are faced with the absolutely serious issues of life and death, and gods who can risk nothing, once again underlines what it means to be human and how serious a matter that is.[2]

The *Iliad* reveals a hidden truth that many people today do not recognize. Understanding this hidden truth is necessary to know what it means to be human and fully walk the road to peace. This truth is that the only reason human beings are capable of being courageous, self-sacrificing, and heroic—the qualities we admire most about human beings—is that we are mortal. The Greek gods are like us in so many other ways, but because they cannot be killed or seriously injured, they cannot be courageous. As Elizabeth Vandiver mentioned, an immortal being that risks nothing* and cannot be killed or seriously injured is incapable of being courageous.

Many adjectives are used to describe God in the Bible, but because he is immortal and invulnerable, he is never described as being courageous. Never does he display courage, the most widely admired human virtue. In fact, it is absurd to think of the biblical God as being courageous, because according to Christian theology, why would an immortal and all-powerful being that cannot be hurt need courage?

* In the *Iliad* aren't the Greek gods risking the lives of their mortal children? It is questionable whether the Greek gods feel real parental love for their mortal children. The only obvious exception is Thetis, who displays motherly love for her son Achilles. However, Thetis is a minor sea goddess and is not an Olympian. In his book *Homer on Life and Death*, Jasper Griffin says Thetis who "is not at home on Olympus" is the only Greek deity in the *Iliad* "who mourns as a mortal mourns." Where the Olympians are concerned, although Aphrodite is an immortal being who cannot be seriously injured or killed, she abandons her son Aeneas on the battlefield when Diomedes wounds her hand. Zeus is fond of his son Sarpedon, but compare his reaction of watching his son die in battle to Priam's reaction of seeing Hector killed in combat. In Greek mythology, the Olympians do not seem to place as high a value on mortal life as humans do.

In the Bible, the Jewish prophets can be courageous (by putting themselves at risk when they oppose injustice), but God cannot. Because of God's immortality and invulnerability, he can only display courage in the Bible by taking human form, when he becomes Jesus. Like human beings, Jesus can be courageous and self-sacrificing. Because he has a mortal body, Jesus can be tortured, seriously injured, and killed. As a result, Jesus possesses qualities such as heroism that the gods in the *Iliad* cannot achieve. Jesus has far more in common with Homer's human characters in the *Iliad*, who are striving heroically to navigate the painful struggle of life and death, than with any of Homer's immortal gods.

When people admire soldiers, firefighters, and nonviolent activists, they often admire the courage it takes to risk one's life for others. Sergeant First Class Alwyn Cashe, an American soldier mortally wounded in Iraq while risking his life to save his comrades, demonstrated how courage, self-sacrifice, and heroism are only possible because we are vulnerable to serious injury and death. Journalist David Zucchino explains how Cashe was mortally wounded while risking his life for others:

> [Sergeant First Class Alwyn] Cashe, his uniform soaked with fuel, had plunged into a burning vehicle in Iraq on Oct. 17, 2005, to rescue soldiers who were on fire . . . Cashe rescued six badly burned soldiers while under enemy small-arms fire. His own uniform caught fire, engulfing him in flames. Even with second- and third-degree burns over three-fourths of his body, Cashe continued to pull soldiers out of a vehicle set ablaze when a roadside bomb ruptured a fuel tank . . .
>
> Nine years after the Iraq bomb attack, retired Sgt. Gary Mills [recalls what happened] . . . Mills was inside the stricken Bradley fighting vehicle that day. He was on fire, his hands so badly burned that he couldn't open the rear troop door to free himself and other soldiers trapped inside the flaming vehicle.
>
> Someone opened the door from outside, Mills recalls.

> A powerful hand grabbed him and yanked him to safety. He later learned that the man who had rescued him was Cashe, who seconds later crawled into the vehicle to haul out the platoon's critically burned medic while on fire himself.
>
> "Sgt. Cashe saved my life," Mills said. "With all the ammo inside that vehicle, and all those flames, we'd have all been dead in another minute or two."
>
> Four of the six soldiers rescued later died of their wounds at a hospital. An Afghan interpreter riding in the Bradley died during the bomb attack. Cashe refused to be loaded onto a medical evacuation helicopter until all the other wounded men had been flown.
>
> A citation proposing the Medal of Honor for Cashe reads: "SFC Cashe's selfless and gallant actions allowed the loved ones of these brave soldiers to spend precious time by their sides before they succumbed."
>
> Cashe's sister, Kasinal Cashe White, spent three weeks at her brother's bedside at a military hospital in Texas as doctors treated his extensive burns. She knew nothing of his actions during the bomb attack until a nurse asked her, "You know your brother's a hero, don't you?"
>
> When Cashe was able to speak, White said, his first words were: "How are my boys?"—his soldiers, she said.
>
> Then he began weeping, she said. He told her: "I couldn't get to them fast enough."
>
> Cashe died Nov. 8, 2005.
>
> "My little brother lived by the code that you never leave your soldiers behind," White said. "That wasn't just something from a movie. He lived it."[3]

Stories like this have enormous inspirational power, yet a person does not have to die a painful death while saving others to display self-sacrifice. Because human beings have a limited lifespan, dedicating most of your life, or even a much smaller amount of your time to serving others, can be an act of self-sacrifice. Because the gods in the *Iliad* are immortal, dedicating even a thousand years to something is not an act of self-sacrifice for them, since they have an infinite amount of time to spare. When a divine being is immortal, time becomes a meaningless feature within the endless landscape of eternity. But because human beings are mortal, every moment is precious and something we can never get back. Lieutenant Colonel Dave Grossman reminds us, "Sometimes the ultimate love is not to sacrifice your life, but to live a life of sacrifice."[4]

Furthermore, a person does not have to risk dying a painful death to be courageous. In *Peaceful Revolution* I define bravery as overcoming the feeling of fear. Courage, however, has a broader meaning because it can be moral as well as physical. As I will discuss later in this book, living courageously is a way of life that allows us to achieve our highest human potential and improve the well-being of any community we interact with. When a person lives courageously, bravery can come more naturally.

Many of us assume that people who possess immense material wealth and luxury have lives similar to those of immortal gods, because luxury offers so much physical comfort that people can live under the illusion that they are immune to pain and death. But we are different from the Greek gods not only because we are mortal, but also in another significant way. As I explain in *The Cosmic Ocean*, human beings have cravings that are not physical. These cravings include our hunger for purpose, meaning, belonging, self-worth, and transcendence.* We must find ways to fulfill these cravings just as other animals must find food and water.

Human beings are the only species on the planet that can become depressed, addicted to drugs, and suicidal, even when we have freedom, a belly full of food, good health, family, and the physical comfort of luxury. Because we can be so greatly tormented by our very existence, there is a part in the *Iliad* where Zeus, the king of the gods, looks upon human beings and says, "There is nothing alive more agonized than man of all that breathe and crawl across the earth."[5]

* We have additional cravings that are not physical, which I describe in *The Cosmic Ocean.*

Unlike humans, the immortal gods in the *Iliad* do not struggle with a need to find purpose and meaning in their lives, the desire to belong, low self-worth, or the yearning to transcend time. Humans crave purpose and meaning so desperately that we can be drawn to many forms of fanaticism, but the Greek gods know that their purpose is to rule the world as divine beings. Humans will die without access to a human community,* which is why we crave belonging, but the Greek gods cannot die. Humans can feel low self-worth because of the way we look, how much money we make, and having characteristics that our society deems imperfect. But the Greek gods do not age, they need no money, and they are perfect in ways that humans can never be. Humans have a craving to transcend the limitations of time, but the Greek gods effortlessly exist beyond these limitations.

The immortal Greek gods also seem immune to the kinds of trauma that so often devastate the human mind. Therefore, the Greek gods in the *Iliad* do not suffer from problems that can result from childhood trauma and our unfulfilled human cravings, such as alcoholism, drug addiction, eating disorders, a desire to numb the mind, a midlife crisis, or suicidal thoughts. If luxury solved all of our human problems, then every successful Hollywood celebrity would never suffer from psychological problems and would instead be completely happy every moment of every day.

In addition to our cravings for purpose, meaning, belonging, self-worth, and transcendence, human beings also crave explanations. As far as we know, when lightning strikes the ground we are the only species that asks why, and we are the only species that tries to answer this question with religious and scientific explanations. Only human beings, not Greek gods or wild animals, create religions and science to explain the mysteries of our universe.

Time is a great mystery that all cultures have tried to understand. An allegory about Zeus's father, Cronos, the god of time, can help us better understand the mystery of time. In the *Iliad* the Olympians, a race of Greek gods that includes Zeus, Poseidon, Hera, Athena, Aphrodite, Ares, and many others, cannot be killed or seriously injured. If they are physically

* Even hermits, in order to survive alone, must rely on the knowledge they gained from a community. If a two-year-old child is abandoned in the wilderness and denied access to a human community, that child will not survive for long.

wounded, their wounds are easily and quickly healed.*

According to Greek mythology, the Titans are an earlier race of Greek gods who rule the world before the events in the *Iliad* take place. Like the Olympians, the Titans also cannot be killed or seriously injured. The Titans include Cronos (the father of the first Olympians), Prometheus (who steals fire from the gods and gives it to humanity), and Atlas (who holds the sky on his shoulders). The first Titans were born from the primeval deities, an even earlier race of gods that include Gaia (a goddess who personifies the earth) and Ouranos (a god who personifies the sky, better known by his Latin name *Uranus*).

Unlike the Olympians and the Titans, the primeval deity Ouranos can be seriously injured in ways that don't seem to heal, although he, like the Olympians and the Titans, cannot be killed. The following allegorical story about the birth of time shows how people in ancient Greece tried to explain the mystery of time. Surprisingly, this ancient story agrees in some ways with modern science. Elizabeth Vandiver recounts how the ancient Greek poet Hesiod described Gaia and Ouranos giving birth to time:

> Gaia and Ouranos mate and produce these twelve children [Titans], but all is not well, because Ouranos does not allow the children to be born. He pushes each one back into Gaia's womb as each child is born . . . This causes Gaia great pain as well as causing her great anger, and therefore she conspires with her youngest son, a Titan named Cronos, to overthrow Cronos's father Ouranos. Gaia produces a sickle [that she gives to Cronos] . . . Cronos hides inside Gaia's body, and the next time Ouranos comes to have sex with Gaia, Cronos from inside Gaia's womb grasps hold of Ouranos's genitals and cuts them off . . .
>
> At this point Ouranos retreats from Gaia and becomes

* In the *Iliad*, the god Hephaestus has disabled legs, but he was born like this, according to book 18 of the *Iliad*. He is the only Greek god who is not physically perfect, and this imperfection resulted from Hera trying to conceive him alone without Zeus. Also, in some religions and mythologies gods can die (Nordic gods such as Odin and Thor are killed in the battle of Ragnarok), but Homer's gods are immune to death. The *Iliad* can be seen as a meditation on human mortality.

the dome of the sky. He never again takes any very active part in anything that happens . . . He cannot be killed . . . A god by definition cannot be killed. What Cronos has done is the next best thing, has disempowered, disabled his father, by castrating him. Obviously, if you can't kill a god, what you are going to do is deprive him of his power to the greatest extent possible, and depriving him of his masculinity is a very clear symbolic way of depriving him of his power.

So Ouranos becomes the dome of the sky that touches Gaia on all sides . . . This also leaves room, physical room, for the children to be born. The picture that Hesiod seems to be presenting here is before the castration of Ouranos [he] was not yet the dome of the sky with which we are all familiar. He was pressing down on Gaia. He was flat on Gaia. There was no separation in-between them, quite literally no room for those children to develop. It's only when Ouranos retreats and becomes the sky as we know it that the Titans, the children, can spring forth from Gaia and become powerful entities in their own rights . . .

This story of Cronos castrating his father also lends itself remarkably well to allegorical interpretation due to the resemblance of Cronos's name to the Greek word for time [*chronos*] . . . Now if we go with the allegorical interpretation that this similarity of the name Cronos and the word for time seems to imply, we can say that when Cronos was freed from Gaia's womb after he castrated his father Ouranos, time itself came into being. On this interpretation, we're really dealing with a fairly sophisticated concept here. Not only is it necessary for there to be space for Gaia's children to develop in, not only must Ouranos back away and leave room for the children to develop, time is also necessary. You've got to have space, you've also got to have time, for development to take place.

And so only when Cronos, only when time, has come

> into true being, according to this allegorical interpretation . . . can the world come into full functioning order [and create the conditions for plants, animals, and humans to exist] . . . I like to point [this allegory] out because again it does show the level of sophistication that can be working under the surface of what at first sight is a rather horrifically gory and outré story, the castration of Ouranos by Cronos.[6]

Time is a great mystery that scientists may never fully comprehend. Metaphors and allegories are useful because they help us understand how the human condition is shaped by this mysterious force we call time, which makes existence possible while transcending human comprehension. Similar to the allegorical interpretation of Cronos's birth, modern science also acknowledges that space and time are necessary for existence to unfold. Many physicists call this *space-time*. The allegory of Cronos's birth* goes a step further by depicting time as a ruthless being that cuts off his father's genitals.

Perhaps the most ruthless depiction of time is found in Hinduism. Kali is a Hindu goddess who symbolizes time. She is also a metaphor for time's ruthlessness, because if we are lucky enough to live a long and fulfilling life, time will take away our loved ones, wrinkle our skin, turn our hair gray, cause our flesh to sag, make us ill, and then after all that, time will kill us. That is, *if* we are lucky enough to live a long and fulfilling life. To symbolize how time kills children and adults with diseases, accidents, and violence before they can experience old age, Kali wears a necklace of decapitated heads, a girdle of hacked-off arms, and earrings made from children's corpses. Hinduism does not sugarcoat its depiction of time.

* Cronos can also be spelled as Cronus. Regarding the similarities between Cronos the god and chronos the Greek word for time, Elizabeth Vandiver adds, "Now these two words, Cronos the name of the god and chronos meaning time, are not actually etymologically related to one another. They come from two entirely different roots; they're not really two versions of the same word. I personally don't think that necessarily invalidates allegorical interpretation, if Hesiod and his audience thought they came from the same word, then that allegory can be working there even though modern linguists know that the resemblance of sound is purely coincidental. This allegorical interpretation by the way was first suggested as early as the sixth century BC."

Although the struggles caused by Kali (time) affect people in different amounts, no person is completely immune to time. How does recognizing the full extent of time's ruthlessness help us wield the weapon of nonviolence with maximum force? As I mentioned earlier, by being fully aware of time's ruthlessness and not repressing this reality, I am able to recognize and feel deeply connected to the vulnerability and fragility of life. This motivates me to be kind and gentle in all the ways time cannot. Because time is so ruthless to all forms of life, we all have an incentive to become kinder, more compassionate, and gentler in our interactions with others.

To show how practical this attitude really is, ask yourself this: do you want to be around people who behave ruthlessly like time, having absolutely no compassion for you, or do you want to be around people who treat you kindly, mercifully, and with a type of gentleness built on the force of respect?

What is gentleness built on the force of respect? West Point graduate General Douglas MacArthur discussed gentleness in leadership and the importance of not running away from struggle in a speech he gave at West Point in 1962. West Point's ideals helped me understand the meaning of gentleness, and in General MacArthur's speech he said that the ideals of West Point "teach you to be proud and unbending in honest failure, but humble and gentle in success; not to substitute words for action; not to seek the path of comfort, but to face the stress and spur of difficulty and challenge; to learn to stand up in the storm, but to have compassion on those who fall; to master yourself before you seek to master others; to have a heart that is clean, a goal that is high; to learn to laugh, yet never forget how to weep; to reach into the future, yet never neglect the past; to be serious, yet never take yourself too seriously; to be modest so that you will remember the simplicity of true greatness, the open mind of true wisdom, the meekness of true strength."[7]

Peter Cullen was the voice actor for Optimus Prime in the 1980s cartoon *Transformers*, a cartoon I watched often as a child. Optimus Prime, the leader of the heroes in the cartoon, was a robot who could transform into a truck. Cullen describes how his brother (a marine and Vietnam veteran) told him about the importance of gentleness:

My brother Larry was a marine who fought in Vietnam, and he was an officer and he was given the Bronze Star for valor [and] a couple of purple hearts. Larry was thirteen months older than me, and he was my hero since we were growing up as kids . . . He did everything, played professional football as well before being in the Marine Corps . . .

And when we were living together in Hollywood, I was going through a little change in my life, and he asked me, "Peter, where are you going?"

I said, "I'm going to an audition."

He said, "Yeah? What are you auditioning for, Pete?"

I said, "I'm auditioning for a truck."

[Larry laughed,] "A truck?"

"But he's a hero truck, Larry . . . What I mean is, I don't know much about it, Larry. I just know he's a truck and he's a leader, he's a hero." And I was getting a little nervous and wanting to get in the car and get out.

And he said, "Peter, if you're going to be a hero, be a real hero." And he got very very calm, and he said, "Don't be shouting and posing and pretending and yelling and acting tough. Heroes don't do that. If you're going to be a hero, be a real hero. Be strong enough to be gentle, and be humble, be courageous, be proud."

And those words hung on me . . . It was so important to me and I thought about those words when I went to the audition. And when I got into the little cubicle, I had the pages in front of me and I had gone over them, but I hadn't done my voice for them yet, but I just remember Larry saying, "Peter, if you're going to be a hero, be a real hero, be strong enough to be gentle." And I just took that softness into the microphone [and said,] "My name is Optimus Prime." And then I read.[8]

We must "be strong enough to be gentle." True gentleness requires the strength of courage, respect, and compassion. In all of human history I don't think anyone has ever seriously said, "I want to be around people who treat me without respect and compassion." If we were supposed to behave ruthlessly, why would people respond so well to being treated with respect and compassion, and why would we respond so badly when our fellow human beings treat us ruthlessly with absolutely no regard for our thoughts, emotions, or well-being?

Recognizing the full extent of time's ruthlessness also helps us dispel the popular myth that peace is the absence of struggle. When we gain literacy in the nature of reality, we understand that this myth of peace is not possible, because as long as time exists, struggle will also exist. Today many people see peace as merely the absence of struggle, which is the most common depiction of peace in the world today. However, the unrealistic depiction of peace as the absence of struggle prevents us from achieving a realistic form of peace based on empathy, understanding, justice, and so much more.

Realistic peace is not the absence of struggle, but the process of transforming struggle into purpose, meaning, empathy, understanding, justice, gentleness built on the force of respect, and the many conditions needed for survival and prosperity. The art of waging peace is a strategic method for activating this peace process in our personal lives, among our local communities, throughout our nations, and around the world. The popular notion that peace is the absence of struggle turns people away from the idea of peace by making it sound naive and unrealistic. The popular notion that peace is the absence of struggle also defies the laws of nature.

Predating humanity, struggle is a part of nature that every creature contends with. Struggle and adversity are laws of life. Even if humanity abolishes war between countries, people will still have to overcome many challenges during our fragile future, and every future generation will also have to struggle to achieve purpose, meaning, belonging, self-worth, transcendence, and the other "spiritual cravings" I describe in *The Cosmic Ocean*.

The star of struggle is a necessary light in the constellation of peace, because creating peace requires us to willingly confront and move toward struggle, rather than run away from struggle. One reason realistic peace has so much difficulty flourishing in our world is that countless people run away from struggle and avoid conflict, which allows apathy and injustice to flourish. A quote attributed to Edmund Burke reminds us, "All that is necessary for the triumph of evil is that good men do nothing."[9]

People often ask me how I gained an understanding of peace and transformed from a soldier in war to a soldier of peace. People also ask me how I transformed my rage into radical empathy. Although all of my books contain stories that illustrate my lifelong journey to find and walk the road to peace, the simplest answer I can provide is that I learned to embrace peace as a process, lifestyle, and way of being.

Because I have embraced peace as a process, I strive every day to transform the struggles I experience into purpose, meaning, empathy, and understanding. In every conflict I experience, I strive to increase justice for everyone involved and become gentler along the way. I also study the art of waging peace so that I can help people come together and apply the peace process on a local and global level.

The global peace process is symbolized by our journey to sail the sea of time on a course toward survival, prosperity, and a sustainable biosphere. As I mentioned earlier, time is a ruthless sea, and humanity is bound together on one ship, the planet Earth. Humanity will go extinct or survive depending on how well we navigate the dangerous waters ahead.

As our ship the Earth sails through time, surging into the future, it is easy to lose sight of the way to peace. The constellation of peace is a beacon to help us navigate the ruthless sea of time so that we do not become lost, but remain empowered and proactive as we journey to peace. In the following quote, Martin Luther King Jr. explained why we must never apathetically leave our global problems in the hands of time, but proactively wage peace to solve these problems before they drive humanity extinct. Throughout his life, King saw so many kind people avoid rather than embrace struggle, but peace cannot exist without struggle.

> We must get rid of the false notion that there is some miraculous quality in the flow of time that inevitably heals all evils. There is only one thing certain about time, and

> that is that it waits for no one. If it is not used constructively, it passes you by.
>
> In this generation the children of darkness are still shrewder than the children of light. They are always zealous and conscientious in using time for their evil purposes. If they want to preserve segregation and tyranny, they do not wait on time; they make time their fellow conspirator. If they want to defeat a fair housing bill, they don't say to the public, "Be patient, wait on time, and our cause will win." Rather, they use time to spend big money, to disseminate half-truths, to confuse the popular mind. But the forces of light cautiously wait, patiently pray and timidly act . . .
>
> We can no longer afford to worship the God of hate or bow before the altar of retaliation . . . We are now faced with the fact that tomorrow is today. We are confronted with the fierce urgency of *now*. In this unfolding conundrum of life and history there is such a thing as being too late. Procrastination is still the thief of time. Life often leaves us standing bare, naked and dejected with a lost opportunity . . .
>
> We may cry out desperately for time to pause in her passage, but time is deaf to every plea and rushes on. Over the bleached bones and jumbled residues of numerous civilizations are written the pathetic words: "Too late." . . . We still have a choice today: nonviolent coexistence or violent coannihilation. This may well be mankind's last chance to choose between chaos and community.[10]

To discuss the many ways time affects the human condition, in this chapter I have described time as an enemy, thief, untrustworthy custodian of human problems, blank canvas where the masterpieces of human existence can be painted, source of mortality that enables the virtues we admire most in human beings, great mystery, ruthless force that motivates me to behave gently in all the ways time cannot, and the reason we must wage peace with urgency and effectiveness.

As we will discuss next, our strange relationship with time has also resulted in human beings possessing a remarkable ability. We can choose to respond to struggle in a seemingly infinite number of ways, which is an ability that no other species on the planet seems to possess. Some choices leave us defeated and in despair. Other choices lead to glory and greatness. By learning how to put time and struggle to good use, we can empower ourselves with the skills that make glory and greatness more likely.

Glorious through Hera

Time may seem to affect human beings in ruthless ways, but it affects other animals that inhabit our planet in ways that seem even more ruthless. Humanity has created hospitals where people can receive medical treatment if they are seriously wounded. But animals in the wilderness do not have this luxury. When a wild animal breaks a leg, gets an infection, or suffers a life-threatening injury, there are no emergency rooms in nature.

Technology not only gives us a more accurate way than ancient methods such as animal sacrifice to predict future events, but it also allows us to correct mistakes from the past. If you are in a serious accident or someone stabs you in the stomach, medical technology might give you a second chance at life. Many people are working hard to create a world where every person has access to medical technology, and many people are trying to improve this technology so that it can save more lives. Animals in the wild are not so fortunate. For them the smallest mistake, such as not being vigilant for one second, can mean the difference between being eaten by a predator or surviving. If predators make a tiny mistake while hunting, they can be gravely injured or lose their next meal, putting them at risk of starvation.

Today it is common to romanticize nature as a benign and all-loving mother, but when we recognize that time is a fundamental law of nature, we can see the reality suppressed by this romanticizing. We can see that

Mother Nature in many ways resembles ruthless Kali. The reality is that time drives nearly every species, eventually, into extinction. Nature can be depicted metaphorically as a mother who eats her own children, because scientists estimate that over 99 percent of the species that ever existed have gone extinct.

In *The Cosmic Ocean* I discuss how people can see nature as benevolent or destructive, and both perspectives contain a piece of the truth. However, modern technology has given us so much comfort, which has insulated us from so many of the harsh realities of nature, that countless people today romanticize nature to an extreme degree and forget the truths our ancient ancestors knew. Ancient civilizations around the world understood truths about the ruthlessness of nature and time, which have been suppressed by romanticized notions of Mother Nature today. Psychologist Erich Neumann explains:

> This Terrible Mother [Nature] is the hungry earth, which devours its own children and fattens on their corpses; it is the tiger and the vulture, the vulture and the coffin . . . It is in India that the experience of the Terrible Mother has been given its most grandiose form as Kali, "dark, all-devouring time, the bone-wreathed Lady of the place of skulls." . . .
>
> The need for fecundating and reviving the feminine earth with blood, death, and corpses—this conception, perpetually reinforced by the flow of life and death in nature, constellates the Great Mother as terrible, killing, and dismembering. That is why the great goddesses [in ancient civilizations around the world] are goddesses of the hunt and of war, dealers in life and blood. That is why the great Aztec Mother Goddess is also the goddess of the obsidian knife with which bodies are dismembered, and why in her aspect of moon goddess she is called the "white stone knife."[11]

To better understand how nature is far from benign, it is just a matter of time before another large asteroid impacts our planet, which will drive much of the life on Earth extinct. This happened millions of years ago to the dinosaurs, and at some point in the future a major asteroid impact will happen again. In addition, the sun gets hotter as it grows older, and the sun will eventually get so hot that it will cause the Earth's oceans to evaporate.* Scientists have also discovered that our sun will expand and destroy the Earth billions of years from now. That may seem like a long time away when we look at it from our everyday human perspective, but billions of years is a tiny amount of time when compared to the endless landscape of eternity. Time, incapable of feeling compassion and mercy, will eventually destroy all life on Earth. It is only a matter of time.

Actually, it is only a matter of time unless humanity does something about it. Human beings are the only species on the planet that can stop a large asteroid from hitting the Earth by using our technology to deflect the asteroid from its path. And when all life on Earth is at risk of being destroyed by the sun in the distant future, human beings may have the technological ability to save some life on Earth, and perhaps the Earth itself. If our planet in the distant future is not inhabited by human beings, or a species similar to us, all life on Earth will be destroyed.

Right now human beings have a unique and far more urgent problem, because today we have become our own greatest threat to our survival. Our technology, which has served many useful functions such as helping to protect us from time's ruthlessness, now threatens to drive us extinct. Humanity may end up becoming a species that uses its technology to create clean forms of energy, embracing ideals that encourage us to treat our environment with an attitude of respect and responsibility. Because our delicate biosphere is so fragile, if we do not treat our environment with an attitude of respect and responsibility, we will endanger the survival of humanity and most life on Earth.

I see four likely options for humanity's future. The first option is that humans become protectors to life on Earth, the Earth's defense against

* We are not sure when the sun will become so hot that it will evaporate the Earth's oceans. It probably won't happen within the next five hundred million years.

asteroids and the threats the sun will eventually pose, stewards who empathize with the other species on our planet that are also subject to time's ruthlessness, guardians who allow creation to unfold in the wilderness according to nature's laws, interfering only to correct the harm we cause or to stop time's ruthlessness from seriously damaging our delicate biosphere. The second option is that humanity destroys itself and most life on Earth. The third option is that humanity implements much of the second option, causing a mass extinction that destroys most life on Earth, then transforms our civilization to align with the first option. The fourth option is that we destroy our biosphere, forcing us to live in self-contained, restricted, artificial environments, similar to underground shelters. If this happened, our ship (the Earth's biosphere) would metaphorically sink, and we would have to make our home in a metaphorical submarine. As I will explain in the last book of this series, there are no guarantees that humans could survive long-term in those restricted conditions.

Our planet gave birth to humanity, like a metaphorical mother. If we choose the first option by becoming a protector of this planet, we will be like a child who grows up to protect our mother, appreciating the many challenges our mother put us through, since nature's ruthlessness was necessary to give us the strength we have today. If we choose the second option by destroying our planet's delicate biosphere along with ourselves, we will be like a child who causes our mother to die in childbirth, where both the child and mother perish together. Similar to a dangerous childbirth, the birth of our global civilization has been a dangerous transition for our planet. If we choose the third option by causing a mass extinction and then becoming protectors, we will be like a child that almost causes our mother to die during childbirth, but the mother survives, severely weakened and in greater need of care. If we choose the fourth option by destroying our delicate biosphere and being forced to live in self-contained, restricted, artificial environments, future generations will mourn the loss of our mother in ways people today cannot even imagine, and perhaps our species will never stop mourning, because unlike babies that have no choice in whether they kill their mother during childbirth, we humans do have a choice.

If we want to become fully empowered to choose the first option, we must discuss why humanity can choose such diverse options in the first place. We are the only species on the planet that can choose to drive itself and most other species extinct, or protect the Earth, travel to other planets, and survive as long as the universe exists. To understand why we can choose such diverse options, we must explore the nature of human struggle. An allegory that can help us do this is the story of Hera and Heracles.

In Greek mythology Hera was an immortal goddess, an Olympian. Her father was the Titan Cronos, the god of time. Hera can be seen as a metaphor for struggle. Just as struggle is a manifestation of time, Hera is a child of Cronos.

However, Hera symbolizes a certain kind of struggle, the form of challenge that gives us purpose and meaning, that leads to glory and greatness. This is the kind of struggle humanity must embrace to survive during our fragile future. This is the kind of struggle that is a star in the constellation of peace.

Heracles (better known by his Latin name, Hercules) is the most famous Greek hero. Possessing superhuman strength, he traveled with Jason and the Argonauts, went on many other adventures, and overcame significant challenges. Heracles was the son of Zeus, the king of the gods, and a mortal woman named Alcmene. Hera was Zeus's wife, and she hated her husband's adulterous affairs. She especially hated Heracles, who was born from Zeus's affair with Alcmene. Hera was determined to take her wrath out on Heracles, causing him severe struggle and suffering.

How severe was his struggle and suffering? Heracles was supposed to inherit a kingdom, but Hera prevented this. She also inflicted him with temporary insanity, causing him to murder his wife Megara and their three children.* To atone for this crime, Heracles had to undertake twelve labors, dangerous and difficult tasks that included slaying monsters. Heracles twice became a slave, and after completing his twelve labors he died after a poison covered his body and consumed his flesh. The poison did not kill him, but ate away his flesh to the point where his bones were exposed. To end his

* There are different versions of this story. In some versions Heracles just kills his children but not his wife, and the number of children can also vary.

agony, Heracles committed suicide by burning himself alive on a flaming pyre.

Obviously, this is not the story portrayed in the Disney animated film about Heracles (*Hercules,* 1997), nor in any other film that I am aware of. Modern depictions of Heracles are greatly sanitized, ignoring his tremendous suffering. But in Greek mythology, the severity of his struggle was crucial to his story. After Heracles died, he became an Olympian because he endured so much struggle. When he ascended to Mount Olympus as a god, Hera, the source of Heracles's immense suffering, allowed him to marry her daughter Hebe, which symbolized a reconciliation between Heracles and the source of his suffering.

Ironically, Heracles owes his divine status to Hera, who tried to destroy him. Heracles became an Olympian, achieving glory and greatness, because of the severe struggle and suffering that Hera caused him. To reflect Hera's role in his achievement of glory and greatness, the first part of his name, "Hera," derives from the name of the goddess who tormented him, and the second part of his name, "cles," derives from the word *kleos*, the Greek word for glory. In ancient Greece, his name was widely understood to mean "glorious through Hera."

The Oxford Encyclopedia of Ancient Greece and Rome explains how Heracles got his name:

> [Heracles is] an ideal everyman, who endures the greatest humiliations and sufferings during his lifetime, and consequently becomes one of the Olympian gods. Of all the great Greek heroes, he is the only one who can be said to have conquered and transcended death.
>
> Although linguists disagree about its etymology, the Greeks interpreted the hero's name as "the glory of Hera" or "glorious through Hera." . . . His name links him to the goddess who is his antagonist and torments him during his lifetime. Yet Hera also spurs him to accomplish the great deeds and experience the sufferings for which he gains his subsequent glory.[12]

Just as Heracles became glorious through Hera, we as human beings can become glorious through struggle. Hera, as a metaphor for struggle, can symbolize many forms of adversity. For my African American ancestors, Hera was state-sanctioned slavery and segregation, which led to the glory and greatness of countless black activists, including the many activists who participated in the civil rights movement.

If someone living in 1900 were to look at African American history, it could seem like nothing but tragedy. In 1900 African American history consisted of hundreds of years of slavery, followed by the "failure" of Reconstruction after the Civil War. Although the United States in the twenty-first century still has a long way to journey on the road to racial justice, we have made progress, because African Americans in 1900 were subjected to a degree of violence, terrorism, and subhuman status that most Americans today cannot imagine.

When people are surrounded by the darkness of injustice they can surrender to the night or work to create light. In 1935 Reverend Howard Thurman, his wife, Sue Thurman, and two other members of a Negro delegation to India became the first African Americans to meet Mahatma Gandhi. Believing that Gandhi's method of nonviolent resistance could help African Americans gain their human rights, Sue Thurman told Gandhi, "We want you to come to America . . . not for White America, but for the Negroes, we have many a problem that cries for solution, and we need you badly."[13]

Gandhi replied, "How I wish I could . . . [but] I must make good the message [of nonviolence] here before I bring it to you. I do not say that I am defeated, but I still have to perfect myself. You may be sure that the moment I feel the call within me I shall not hesitate."[14] Among his final comments to the African Americans who had traveled so far to meet him, Gandhi said something prophetic: "It may be through the Negroes that the unadulterated message of nonviolence will be delivered to the world."[15]

Howard Thurman became a mentor to Martin Luther King Jr. and other leaders in the civil rights movement. Gandhi never received the Nobel Peace Prize, but when King was awarded the prize in 1964, it symbolized that the world had taken a step toward recognizing the worth and power of nonviolence. The civil rights movement created light in the darkness of injustice, helping to inspire nonviolent movements around the world. Every David versus Goliath story that inspires us, such as the civil rights movement's fight against racism, is based on struggle. In fact, every story that inspires us is based on some kind of struggle. Without struggle there is no story.

For athletes, artists, or anyone to become more skilled at their craft, they must learn and grow through struggle. Skill is a plant that grows when it is watered by struggle. Struggle also waters every movement for justice. I am deeply inspired by the early women's rights activists and their heroic efforts to create one of the most incredible revolutions in world history, but the glory and greatness of the women's rights movement resulted from their challenging struggle against sexism. Countless people are inspired by nonviolent movements, but without the need to struggle against injustice, there would never have been a nonviolent movement anywhere in the world. The nature of reality is that inspirational stories, along with every example of significant physical, mental, and spiritual growth, cannot exist without the star of struggle.

Frederick Douglass, an escaped slave, abolitionist, and women's rights activist, explained how struggle is an essential part of peace, because embracing struggle is necessary for justice and all forms of progress:

> If there is no struggle, there is no progress. Those who profess to favor freedom, and yet depreciate agitation, are men who want crops without plowing up the ground. They want rain without thunder and lightning. They want the ocean without the awful roar of its many waters. This struggle may be a moral one; or it may be a physical one; or it may be both moral and physical; but it must be a struggle. Power concedes nothing without a demand. It never did, and it never will.[16]

Again, this is why seeing peace as the absence of struggle, which is the most common way peace is viewed today, is so dangerous. If we do not embrace struggle as a star in the constellation of peace, we cannot solve our most serious human problems and create the progress our world needs most. Furthermore, without struggle we cannot strive toward our highest human potential.

As symbols of our highest human potential, ancient figures such as Socrates, Jesus, and Buddha also achieved glory and greatness through struggle. Socrates struggled to promote truth and justice, Jesus struggled to spread a revolutionary message of love, and Buddha struggled for enlightenment in the midst of suffering. Their highest ideals live on because we continue to be inspired by their struggles. Thousands of years later, we also continue to learn from their struggles.

Jesus told us to love our enemies and not judge, but one reason so few Christians do this is that it is such a significant struggle. Buddha symbolizes being respectful, gentle, and compassionate to many forms of life, not just human life, and even to those who hate us. But the challenging spiritual journey that allows us to attain this deep form of love is not easy.

Learning to love in the midst of conflict, where love is needed most, is certainly challenging. Struggle is a star in the constellation of peace, because if we run away from the struggle required to love deeply and grow spiritually, we cannot create realistic peace. In the next chapter we will discuss how to maintain empathy and calm during those turbulent moments when it seems most difficult to do so. We will also discuss techniques that can help us love deeply and grow spiritually. When I use the word "spiritual," I am not referring to a supernatural spirituality, but an intellectual, emotional, and philosophical spirituality.

History is filled with people who achieved glory and greatness through struggle, but how do I define glory and greatness? In ancient Greece, glory referred to the ability to transcend time, which the Greeks believed could be accomplished through everlasting fame. I also define glory as the ability to transcend time, but as I will explain in the last book of this series, there are more fulfilling ways than fame to transcend time. When we embark on a spiritual journey that increases our purpose, meaning, understanding, empathy, gentleness, and service to others, we can transcend time in deeply fulfilling ways.

I define greatness as our ability to fulfill our human potential. When we strive for greatness in the context of waging peace, we are not striving to become superhuman like Heracles, but fully human. When we strengthen the muscles of our shared humanity, which include hope, empathy, appreciation, conscience, and reason, we make progress on the path to becoming fully human.

When glory and greatness are achieved through waging peace, it creates more prosperity in our society. I define prosperity not in narrow material terms, but in broader human terms. Prosperity not only consists of access to basic physical necessities, but the conditions that help us achieve a meaningful life and become fully human. A truly prosperous society trains us to live according to our highest ideals and cultivates the full development of our humanity.

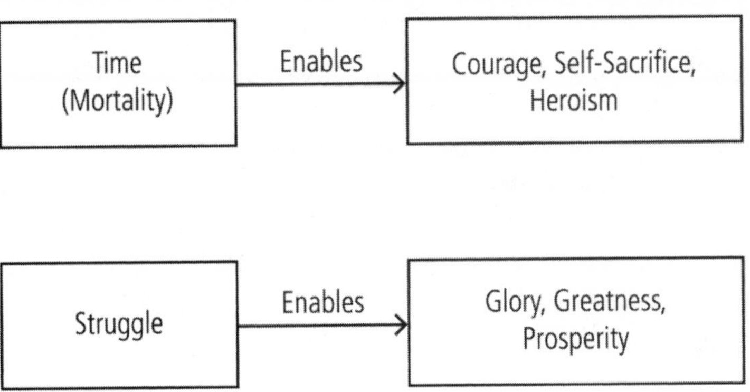

Figure 1.1: The Treasures of Time and Struggle

Hera, as a metaphor for the struggle that enables glory, greatness, and prosperity, can symbolize many different forms of adversity. If you think about the experiences in your life that allowed you to grow the most, they probably involved some form of struggle, some aspect of Hera. In *The Cosmic Ocean* I wrote that trauma has been my greatest teacher. For me, Hera is the trauma that allowed me to develop realistic hope, radical empathy, and revelatory understanding. Hera is also the racism I experienced as a child, which led me to understand our shared humanity. Hera is my experience in war, which deepened my commitment to waging peace. Hera is the reason I wrote these books and learned to walk the road to peace.

While Greek mythology symbolizes struggle as Hera, Buddhism symbolizes struggle as mud. Just as Heracles achieved glory and greatness through Hera, Buddhist philosophy teaches that the beautiful lotus flower, a symbol of spiritual growth, arises out of mud in a pond. These metaphors can be instructive and inspiring, but we should never forget that mud in Buddhism, along with Hera in Greek mythology, symbolize agony to millions of people. We should not romanticize struggle to the point where we trivialize anyone's suffering, but use the adversity in our life to expand our empathy for all who suffer.

Struggle can give us an opportunity to grow, but struggle can also kill us. I have often heard a popular cliché: "God does not give us more than we can handle." This cliché, which is easily refuted by reality, is based on a misinterpretation of the Bible. There are so many examples where people are given more struggle than they can handle, such as the countless people who have died from famine, war, genocide, slavery, suicide, alcoholism, cancer, drug overdoses, plague, and childhood diseases, just to mention a few examples. Reality can be so incredibly harsh and unforgiving that we as human beings should be protectors rather than tormenters of our fellow living creatures. We should not try to play the role of Hera by being ruthless and devoid of empathy, but leave that job to time and reality.

When understanding the force of nature that is struggle, the metaphor of Hera and the metaphor of mud both have their uses. The metaphor of Hera encourages me to help others, have compassion for them, and not trivialize their pain. Since even a demigod like Heracles had some help during his journey to overcome Hera, it is even more important that we as mere humans help each other. Because pond mud seems harmless, static, and passive, it can cause us to underestimate the pain people go through during their struggles, whereas the metaphor of a goddess inflicting insanity and tragedy on someone better captures the agony that extreme trauma and other problems can inflict on people. When I feel at peace with the wounded parts of myself, I see the flowers that have risen from the mud.

Although my books use metaphors from various religions and cultures, there are four reasons why Greek mythological characters in particular can help us gain a deeper understanding of peace. The first reason is that these characters are useful metaphors for so many aspects of the human condition and the nature of reality. The second reason is that Greek mythological characters are known in many parts of the world, which makes them accessible to a wide variety of people. These characters can even be seen in films and video games popular in many countries.

The third reason is that Greek mythological characters have a surprising ability to help people in numerous cultures and time periods better understand their problems, and a better understanding is necessary for creating effective solutions. I have met people who say we should not study the ancient Greeks, because this is "Eurocentric" and we need to stop studying "dead white men." But these claims are greatly misleading, because the ancient Greeks did not see themselves as "white people," and they would have considered it an insult to be associated with the "barbarian" tribes living in Western Europe during that time.[17] In fact, ancient Greece was not "European" in culture (there was no concept of "European culture" back then), but borrowed heavily from other parts of the world. Ancient Greek religion and culture borrowed from areas outside of Europe such as the Near East and North Africa, the Greek phonetic alphabet derived from the Phoenicians, and many Greek texts were preserved not by western Europeans, but by people from the Middle East.[18]

The fourth reason Greek mythological characters are helpful for understanding peace is the current lack of religious dogma surrounding these characters. I have met some people who do not realize "Greek mythology" was actually "Greek religion," nor do they realize Heracles was a religious figure that people prayed to. Most people today think of Heracles as a character in a Disney cartoon or action film. When you discuss other religious figures and people's cherished cultural stories, people from that religion or culture can be easily offended if you are not careful about what you say, but a discussion about Greek mythological characters can be free to explore the human condition and the nature of reality without being constrained by these sensitivities.

I do not use metaphors of Hera and mud to romanticize suffering, but to depict struggle realistically so that we can wage peace more effectively. Despite the widely believed myth that peace is the absence of struggle, embracing struggle is necessary to achieve and maintain peace and progress. That is a fact of reality. Despite the widely believed myth that time can be trusted to heal wounds and solve our problems, having this apathetic attitude toward struggle endangers our communities and entire planet. That is another fact of reality. Despite the widespread tendency to romanticize struggle and ignore its dark side, struggle is also messy, filled with mistakes, painful to many, and not without setbacks. That is also a fact of reality.

In *The Grapes of Wrath*, John Steinbeck says that we should not fear the messy struggle needed to create progress, which he calls the "stumbling-forward ache." Instead, we should fear the day when people no longer embrace struggle. We should fear the day when humanity (which he refers to as "man" and "Manself") will no longer die for an idea. According to Steinbeck, every bomb dropped is proof that the stumbling-forward ache of struggle and progress are alive:

> For man, unlike any other thing organic or inorganic in the universe, grows beyond his work, walks up the stairs of his concepts, emerges ahead of his accomplishments . . . Man reaches, stumbles forward, painfully, mistakenly sometimes. Having stepped forward, he may slip back, but only half a step, never the full step back. This you may say and know it. This you may know when the bombs plummet out of the black planes on the market place, when prisoners are stuck like pigs, when the crushed bodies drain filthily in the dust. You may know it in this way. If the step were not being taken, if the stumbling-forward ache were not alive, the bombs would not fall, the throats would not be cut.
>
> Fear the time when the bombs stop falling while the bombers live—for every bomb is proof that the spirit has not died. And fear the time when the strikes stop while

> the great owners live—for every little beaten strike is proof that the step is being taken. And this you can know—fear the time when Manself will not suffer and die for a concept, for this one quality is the foundation of Manself, and this one quality is man, distinctive in the universe.[19]

Training in the art of living and the art of waging peace can help us survive the stumbling-forward ache of struggle and progress. By exploring the star of training in the next chapter, we will learn how to see struggle as an opportunity, use adversity to become more fully human, and increase our purpose, meaning, empathy, understanding, and gentleness. As humanity stumbles forward painfully on the road to peace, the star of training can help us remain standing and surviving, instead of falling into despair and extinction.

Chapter 2

The Star of Training

Becoming Fully Human

During my childhood I often heard people say, "Sticks and stones may break my bones, but words will never hurt me." In *The Cosmic Ocean* I discuss why words in the form of verbal abuse and bullying can harm our psychological health. This chapter will go a step further by explaining why words can be considered humanity's most dangerous weapon.

Before humans can commit organized violence or oppression, they must first communicate with words. Genocide cannot happen without words that spread hate and irrational fear. State-sanctioned slavery cannot exist without words that justify slavery. Words are also necessary to coordinate the buying, selling, and transport of slaves. People use words when they want to incite the hostility needed for mob violence, and religious fanaticism requires words that teach fanatical points of view. Words can tell us lies, such as "those people are subhuman and born to be slaves," "women are intellectually inferior to men," and "time heals all wounds."

A war between countries cannot happen without words. Adolf Hitler was not physically intimidating. He was not exceptionally strong or tall, nor was he a good fighter. But he was extremely dangerous because of his ability to use words, which allowed him to manipulate millions of people and motivate them to commit violence. I have heard many people fantasize about a time traveler going back in time to 1920 and killing Hitler before he could rise to power. But a time traveler would not have to kill Hitler to stop him from committing atrocities. If a time traveler had technology that could prevent Hitler from using words in any way, then Hitler would have lost his greatest weapon. Without the weapon of words, Hitler would have been practically harmless.

Words also have the power to make an enormous positive difference. Before humans could organize the anti-slavery movement, women's rights movement, civil rights movement, or any movement for justice, they first had to communicate with words.

I learned about the positive difference words can make when I was fifteen years old. Back then a few simple words changed my life, and I don't think I would be alive today if those words had not been spoken to me. After I wrote a short story for an English class, my tenth-grade English teacher, Janice Vaughn, said, "I really liked your story. You should think about being a writer." I had never thought about being a writer before, because I had never liked reading books. But I pondered what she said and realized I had enjoyed writing that story. So I wrote another, and another, and another. I began writing obsessively, and when I went to West Point I spent more time writing than doing my homework.

Even though I did not like reading books as a fifteen-year-old, our society's education system had given me a strong foundation to help me become a writer. At age fifteen I had been learning to write for twelve years, beginning with the alphabet and simple words in preschool. Our society invests significant resources toward helping people become literate and communicate well, because our society recognizes the importance and difficulty of mastering language. If mastering language were easy, then people would be master writers by the time they entered college, but many American high school students still have low reading comprehension and poor writing skills after many years of English classes, and most college students do not communicate nearly as well as professional writers and speakers who have been honing their communication skills for decades.

There are many reasons why high school and college students can have poor communication skills, but the main point I am making is that mastering language is not easy, and this is why our society recognizes the need to invest significant resources to help people master language. Most people are able to master walking by around age five without ever taking a walking class in school, but language is much more complex than walking. In a job interview or college application essay, a good communicator is going to have a major advantage over someone who mangles grammar.

In ancient Greece and Rome, rich people hired tutors to educate their sons in the skillful use of language, because they wanted their sons to have every possible advantage (back then girls were not given the same educational opportunities as boys). King Philip II of Macedon had the famous philosopher Aristotle tutor his son, who later became known as Alexander the Great. But most Americans do not have the resources to educate their children with elite private tutors, instead relying on our society's education system.

It took encouraging words from my teacher, along with dedication on my part, to become a writer. But it also took the training that our society's education system had given me in the art of writing and communication. Imagine if an English teacher had told my ancestor Wyatt Chappell (born a slave in Alabama in 1835) when he was fifteen that he should be a writer. Instead of his society investing significant resources toward literacy for all, his society made it illegal for slaves to learn to read and write. Even if someone had encouraged him to be a writer and it had been legal for him to do so, he would have had to walk a much harder path to become a writer at age fifteen than I did, because at that age I had twelve years of writing training that he did not have.

My society had given me a foundation of literacy, which I built on to harness the power of words, but in other important areas my society had given me no foundation at all. As I explain in *The Cosmic Ocean*, in high school I often fantasized about committing a mass shooting. This was due to extreme childhood trauma that had filled me with homicidal rage. To better understand how pain can breed violence, imagine having the best day of your life. When you are filled with overwhelming joy, you usually don't want to hurt anyone. On the other hand, if you want to murder people who have never done any harm to you, and you even want to murder people who have been kind to you, then you are in a lot of agony.

At age nineteen I made a serious commitment to heal my rage. But the education system had not given me a single hour of training to help me understand the nature of rage. When I realized that I would need to strengthen my empathy, conscience, and sense of purpose to heal my rage,

I realized that the education system had not given me a single hour of training to help me fully develop those qualities. In fact, much of what I learned in school taught me to suppress my empathy and conscience, and to view purpose in the narrow context of accumulating material wealth.

What if the education system had put as much effort toward cultivating my muscle of empathy as it did toward cultivating my muscle of language? What if I had learned as much about rage, conscience, and conflict resolution as I had about grammar, punctuation, and sentence structure? Three thousand years ago, societies did not invest any resources toward universal literacy in reading and writing. Back then probably less than 1 percent of the global human population was literate, compared to around 83 percent of the global population today. Today it would sound absurd for anyone to say our society should not aim for universal literacy. Today we realize that when people are not literate in reading and writing, they are at a severe disadvantage. This is why American slave owners made it illegal to teach slaves to read and write: they wanted their slaves to remain at a severe disadvantage. This is why our society today recognizes that it is a problem when high school students read at an elementary school level.

If humanity is going to survive during our fragile future, we must recognize that although it would be absurd to not teach literacy in reading and writing in schools today, it is just as absurd to not teach peace literacy skills in schools today. Illiteracy in reading and writing puts people at a severe disadvantage, but when people are not literate in peace, this also puts them and our entire planet at a severe disadvantage. Humanity will not be able to solve the global problems that threaten our survival and the health of our planet unless we become peace literate. As I will discuss later in this chapter, peace literacy also reduces the harm caused by the weapon of words, because the more peace literate people become, the more difficult they are to manipulate with words, and the greater their immunity to words that spread hate, irrational fear, and propaganda.

A lack of peace literacy can also put workplaces at a severe disadvantage. Would you rather work for a boss who has peace literacy skills such as the ability to lead through being respectful, listening with empathy, living with integrity, and putting the well-being of the group above selfish interests, or would you rather work for a boss who disrespects you, does not listen to you, lacks integrity, and would throw you under a bus to get ahead? Peace literacy helps us increase peace in our personal lives, relationships, families, workplaces, communities, country, and throughout our world.

Today many people say that it is up to parents to teach empathy. However, many parents are not skilled in empathy, and this skill is too important for the well-being of our country and planet to be left just in the hands of parents. Some children learn good empathy skills from their parents, but many children learn harmful habits from their parents. In a similar way, in the eighteenth century many Americans said it was up to parents to teach English, and that grammar schools should not teach English.* Today American students learn English from preschool through college, and it would sound absurd to say that English should not be taught in American schools today. If English was not being taught in American grammar schools during the eighteenth century, then what was being taught? Historian Carl J. Richard explains:

> The Founding Fathers encountered most of these ancient historians and orators at an early and impressionable age, in grammar school and at college. In fact, the "grammar" in "grammar school" referred to Greek and Latin grammar, not English grammar; the mother tongue was not taught in American grammar schools until after the Revolutionary War, since most eighteenth-century Americans believed that precious school time should be reserved for serious academic subjects like the classical languages, not wasted on knowledge the child could learn at home.[1]

* This does not mean that no schools in early America taught English, but that most people did not view English as something that all children should learn throughout their childhood from an education system. Back then many children did not learn English in school (in fact, many children did not go to school), and some schools might only provide children with a couple of years of English training, unlike our current system that teaches English from preschool through college.

Someone might say that my ability to write this book disproves the need for peace literacy in our education system, because if I could learn peace literacy skills on my own without the help of the education system, then why do we need schools to teach peace literacy? That would be like saying, "Since Frederick Douglass mostly taught himself to read and write, why do we need schools or parents to teach children how to read and write?" At West Point I never heard anyone say, "Alexander the Great learned the art of war without going to a military academy, so let's not give military officers today any formal training."* The truth is that peace literacy is even more complex than literacy in reading and writing, and the art of waging peace is even more complex than the art of waging war, because the art of waging peace confronts the root causes of our problems rather than merely addressing surface symptoms, empowers us to become fully human,** and reshapes our world in the image of justice.

The art of living, one of the seven forms of peace literacy, is the most complex art form, yet most of us are not taught how to live. Just as we must learn any art form, we must also learn how to live. But unlike other art forms, the art of living transforms us into both the sculptor and the sculpture. We are the artist and our life is the masterpiece.[2] As a child I was never taught the art of living. For example, I was never taught how to overcome fear. Wouldn't this be an incredibly useful thing to know? In fact, overcoming fear is one of the most important life skills we can have. Nor was I ever taught how to calm myself and other people down. This is another essential life skill.

As a child I was never taught the many essential life skills that are

* Military schooling for officers goes beyond commissioning sources such as West Point, ROTC (Reserve Officers' Training Corps), and OCS (Officer Candidate School), because there are also schools that lieutenants, captains, and higher-ranking officers must go through. This kind of schooling did not exist during the eras of Alexander the Great and Hannibal, who were arguably two of the greatest military geniuses in history. Even Spartan military training was very limited. During their formal military education, Spartan officers spent many years learning discipline and the combat skills needed on the battlefield, but they did not study strategy, which is considered a necessity for high-ranking military officers today. As Gandhi realized, if peace schooling was taken as seriously as military schooling, our world would be a much different place.

** In *Peaceful Revolution* I discuss what it means to be fully human. This chapter focuses on how training in the form of peace literacy gives us a path to becoming fully human.

part of the art of living. I was never taught how to resolve conflict peacefully, make the most of adversity, listen deeply, focus my mind, inspire people to overcome long-term challenges, lead from a foundation of respect rather than intimidation, develop my full capacity for empathy, be a good friend, have a healthy relationship, challenge injustice, be happy, find purpose and meaning in life, develop my sense of self-awareness so that I could critique myself honestly, and help humanity create a more peaceful and just world.

Some children learn these skills from their parents, but many parents do not know how to listen well or handle conflict without yelling, causing children to learn harmful habits. When people watch cable news, reality shows, and other forms of media entertainment, how often do they see someone who listens well and resolves conflict calmly and respectfully? More people in our society are taught to resolve conflict through aggression than through the power of respect.

Imagine if you watched a basketball game, but nobody on either team had ever been properly taught how to play basketball. It would be a mess. Imagine if you listened to an orchestra play Beethoven's Ninth Symphony, but nobody in the orchestra had been properly taught how to play their instruments. It would also be a mess. Since living is far more complicated than playing basketball or Beethoven, when our society is filled with people who have not been taught the art of living, life becomes a lot messier than it needs to be. Living will always be somewhat messy because it is the most difficult art form, but when we are trained in the art of living we gain the skills to prevent unnecessary conflict, violence, misunderstanding, suffering, and trauma. And we become empowered to solve these and other problems when they arise.

As I mentioned earlier in this book, an oak tree knows how to be an oak tree. It doesn't need a mentor or role model to guide it. A caterpillar knows how to turn into a butterfly and thrive in the world. It doesn't have to attend school or be instructed by its parents. But human beings, more than any other creature on the planet, must learn to be what we are. We must learn to be human. The star of training is a metaphor for the fact that reality causes all species to have a full potential, but achieving our full potential as human beings requires training.

Humanity is not the only species that needs training from its community (many mammals learn survival skills from their parents), but no species requires as much training as we do. Because our brains are so complex and take so long to develop, human children remain helpless longer than the offspring of any other animal, and our brains are like sponges designed to soak up training. The interplay of training involves teaching and learning. Our early ancestors spent many years teaching their children how to speak, make a wide variety of tools, forage for food, hunt, build reliable shelters, make items to protect or decorate their bodies (such as clothes, jewelry, and face paint), perform rituals, use fire, cook food, prepare dead bodies for burial, and much more.

Just as there was a time when brilliant adults in preliterate societies could not teach children how to read, today we live in a society that is largely preliterate in peace, where many brilliant adults are not skilled in the art of waging peace, the art of living, and the ability to perceive our shared humanity. How many adults today know how to resolve conflict peacefully, listen deeply, treat all people with respect, confront the root causes of our problems rather than merely address symptoms, reduce dehumanization in our society, cultivate realistic hope, and have a calm discussion with someone who passionately disagrees with them on a controversial issue? When I say that our society does not train people in the art of living, I am not saying that people don't know how to live at all, but that most people don't know how to live in ways that unlock their full human potential. The art of living means having the skills that empower us to confront the root causes of our problems, become fully human, and increase realistic peace (which is far more than just the absence of war).

In the distant past, literacy in reading was a waterless desert, because there was a time in early human history when no societies had written languages. But in the distant past, literacy in peace was a trickling stream, because the seven forms of peace literacy emanate from our shared humanity, and early figures such as Socrates, Buddha, Lao-tzu, Jesus, many elders of indigenous tribes, and people from various walks of life were able to master aspects of these seven forms.

Today we must turn this trickling stream into a broad river of peace literacy that can nourish our society and the world. The key to accomplish this is training, which is what reality requires of us to achieve our full potential. In the previous chapter I quoted Buddha, who said, "Gray hairs do not make a master. A man may grow old in vain."[3] Training, which we can also call "education," helps us to not grow old in vain by empowering us to become fully human. Education should increase our skills, especially our skill at living. Before Buddha's birth in the sixth century BC, the ancient Greeks also realized that in our quest to unlock our full potential, our skill at living mattered more than having gray hairs.

In Greek mythology, Nestor is a Greek soldier who traveled with Jason and the Argonauts. Many years later when the events in the *Iliad* begin, Nestor has grown older and learned much from his life experiences, becoming an elder regarded as the wisest man in the Greek army. When there is a chariot race toward the end of the *Iliad*, Nestor's son Antilochus is the youngest person to enter the race, and his horses are slower than the others competing. Nestor tells his son that he can win the race, even if the other charioteers are older and possess faster horses. According to Nestor, skill is more important than age and physical prowess. Nestor tells his son that skill matters in all areas of life:

> Antilochus, you are young indeed, but Zeus and Poseidon have loved you and taught you horsemanship in all of its aspects. Therefore there is no great need to instruct you; you yourself know well how to double the turning-post . . . The horses of these men are faster, but they themselves do not understand anymore than you of the science of racing. Remember then, dear son, to have your mind full of every resource of skill, so that the prizes may not elude you. The woodcutter is far better for skill than he is for brute strength. It is by skill that the sea captain holds his rapid ship on its course, though torn by winds, over the wine-blue water. By skill charioteer outpasses charioteer.[4]

The passage of time gives us many opportunities to increase our skill, understanding, and wisdom. If we use our time well, we can grow wiser with age, accumulating a wealth of wisdom not available during our youth. In the *Iliad*, Nestor (who is likely in his seventies) is too old to fight in the front ranks with the younger men. When King Agamemnon, the commander of the Greek army, expresses his regret that Nestor is elderly and no longer in his physical prime, Nestor responds with the attitude that aging can be a blessing. According to the *Iliad*:

> The old soldier [Nestor] spurring his men with skills from a lifetime spent campaigning, battles long ago. And King Agamemnon, thrilled to see his efforts, cheered him on with a flight of praise: "Old war-horse, if only your knees could match the spirit in your chest and your body's strength were planted firm as rock, but the great leveler, age, has worn you down. If only some other fighter had your years and you could march with the younger, fitter men!"
>
> And Nestor the seasoned charioteer replied, "True . . . if only I were the man I was, years ago . . . but the gods won't give us all their gifts at once."[5]

By using his time well, Nestor traded his physical prime for increased wisdom and understanding. By using time to increase his wisdom and understanding, Nestor created a positive purpose out of time's ruthless flow, allowing him to wear the physical signs of time's passage proudly. When we use our time well and create a positive purpose by becoming more peace literate, we can become effective soldiers of peace in humanity's struggle to solve our global problems and create a more peaceful world. In this way, time can become our ally, because the more time that passes, the more peace literate and fully human we can become.

Not enough activists today emphasize the importance of training for creating peace. Activism is perhaps the only endeavor where numerous people believe they can just show up to a protest without any training, write something on a sign, and be effective. Imagine if a group of musicians, martial artists,* or athletes showed up to one of their events without any training. They would not perform anywhere near their potential, and would likely perform poorly. Musicians, martial artists, and athletes know that in order to do well, just showing up is not enough. In a similar way, if we want to create realistic peace, just showing up is also not enough. We must be well trained and highly skilled.

People realize that music, martial arts, and sports are art forms that require training. Therefore, if people want to become competent in any of these arts, they realize they have to get some kind of training. But waging peace is also an art as well as a science, so why wouldn't we also need training? Waging peace is extremely challenging, because it strives to defeat powerful unjust systems, transform how people think about the most controversial issues in the world, and overcome mighty enemies such as hatred and ignorance. The more challenging something is, the more important training becomes.

Today the forces of injustice have far more money and external power than the forces of justice, but thankfully training is the great equalizer. Just as Nestor realized that skill can overcome advantages in age and physical prowess, effective social movements throughout history have shown that skill in waging peace can overcome advantages in money, external power, and even military might (in chapter 4 I will discuss how waging peace can strategically overcome a militarily superior adversary).

West Point taught me that training is the great equalizer, and that training's ability to remove disadvantages applies to all areas of life. Why was Rome, which started out as a small city on the Italian peninsula, able to create one of the largest empires in history? A primary reason is that the Roman military had the best training in the world. To understand how training was the great equalizer in ancient warfare, we must first understand the importance of size and strength in close combat.

* Although martial artists can be considered athletes, many martial arts schools teach that being a martial artist requires more than just being an athlete; it also requires adhering to various ideals of martial arts philosophy.

In ancient warfare where soldiers used spears and swords, size mattered. Physical strength allowed people to wear heavy armor and wield their weapons with greater force, and being tall allowed soldiers to more easily intimidate their adversaries during close combat. Intimidation is a form of psychological warfare. This is why the ancient Greeks wore big helmets that made them appear taller than they really were.

Tragically, child soldiers have become common during the age of rifles and machine guns, but ancient armies did not use child soldiers partly because it would have been impractical. A young teenager can use a lightweight rifle to kill grown men, but children do not have the upper-body strength needed to effectively wield a sword and shield against an armored opponent, let alone carry their own set of heavy armor. A man in his fifties, if he was well trained and in good shape, could wield a bladed weapon with the strength necessary to kill an armored adversary. Leonidas, the famous Spartan king who led three hundred Spartan soldiers and their allies against the Persians during the battle of Thermopylae, died in battle at age sixty.

In the ancient world where size mattered in battle, it is even more surprising that the Romans developed the most powerful army in the world, because the Romans were often physically smaller than their opponents. Commenting on his military campaign in Gaul (a region that included modern-day France), Julius Caesar said, "All the Gauls are inclined to be contemptuous of our short stature, contrasting it with their own great height."[6]

Describing how a Germanic tribe called the Atuatuci looked down on the Romans because of their short stature, Caesar recounted how the Atuatuci reacted when they saw the Romans setting up a siege tower to overtake the Atuatuci's defensive fortress wall: "When [the Romans] began to erect a siege tower at some distance, the [Atuatuci] defenders on the wall at first made abusive remarks and ridiculed the idea of setting up such a huge apparatus so far away. Did those pygmy Romans, [the Atuatuci] asked, with their feeble hands and muscles, imagine that they could mount such a heavy tower on top of a wall?"[7]

Why were the Romans able to conquer so many nations? As I already mentioned, a primary reason is that they had the best military training in the world. Caesar described how the Atuatuci reacted when the well-trained and highly skilled Romans quickly moved their siege tower toward the Atuatuci's defensive fortress wall: "But when [the Atuatuci] saw the tower in motion and approaching the fortress walls, the strange, unfamiliar spectacle frightened them into sending envoys to ask Caesar for peace. The envoys said they were forced to the conclusion that the Romans had divine aid in their warlike operations, since they could move up apparatus of such height at such a speed."[8]

Roman military historian Vegetius, who lived during the latter period of the Roman Empire, described how training allowed his people to create a massive empire during an era when size mattered. As Vegetius explained, training was a key factor that allowed the Romans to conquer adversaries who were superior in size, physical strength, numbers, resources, and other advantages:

> We find that the Romans owed the conquest of the world to no other cause than continual military training, exact observance of discipline in their camps and unwearied cultivation of the other arts of war. Without these, what chance would the inconsiderable numbers of the Roman armies have had against the multitudes of the Gauls? Or with what success would their small size have been opposed to the prodigious stature of the Germans? The Spaniards surpassed us not only in numbers, but in physical strength. We were always inferior to the Africans in wealth and unequal to them in deception and strategy. And the Greeks, indisputably, were far superior to us in skill in arts and all kinds of knowledge.[9]

Training is a great equalizer that makes up for a certain degree of disadvantage, but it is not a magic bullet that makes up for *any amount* of disadvantage. For example, a ten-year-old child with martial arts training is not going to win a fight against a massive NFL player who lacks martial arts training. In addition to having excellent training, the Romans also possessed their own territory, a population large enough for substantial military recruitment, a high degree of resourcefulness, and superior military equipment. A Roman army could have the best training in the world, but if that army lacked military equipment and supplies, they would have been easily defeated in battle.

In a similar way, soldiers of peace can have excellent training, but they also require other ingredients to be successful. If soldiers of peace do not combine the star of training with the star of truth and the star of strategy (which we will explore in the next two chapters of this book), they will not be able to wield the weapon of nonviolence with maximum force. When we embrace struggle, training, truth, and strategy, we can defeat the largest unjust systems in the world.

Gandhi realized that realistic peace is rare in our world because those who serve evil recognize that training is needed to accomplish one's goals, but those who serve good often do not. Gandhi also realized that if we want to create lasting peace and justice, we should train to wage peace as seriously as successful militaries throughout history (such as the Romans) trained to wage war.

Yet, again, the myth that peace is the absence of struggle deceives us, because training does not seem necessary if peace is the absence of struggle. But soldiers know that struggle is an inseparable part of war, so they dedicate a lot of time to the training that enables them to overcome significant struggle. In a similar way, Gandhi, Martin Luther King Jr., and other effective peacemakers knew that struggle is an inseparable part of creating realistic peace, so they understood the importance of training to overcome the many obstacles that block the path to peace. If our society recognized the necessity of peace literacy for human survival, healthy democratic systems, and protecting the health of our planet, we could begin taking the practical steps that would allow us to train people as effectively in peace, democracy, and human survival as the Romans trained their citizens in waging war.

Like the Romans, the Nazis also succeeded in war partly because of their exceptional training. In 1940 Gandhi realized that if activists became as committed to training themselves in waging peace as the Nazis were to training themselves in waging war, realistic peace would become far more common throughout our world. Gandhi thought Hitler's actions were terrible, but

Gandhi was very practical and not naive. He realized Hitler was succeeding largely because he possessed the kind of focus that helps people accomplish challenging goals, the kind of focus that many activists lacked. Frustrated that most activists did not approach waging peace with the same focus, discipline, and dedication as Hitler approached waging war, Gandhi said:

> We have to live and move and have our being in ahimsa [nonviolence], even as Hitler does in himsa [violence]. It is the faith and perseverance and single-mindedness with which he has perfected his weapons of destruction that commands my admiration. That he uses them as a monster is immaterial for our purpose. We have to bring to bear the same single-mindedness and perseverance in evolving our ahimsa. Hitler is awake all the 24 hours of the day in perfecting his sadhana [method]. He wins because he pays the price. His inventions surprise his enemies. But it is his single-minded devotion to his purpose that should be the object of our admiration and emulation . . . A mere belief in ahimsa . . . will not do.[10]

When Gandhi said a mere belief in nonviolence would not do, he acknowledged that if we want to create a better world, good intentions are not enough. Gandhi realized that people also need training and skills to effectively wage peace. If good intentions were enough, then world peace would have happened a long time ago. Recognizing that good intentions without deep understanding and skill often causes more harm than good, an old adage tells us, "The road to hell is paved with good intentions."

Many people in our society romanticize peace as a mere belief, when peace is actually an art and a science that requires training, skills, deep understanding, and effort. This romanticized view of peace misleads people with the illusion that peace will happen if enough people simply believe. But realistic peace requires far more than just belief. Realistic peace also requires the stars of struggle, training, truth, and strategy. Romanticizing peace as a mere belief is one of the greatest dangers to realistic peace. In a world where human survival depends on people doing the hard work necessary to create and sustain realistic peace, romanticizing peace as a mere belief paves the road to hell.

When I say that our society is preliterate in peace, I am not saying that most people do not have good intentions or do not want peace. Instead, being preliterate in peace means that most people in our society do not have the skills to confront the root causes of our problems, become fully human, and increase realistic peace. A peace literate society creates new possibilities for humanity's future that many people today cannot even imagine.

Another old adage tells us, "Don't throw the baby out with the bath water." Should a person who opposes war also reject courage, discipline, strategic thinking, and training, just because soldiers realize that embracing these strengths is needed to overcome significant struggle? Many effective nonviolent movements in history have understood the importance of courage, discipline, strategic thinking, and training. James Lawson, whom Martin Luther King Jr. called "the leading theorist and strategist of nonviolence in the world," said, "The difficulty with nonviolent people and efforts is that they don't recognize the necessity of fierce discipline, and training, and strategizing, and planning, and recruiting."[11]

Today more and more activists are realizing the importance of training. How often do you see basketball players compete in a tournament or musicians play in a concert without training themselves through practice? When human survival is at stake, shouldn't training in waging peace be even more important? The forces of injustice are so powerful, and the dangers confronting humanity and our planet are so severe, that we cannot afford to neglect training. People working for peace and justice are struggling against systems that possess immense amounts of money and external power, and one of the few things we can control is how strategic, disciplined, determined, creative, and well-trained we are.

If we meet activists who belittle the importance of training, we should have empathy for them by realizing that their attitude reflects a larger cultural problem in our society. Our society not only promotes the myth that peace is the absence of struggle, but our society also conditions us to look for quick fixes and easy answers. Training is anything but quick and easy. It requires hard work. To show how practical this hard work is for improving our lives, I will discuss an art where training is essential today, an art that is also becoming more and more neglected in the twenty-first century—the art of listening.

The Art of Listening

To wage peace well and live well, I first had to learn how to listen well. One thing most people can agree on is that our world would be much better off if more people knew how to listen well. In any kind of conflict, whether within a friendship, family, relationship, or workplace, I don't think anyone has ever cited good listening as the cause.* I don't think anyone in human history has ever seriously said, "The reason I am so angry is because when I was speaking to him, he was listening to me." On the contrary, most people cite *not being listened to* as a major reason why they get angry, feel disrespected, and have conflict. The art of listening not only empowers us to resolve conflict and better understand the pain and aggression in others, but to also better understand the pain and aggression within ourselves.

As the following diagram shows, the art of listening is an essential component within the art of waging peace, which are both essential components within the larger art of living. If we cannot listen well, we cannot wage peace well. And if we cannot listen well and wage peace well, we cannot live in ways that empower us to confront the root causes of our problems, become fully human, and increase realistic peace. Because of the modern global problems that threaten human survival, if we do not learn to listen well and wage peace well, our species will descend toward extinction, preventing humanity from living at all.

* Obviously, eavesdropping (which occurs when someone tries to hear us against our wishes) can cause conflict, but when we intend to communicate with someone in particular, that person's intent to listen to us is not seen as disrespectful. Eavesdropping is of course different from listening, because listening implies consent, whereas eavesdropping implies lack of consent.

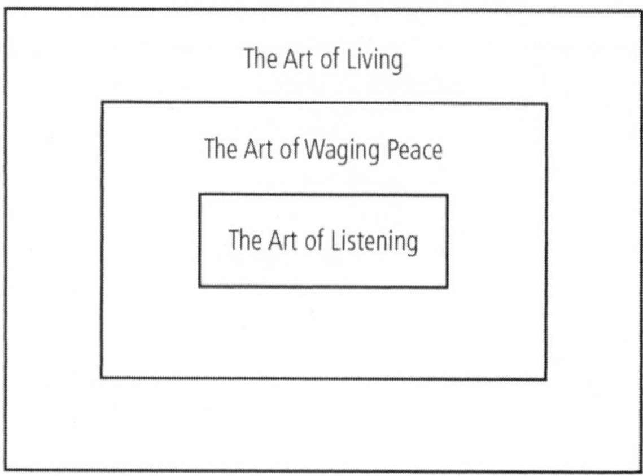

Figure 2.1: The Arts of Listening, Waging Peace, and Living

Listening is so vital to a healthy human community that every culture in history has viewed listening as respectful and not listening as disrespectful.* In fact, all people like to be listened to. In all of human history, I don't think anyone has ever seriously said, "I hate it when people listen to me!" I don't think anyone has ever complained, "My spouse and I need to go to marriage counseling, because my spouse listens to me all the time and I can't stand it anymore!"

The first step to listening is empathy. To *truly* listen to others, we must develop empathy. If we do not empathize with people we cannot really hear what they are saying. When we do not listen with empathy we hear only their words. But when we listen with empathy we also hear their emotions, hopes, and fears. We hear their humanity.

When we do not listen with empathy our conversations often become barriers that alienate us from the humanity of others. But when we listen with empathy our conversations become bridges that connect their humanity

* "Conditioned inequality" (which I discuss in *Peaceful Revolution*) can create the illusion that some people are inferior and should not be listened to. In the next chapter we will discuss how waging peace has expanded our perception of who should be listened to in a society. Male citizens in ancient Athens certainly believed that male citizens should be listened to, but most of them did not believe that women and slaves should be listened to.

to ours. The art of listening is an essential life skill that can improve our friendships, relationships, and daily interactions with all kinds of people.

To listen with empathy, we must perceive what is beneath the shallow surface. For example, aggression is always the symptom of a deeper emotion. Aggression is like the scorching heat emitted from a fire. Empathy allows us to perceive the underlying fires that cause aggression, rather than focusing merely on the surface symptom of heat. Empathy gives us a deep perception that allows us to understand the root causes of people's behavior.

What kinds of fires (emotions) can cause the heat of human aggression? One fire that can cause human aggression is fear. If I use the deep perception of empathy to understand that someone is behaving aggressively because of underlying fear, then I can have more empathy for this person. It is easier to have empathy for someone we perceive as afraid, rather than someone we perceive as an "aggressive jerk."

By using the deep perception of empathy to see the underlying fear beneath the shallow surface of aggression, I can also become more effective at peacefully resolving an aggressive situation by asking myself, "Why is this person afraid? What can I do to help reduce this person's fear?" By confronting the underlying fire (the cause rather than the symptom), we can reduce the heat of people's aggression and interact with them in a more productive way.

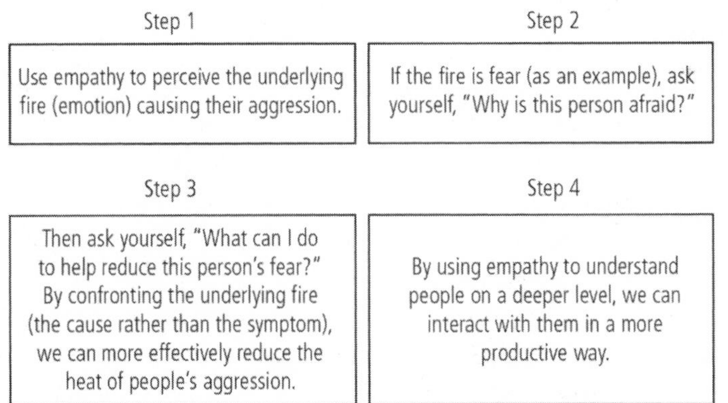

Figure 2.2: Four Steps for Reducing the Heat of Aggression

Aggression can be caused by other underlying fires (emotions), and also by a combination of various fires. What are some other fires that can cause the heat of human aggression? As I explain in *The Art of Waging Peace,* the most common cause of human aggression is feeling disrespected. Take a moment to ponder the times when someone most angered you, and feeling disrespected probably had a lot to do with it. Disrespect is the feeling that another human being has violated us in some way. We can feel disrespected when we feel betrayed, humiliated, ignored, gossiped about, judged, insulted, not listened to, stereotyped, looked down on, and dehumanized, just to mention a few examples.

In *The Art of Waging Peace* I spend several chapters discussing the power and anatomy of respect. I call this power the *infinite shield,* because respect is a force that increases safety in any community. When we treat people with a kind of gentleness built on the force of respect, we increase trust and help prevent the most common cause of conflict: disrespect.

Why does martial arts philosophy teach us to always respect everyone, including our opponents? The reason is that the majority of human conflict comes from people just feeling disrespected. Martial arts philosophy teaches that the best self-defense is not being skilled at punching or kicking, but being skilled at conveying respect. If we are skilled at conveying respect, we not only reduce unnecessary conflict in our lives, but when we do have conflict (which will happen eventually), we dramatically improve our ability to resolve it.

One reason disrespect causes so much conflict is that human beings are very sensitive and vulnerable creatures. You might see a big, muscular, macho guy who has a lot of tattoos and think he is not sensitive, but go up to him and say something bad about his mother, or call him stupid to his face, or spit on him, and see how he reacts. Obviously, don't actually do that! The point I am trying to make is that people are more sensitive and vulnerable than we often admit. Men and women all over the world are very sensitive and vulnerable to feeling disrespected, and in *The Art of Waging Peace* I discuss the three elements of universal respect that all cultures have in common (listening, not being hypocritical, and speaking to people's potential) versus the forms of disrespect that can subjectively change from culture to culture.

After one of my lectures, a teacher asked me, "Every couple of years I get a male student in my class who is extra aggressive. Do you think these students have a gene that causes them to be extra aggressive?" I said, "On the surface it might seem like these children are extra aggressive, but if we look deeper, we can see that they are actually extra sensitive. Their feelings are hurt easily, and our society conditions boys and men to display their pain through acts of aggression. People express aggression because they are feeling uncomfortable emotions, and aggression is a way of communicating the discomfort they are feeling. So children who seem extra aggressive are actually feeling discomfort, and are not skilled in more productive ways to express this discomfort."

During an interview for HBO *Real Sports*, Mike Tyson discussed how his extra aggression is a symptom of the extra sensitivity that resulted from the trauma of being severely bullied as a child. The interviewer asked, "You think you still have the potential to be, forgive me, crazy Mike Tyson, if you got into the wrong company?" Tyson responded, "Absolutely, a hundred percent. I'll be too sensitive. I'll think someone's picking at me or making fun of me, and I'll get sensitive probably . . . I still have that baggage of a little kid being picked on. I still have that baggage. I haven't gotten rid of that yet. So a person can just be looking at me and say, 'Oh that's Mike Tyson,' and I might be offensive. I might think he's laughing at me."[12]

The army taught me that if there is a problem with a person or military unit, to understand what went wrong, where is the first place we should look? The first place we should look is their training. We can gain deeper understanding by applying this army principle to our broader society when there are problems with a person or a group of people. What kind of training did they get in their home, during their time in school, and from the messages they heard throughout our society that pushed them in this direction? This army principle does not mean that people are not held accountable for their actions, but this principle does help us better understand the causes of problems, which allows us to provide more effective solutions.

To apply this army principle to myself, the extreme childhood trauma I experienced led to many behavioral problems during my childhood. I was kicked out of elementary school for fighting, almost kicked out of middle school, and suspended in high school for fighting. Something I distinctly remember is that when I had trouble paying attention in class or acted out aggressively, my teachers would often become angry and yell at me. When I reflect on this today, the thought of an adult getting angry at a small child suffering from trauma seems very odd, but some teachers (who might be feeling pain because of their own problems) seemed to take everything personally. They did not see me as a child in pain, but seemed to imagine that I had woken up in the morning with the goal of making their life difficult. This does not mean that every child with behavioral problems is suffering from the same level of extreme trauma as I was, but recognizing that aggression is caused by some form of discomfort can give us a more realistic understanding of what a child is going through, rather than taking the child's aggression personally.

Today there is a common misconception that people in the modern world are more sensitive and thin skinned than people in the past, but this is not necessarily true. People throughout history have been very sensitive to disrespect. If you disrespect people today they might respond with a rude comment, but if you disrespected a samurai in medieval Japan, a European aristocrat during the Renaissance, or an American during the Revolutionary War era, the person might challenge you to a life-threatening duel, because of the cultural expectation that a man must risk his life to defend his honor. The samurai were far more sensitive to disrespect than many people living today.

Even warriors in the ancient world were very sensitive to disrespect. In the *Iliad*, the Greek soldier known as Little Ajax got into an argument with one of his comrades named Idomeneus because of disrespect. If Achilles had not quickly intervened to break them up, their aggression might have escalated into a fight. Idomeneus insulted Little Ajax by saying, "Ajax [is] stupid too, first and last the worst man in the Argive armies—stubborn, bullnecked fool."[13]

Homer describes what happened next:

> So [Idomeneus] spoke, and swift Ajax, son of Oileus,
> was rising up, angry in turn, to trade hard words with him.
> And now the quarrel between the two of them would have

> gone still further, had not Achilles himself risen up and spoken between them: "No longer now, Ajax and Idomeneus, continue to exchange this bitter and evil talk. It is not becoming. If another acted so, you yourselves would be angry."[14]

I am using examples of conflict from the *Iliad*, which is nearly three thousand years old, to show how timeless the human condition is. By revealing aspects of the human condition that transcend time and culture, the *Iliad* shows that disrespect angered people three thousand years ago in ancient Greece, just as it does today in every society around the world. Similar to the way Idomeneus insulted Little Ajax, if someone called you stupid to your face in front of your colleagues (which can be humiliating) and said you were the worst person in your organization, wouldn't this probably offend you, regardless of whether you are a man or woman?

Unless you have worked on developing your sense of inner peace, then being disrespected like this would probably make you angry. Even if you have developed your sense of inner peace, being disrespected can still be painful, but the deep empathy of inner peace allows us to interpret the event differently. Rather than focusing on the surface heat of people's aggression, empathy allows us to perceive the underlying fire beneath their aggression.

The *Iliad* also shows that people three thousand years ago did not like having their intelligence insulted. This is a timeless aspect of the human condition that is still true in cultures around the world today. When I taught a Peace Leadership workshop in Uganda, one of the participants said that his young nephew had many aggression problems throughout his adolescence. When someone finally asked him why he was so angry all of the time, he said that when he was around six years old, one of the adults in his family said that his head was filled with porridge (suggesting he was stupid), and the other adults who overheard this started laughing. The participant said that his nephew was not able to get over this negative perception of himself, and when he became frustrated he tended to lash out aggressively.

Idomeneus insulted Little Ajax because he thought Little Ajax had insulted him first, but it was more of a misunderstanding. If Little Ajax had used empathy to perceive the underlying fire of feeling disrespected that caused the heat of Idomeneus's aggression, Little Ajax could have used steps 2 and 3 in the Four Steps for Reducing the Heat of Aggression diagram by asking himself, "Why does Idomeneus feel disrespected? Did I do something to disrespect him? What can I do to help him feel respected again?" These empathetic questions give us a deeper perception into reality, which prevents unnecessary conflicts and helps us resolve existing conflicts. Unlike Little Ajax during this conflict, other characters in the *Iliad* seem better able to harness and benefit from the deep perception of empathy.

The following story from the *Iliad* shows an example of a character using empathy to see the underlying fire beneath the heat of someone's aggression. Earlier I discussed the Greek elder Nestor giving his son Antilochus advice on winning a chariot race. During the race Antilochus uses an aggressive technique that some consider a dirty trick to beat Menelaus, an older soldier and king of Sparta who is the brother of King Agamemnon. Menelaus feels disrespected because he believes he has been cheated, and he also feels humiliated because he lost to Antilochus's slower horses and the spectators could not see that Antilochus used a dirty trick. This makes Menelaus very angry. If you believed someone cheated you and caused you public humiliation, wouldn't this probably make you angry? Homer describes the incident that occurred during the chariot race:

> Antilochus saw the narrow place where the road washed out—a sharp dip in the land where massing winter rains broke off the edge, making it all one sunken rut. There [Menelaus] was heading—no room for two abreast—but Antilochus swerved to pass him, lashing his horses off the track then swerving into him neck-and-neck and [Menelaus], frightened, yelled out at the man, "Antilochus—you drive like a maniac! Hold your horses! The track's too narrow here—it widens soon for passing—watch out—you'll crash your chariot, wreck us both!"
>
> So he cried but Antilochus drove on all the wilder,

> cracking his lash for more speed like a man stone deaf . . . So far they raced dead even . . . [But then Menelaus dropped back because] he feared the massive teams would collide on the track . . . As his rival [Antilochus] passed the red-haired captain [Menelaus] cursed him: "Antilochus—no one alive more treacherous than you! Away with you, madman—damn you!" . . .
>
> [After the race] Menelaus rose, his heart smoldering, still holding a stubborn grudge against Antilochus . . . and with all his royal weight [Menelaus] thundered, "Antilochus—you used to have good sense! Now see what you've done! Disgraced my horsemanship—you've fouled my horses, cutting before me, you with your far slower team."[15]

Antilochus responds by apologizing very respectfully, which calms Menelaus down. This also allows Menelaus to see that Antilochus's aggression during the race was caused by the underlying fire of youthful recklessness that desired to win at all costs and please his father, Nestor. Homer describes how Menelaus uses empathy to perceive Antilochus on a deep level immediately after the apology:

> And his heart melted now like the dew that wets the corn when the fresh stalks rise up and the ripe fields ripple—so the heart in your chest was melted now, Menelaus, and you gave your friend an answer, winged words: "Antilochus, now it is my turn to yield to you, for all my mounting anger . . . you who were never wild or reckless in the past. It's only youth that got the better of your discretion, just this once—but the next time be more careful. Try to refrain from cheating your superiors."[16]

When Antilochus offers the prize he received from the race to Menelaus as a form of apology, Menelaus lets him keep the prize. Menelaus says he does this "so our people here will know the heart inside me is never rigid, unrelenting."[17] I am using examples of conflict from the *Iliad* to not only show how timeless the human condition is, but to also show the importance of knowing how to peacefully resolve conflict. This knowledge is useful not only for people in nonviolent movements, but also for people in the military. People from all walks of life can benefit from knowing how to peacefully resolve conflict with friends, family, coworkers, and strangers.

As the *Iliad* shows and my own experiences in the military confirm, knowing how to peacefully resolve conflict has so many practical applications that it is especially useful in the military. In fact, I learned some very effective peaceful conflict resolution techniques while serving in the military. It might seem absurd that soldiers should know how to peacefully resolve conflict, but think about this from a practical perspective. Consider how dangerous conflict can be when you are part of a group where everyone has a weapon and is also a trained killer. If a military commander disrespects his soldiers by bullying or humiliating them, they might shoot him in the back. Commenting on World War I, General Douglas MacArthur said, "There were officers overseas shot in the back by their own men simply because they had been brought up with the mistaken idea that bullying was leadership."[18]

Paradoxically, when a group has a lot of weapons, is well trained at killing people, and must endure severe stress, then peaceful conflict resolution can be even more necessary within that group. In the *Iliad*, King Agamemnon nearly destroyed his army of Greek allies by disrespecting Achilles, who reacted by seriously considering killing Agamemnon. Achilles then broke away from his community of comrades by refusing to fight, which caused such heavy losses to the Greek army that Agamemnon practically begged Achilles to return to battle. The Greek army was nearly annihilated, all because of disrespect.

At West Point I learned that the most effective military commanders lead their soldiers by respecting rather than degrading them. Every freshman at West Point has to memorize a passage from a speech Major General John M. Schofield gave there in 1879. The passage, which explains the practical value of respect, reads: "The discipline which makes the soldiers of a free country reliable in battle is not to be gained by harsh or tyrannical treatment.

On the contrary, such treatment is far more likely to destroy than to make an army . . . He who feels the respect which is due to others cannot fail to inspire in them regard for himself, while he who feels, and hence manifests, disrespect toward others, especially his inferiors, cannot fail to inspire hatred against himself."[19]

In many cultures throughout history, people sometimes dueled when they felt disrespected, because disrespect attacks our sense of self-worth, and it is not uncommon for people to risk their lives to protect their self-worth. Today feeling disrespected is a common cause of assault and murder. Many incidents of gang violence occur because someone feels "dissed" (disrespected). As a result, knowing how to respect people, in the form of the three elements of universal respect that I discuss in *The Art of Waging Peace*, is not about being politically correct. My experiences in the military and training in martial arts have taught me that respect can be a matter of life and death.*

Developing the skills to confront the root causes of aggression is an urgent matter today, because acts of physical aggression are increasing even among women. In his book *Female Serial Killers*, Peter Vronsky says, "Aggression in females slips below the radar because they tend to express early aggression through social and verbal forms. Today few would deny that girls commit physical bullying: Schoolgirl bullies are a huge juvenile issue these days. In the past, females tended to first use gossip and social exclusion as a form of aggression among their peers, but today that expression is frequently a prelude to conventional physical violence."[20]

In addition to fear and feeling disrespected, what are other underlying fires that can cause the heat of human aggression? Frustration is another fire that can cause aggression. Have you ever been frustrated and wanted to yell

* In *The Art of Waging Peace* I show how the three elements of universal respect—listening, not being hypocritical, and speaking to people's potential—promote human survival in any community, from a small tribe to our global community. The discomfort that people feel from being disrespected in these three ways—not being listened to, being affected by hypocritical behavior, being talked down to as if we were worthless—can actually be a good thing, because it can compel us to discourage the behavior that threatens human survival. Of course, we have to know the appropriate time to be listened to. If a married couple is having dinner at a restaurant, I should not sit down next to them and demand that they listen to me talk. If someone else is giving a lecture, I should not start yelling and demand that the audience listen to me, when they are there to listen to the person giving the lecture.

or hit something? Have you ever been frustrated with your computer or cell phone and wanted to throw it across the room? Other fires that can cause human aggression include feeling insecure, humiliated, and betrayed.

Guilt is also an underlying fire that can cause the heat of human aggression. How can guilt cause aggression? Martin Luther King Jr. tells us, "So often people respond to guilt by engaging more in the guilt-evoking act in an attempt to drown the sense of guilt."[21]

To explore what King means, we must first recognize that the underlying fires that cause the heat of human aggression are comprised of uncomfortable emotions. Because guilt is a painful emotion, when we feel guilty we often respond in one of two ways. First, we can try to behave more conscientiously in order to remove the root cause of our guilt. Or second, we can become aggressive and try to punish a person for making us feel guilty, because we perceive the person as causing us pain.* During the civil rights movement, Martin Luther King Jr. saw advocates of segregation react in both ways.

Trauma is also an underlying fire that can cause the heat of human aggression. Because of trauma, adults can react aggressively today because of something that happened to them when they were children. As a source of aggression, trauma can resemble a fiery explosion that causes people to easily erupt in violent rage. The reason I have devoted so much time to developing my empathy is that extreme childhood trauma has given me a high capacity for rage. When I was nineteen I realized that my desire to murder people was getting so out of control that I needed to find a way to protect people from my rage. Strengthening my empathy, finding a positive purpose in life, and increasing my understanding are some of the effective medicines that have helped me soothe my rage.

The vast majority of incidents where people feel disrespected do not result in assault or murder. If someone wants to murder you simply because you behaved disrespectfully, the fire of feeling disrespected has probably combined with other fires, such as the fire of humiliation, betrayal, or trauma,

* There are other ways we can respond to guilt, such as rationalizing our actions in an attempt to suppress the sense of guilt.

resulting in a much larger inferno. In *The Art of Waging Peace* I discuss how humiliation, betrayal, and trauma can cause *berserker rage*. If you disrespect people by betraying or humiliating them, and on top of that they also have severe childhood trauma, do not be surprised if those fires combine into an inferno and the people you disrespect try to hurt or kill you. Again, knowing how to respect people is not about being politically correct, but reducing one of the root causes of violence in our society.

In *The End of War* I describe aggression as freezing cold, but in this chapter I am describing aggression as burning heat. This is not a contradiction, because the causes of aggression, like hell in *Dante's Inferno*, can be described with metaphors of both ice and fire. Just as Dante's depiction of hell contains both "frozen rain" and "burning sands," aggression can be caused by a cold heart and the fire of rage. The warmth of empathy can restore balance by melting the ice and cooling the fire.

The following diagram lists some of the underlying fires that can cause the heat of human aggression. These fires can also combine to create an inferno. This is not a complete list, and I encourage you to ponder what other fires can be added to this list. Having a list of specific words to describe different emotions is much more useful than describing every uncomfortable emotion we experience with the generic word "anger." When people say they are "angry," they are usually describing the surface symptom of aggression, rather than the emotion underneath. Anger can be a useful synonym for aggression, while rage is an extreme form of anger (aggression) that cares more about hurting someone than personal safety. The following list shows some of the underlying fires that can cause the surface heat of anger and rage.*

* When I teach workshops on this subject, people sometimes wonder why I do not add "greed" to this list. But what if greed, like aggression, is also the symptom of much deeper problems? What if greed is also a kind of surface heat caused by various underlying problems? In *The End of War* and *The Cosmic Ocean* I discuss some of the underlying problems that can cause greed, such as a distorted value system (represented by the allegory of Plato's Cave), lack of appreciation, and unsatisfied hunger for purpose, meaning, self-worth, and transcendence.

Fear
Disrespect
Frustration
Insecurity
Humiliation
Betrayal
Shame
Confusion
Guilt
Physical Discomfort
Trauma
Loneliness
Alienation
Low Self-Worth
Disappointment
Despair
Lack of Meaning
Rejection
Our Loved Ones in Danger

Figure 2.3: Some of the Fires That Can Cause Human Aggression

The fires that cause aggression are invisible to our eyes, but they can be seen with the metaphorical eye of empathy. We must learn to see with the eye of empathy so that we can perceive the underlying fires that cause the heat of human aggression. This can create a positive feedback loop, because the more we see with the eye of empathy, the more understanding we gain, and the more understanding we gain, the better we can see with the eye of empathy.

When we perceive the reality beneath the heat of human aggression and understand that a person behaving aggressively is actually afraid, frustrated, humiliated, or reliving childhood trauma, it is much easier to have empathy for the person. This does not excuse people's behavior, and this certainly does not mean that we don't hold people accountable for their actions. Instead, the eye of empathy empowers us with a deep perception that makes us more effective at confronting and healing the root causes of conflict, aggression, and violence.

As a result, the eye of empathy allows us to see that aggression is a distress response caused by some form of underlying pain. Aggression is an expression of pain.* We and those around us benefit when we train ourselves to see aggression as a distress response, and when we also train ourselves to see the underlying causes of people's distress. Peace literacy gives us essential life skills that help us heal the underlying causes of people's distress and confront their distress responses more effectively.

Empathy does not mean that we let people use us as a doormat or that we submit to injustice. Instead, empathy is a skill that allows us to confront the underlying causes of people's pain and the attitudes that sustain injustice. People who have enormous empathy such as Gandhi and Martin Luther King Jr. are often the most intolerant of injustice, and they also have the skills to confront the root causes of our human problems rather than merely addressing surface symptoms.

How do we increase our empathy for people? In *Peaceful Revolution* I have an entire chapter on the muscle of empathy, and in *The Cosmic Ocean* I discuss how I developed radical empathy. The first step on the path to strengthening our empathy for all of humanity is becoming literate in our shared humanity. All of my books express many examples of our shared humanity that we can study and internalize.

So far I have discussed that the first step in the art of listening is empathy. The second step in the art of listening is concentration, because without concentration, we lack the focus necessary to become deeply connected to others. Concentration protects us from the many distractions that disrupt our ability to connect deeply with others, ourselves, our surroundings, and the universe itself.

* Many people use the word "aggression" to describe what we can also call "passion" or "motivation," which does not always result from pain. When I say that "aggression is an expression of pain," I am referring to two kinds of aggression that I define in my other books. In *The End of War* and *The Cosmic Ocean* I distinguish between *warning aggression* (that tries to prevent violence) and *hostile aggression* (that tries to inflict harm), which result from fear and other uncomfortable emotions. When people try to prevent violence by inflicting harm (an example is the Roman Empire's use of crucifixion to deter rebels from revolting), they are combining warning and hostile aggression.

In *Peaceful Revolution* I describe empathy and discipline as metaphorical muscles. Concentration is a vein in the muscle of discipline. Like the veins in an athlete's arm, which become more visible when the athlete's biceps flex and grow, the stronger the muscle of discipline becomes, the more prominent its veins will be. To master the art of listening, we must strengthen our muscles of empathy and discipline.

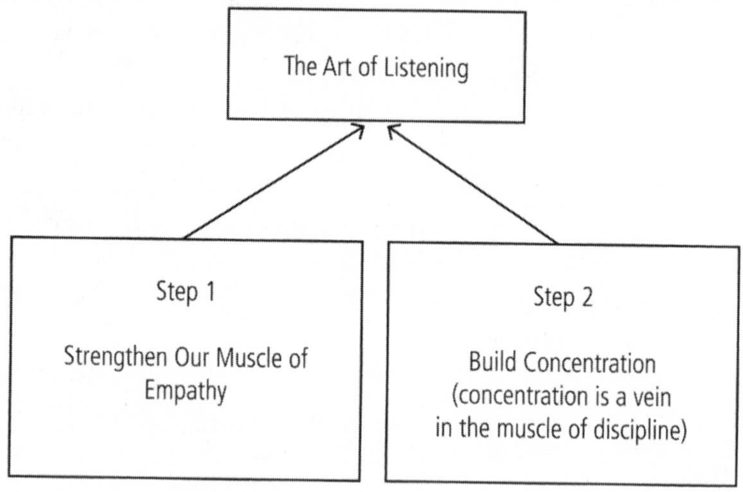

Figure 2.4: The Art of Listening

Building concentration by strengthening our muscle of discipline is necessary to do anything in life to the best of our ability. Psychologist Erich Fromm explains the importance of discipline and concentration for cultivating our unconditional love (a higher expression of empathy) and practicing any art form:

> The practice of any art has certain general requirements, quite regardless of whether we deal with the art of carpentry, medicine, or the art of love. First of all, the practice of an art requires *discipline.* I shall never be good at anything if I do not do it in a disciplined way; anything I do only if "I am in the mood" may be a nice or amusing

> hobby, but I shall never become a master in that art. But the problem is not only that of discipline in the practice of the particular art (say practicing every day a certain amount of hours) but it is that of discipline in one's whole life . . .
>
> In the battle against authoritarianism . . . [people have] become distrustful of all discipline, of that enforced by irrational authority, as well as of rational discipline imposed by [ourselves] . . . Without such discipline, however, life becomes shattered, chaotic, and lacks in concentration.
>
> That *concentration* is a necessary condition for the mastery of an art is hardly necessary to prove. Anyone who ever tried to learn an art knows this. Yet, even more than self-discipline, concentration is rare in our culture. On the contrary, our culture leads to an unconcentrated and diffused mode of life, hardly paralleled anywhere else. You do many things at once; you read, listen to the radio, talk, smoke, eat, drink. You are the consumer with the open mouth, eager and ready to swallow everything—pictures, liquor, knowledge. This lack of concentration is clearly shown in our difficulty in being alone with ourselves. To sit still, without talking, smoking, reading, drinking, is impossible for most people. They become nervous and fidgety, and must do something with their mouth or their hands.[22]

When we concentrate deeply, we transcend our sense of time and become fully absorbed in the present moment. To improve our ability to concentrate, we can exercise our muscle of discipline by focusing our mind on an activity. These *discipline exercises* can take many forms. Buddhists often use Eastern meditation, Catholics can use the rosary to focus their minds and build concentration, and musicians can gain concentration through rigorous practice. You can also build concentration by intently focusing your mind while running, cleaning your home, lifting weights, reading, stretching, cooking, gardening, or sitting quietly and being mindful of your breathing. There are many ways to build concentration.

Some people reading this may think the art of listening sounds great in theory, but is not practical for everyday life. Someone might ask, "What about those people who keep talking nonstop? They just chatter endlessly and don't listen to anything you have to say. If I listened to those people, they would take up so much of my time that I wouldn't be able to get anything done."

That is exactly why our society needs greater literacy in the art of listening: because there are many people who talk a lot and don't listen. Listening with empathy and concentration is about improving the *quality* of our listening. Like most things in life, quality is more important than quantity. None of us can spend all day listening to people, because we have other responsibilities in life, plus we have to sleep, and sometimes we might feel drained and not have the energy needed to listen to the best of our ability. But if we improve the *quality* of our listening, and if more people learn how to listen with empathy and concentration, this would make us much more effective at resolving conflict and healing the root causes of our human problems.

To show how practical the art of listening really is, ask yourself these questions. When *you* speak to people, would you prefer that they listen to you with empathy and concentration? Would our world be better off if more people knew how to listen well? Cooperation is one of our most important human abilities, and does the ability to listen well help or harm cooperation?

The health of our democracy requires us to explore the complex problems threatening our country and planet through the depth of dialogue rather than the shallowness of sound bites. The garden of democracy becomes sick when citizens are unable to listen to each other, and the government is unable to listen to its citizens. The art of listening allows us to listen not only to others, but also to ourselves. Later in this chapter I will discuss how to direct our empathy and concentration inward so that we can listen to what our anger and rage are truly trying to tell us. By directing our empathy and concentration inward, we can unravel the mysteries of our mind and walk the path to becoming fully human.

Another popular misconception is that listening simply means not thinking about what we are going to say when people are talking to us. But listening is so much more than that. It is a way of life. Throughout the day I strive to listen not only to people, but also to the reality around me and the reality within me. When we increase our skill in the art of listening we give others the gift of being listened to, and we give ourselves the gift of deeper understanding. But directing this skill inward gives us another gift—the ability to hear the innermost part of ourselves that desperately wants to be heard.

Odysseus and the Dangers of Language

Among wild animals, size and strength are important. The lion or buffalo that is biggest, strongest, or fiercest can often get its way. But among human beings, physical strength is overrated, because we possess something far more powerful, far more dangerous, than physical strength. We possess a capacity for language that greatly exceeds that of any other species.

Which person is more dangerous, a large and muscular man who is very skilled at killing, or a master of language who can convince a hundred thousand people to kill for him? Throughout human history, the unjust rulers have almost never been the biggest or the strongest. Intelligence and mastery of language give unjust rulers a much greater ability to commit evil than size or strength.

Alexander the Great and Julius Caesar were not the largest men in their armies. But they both possessed something far more dangerous than sheer size; they had incredible intelligence. Napoleon and Hitler were not physically massive either. But they also possessed something far more dangerous than exceptional height and bulging muscles; they were masters at convincing others to kill for them.

The masters of language, more than anyone else, have shaped human history for better and worse. Where waging peace is concerned, people such as Socrates, Jesus, and Buddha were brilliant teachers and effective communicators, able to make complex ideas sound simple by using metaphors, parables, and stories. In the modern world, Gandhi and Martin Luther King Jr. were also masters of language who could inspire people, transform how others think, and motivate many to go to prison and even die for a cause. Good speakers such as Hitler and Mussolini tried to manipulate the masses, while good speakers such as Gandhi and King tried to protect the masses from manipulation.

The muscle of language is a mighty yet dangerous human power, because it has such a high capacity to serve both peace and justice or deception and destruction. In *Peaceful Revolution* I outline seven faculties of the human mind, which I describe metaphorically as muscles of our shared humanity (hope, empathy, appreciation, conscience, reason, discipline, and curiosity). In *Peaceful Revolution* I explain how strengthening those seven muscles encourages us to take ethical actions and gives us the means to create a more peaceful world. Those seven muscles can be thought of as virtues. However, two additional human faculties exist that are not virtues and are extremely dangerous if not guided by those seven muscles. Our two most dangerous human powers are the muscle of language and the muscle of imagination.

This book explores how we can unlock the full potential of human language while protecting ourselves from the dangers of language, and the last book of this series discusses how we can unlock the full potential of the human imagination while protecting ourselves from the dangers of imagination. Before humans can commit genocide, child sex trafficking, fraud, or any premeditated harm, they must first consider the thought in their imagination. Without imagination, humans would be unable to commit premeditated harm that requires long-term planning.

Before we can unlock the full potential of language, we must first understand how the nature of language shapes the human condition. Today I often hear a common misconception, which claims that tribes in early human history were ruled by the biggest and strongest, and that our early ancestors were not sophisticated people but instead relied on brute force to get their way. But in small indigenous tribes around the world, elders who possess experience and wisdom, rather than young people who possess greater physical strength, tend to have the most status. The tribal elder who can persuade, teach, and guide the tribe has abilities that are more crucial to the tribe's survival than raw physical strength, especially since human beings are tool users who can cooperate to a limitless degree, which makes up for our lack of strength.

Even three thousand years ago in ancient Greece where Homeric warrior heroes were idolized, brains were recognized as being more important than brawn. If ever there had been a society where the biggest and strongest should have the most status, it would be the hypermasculine warrior culture depicted in the *Iliad*. But this was not the case. The biggest and strongest Greek warrior was Giant Ajax (not to be confused with Little Ajax), but the most valued warrior was Achilles. He was not as big or strong as Ajax, but he was the most skilled warrior and also a master of language.

Historian James Colaiaco tells us, "Homeric heroes had to be proficient in public discourse; the young Achilles was taught to be not only a man of action, skilled with arms, but also a master of words. Throughout the *Iliad*, Achilles boasts of his rhetorical prowess, duly acknowledged by his associates. And Odysseus proclaims that the people regard the expert speaker as a god."[23]

People living thousands of years ago understood that language is powerful and dangerous. This is a timeless aspect of the human condition, because language is just as powerful and dangerous today as it was in the distant past. Socrates and Plato realized that one reason democracy is such a fragile and hazardous form of government is that a good speaker can manipulate the masses with eloquent speech. This happened often in ancient Athens and the Roman Republic, and it happens all the time in the United States today. The only way to protect people from the manipulation of good speakers is through the form of education that I call peace literacy, which gives us the skills to see through manipulation and illusion.

In a preliterate society where face-to-face spoken language is the most common way to communicate and complex visual propaganda has not yet been invented, language is certainly important. This is demonstrated by the events that cause Giant Ajax to commit suicide in disgrace. After Achilles dies during the Trojan War, the Greeks recognize Odysseus, rather than Giant Ajax, as the most valued soldier in the Greek army, even though Giant Ajax is by far the best warrior in the army after Achilles.[24]

Stocky and muscular, Odysseus is also a skilled warrior, but he possesses an ability much deadlier than prowess on the battlefield. He is the most cunning man in the Greek army. Odysseus is highly intelligent, a clever master of language, and a brilliant tactician, who later thought up the idea of the Trojan horse that won the war.

By voting to award Achilles's armor to Odysseus instead of Giant Ajax, the Greek army acknowledges that brains are more important than brawn, even in ancient militaries. Professor Elizabeth Vandiver explains:

> After the death of Achilles during the Trojan War, the question arose what to do with Achilles's great armor. Achilles had a suit of armor that had been made for him by the god Hephaestus, and so it would be a very great prize of honor for whomever the armor was awarded to after Achilles's death. There were two contenders. Ajax the Greater, who after Achilles's death was the greatest remaining warrior among the Greeks. The other contender was Odysseus, who was the most clever of the Greeks. So the question of who should get the armor is really a question of what does the Greek army value more, valor and prowess in battle, or cleverness and intelligence. The Greeks vote to give the armor to Odysseus, and Ajax commits suicide.[25]

The vote to give Achilles's armor to Odysseus not only attacked Giant Ajax's sense of self-worth, but could also be seen as an act of betrayal by his comrades, because when Achilles refused to fight after King Agamemnon disrespected him, Giant Ajax did more than any other Greek soldier to fend off the rampaging Trojans and protect the Greek army from destruction. Without him, the Greeks probably would have been massacred. Giant Ajax had saved all his comrades' lives, yet despite this they voted to give Achilles's armor to Odysseus, who used his high intelligence to not only be a master of language, but also a master of lies.

Historian Lawrence Tritle describes the betrayal Ajax felt when his comrades chose Odysseus over him: "In his drama *Ajax*, Sophocles [the ancient Greek playwright] tells the story of the great Telamonian Ajax . . . who took his own life when his fellow Greeks denied him the prize of Achilles' armor. His suicide results from his belief that he has been betrayed by those closest to him, his own comrades, and it would seem that he has a point. Ajax's perception of betrayal . . . corresponds well with the diagnosis of PTSD, particularly that aspect of it that focuses on the destruction of the capacity for social trust . . . The suicide of Ajax could be set beside the real-life suicides of many Vietnam veterans, who finally took their own lives, convinced that everyone had abandoned them."[26]

Unlike Giant Ajax, Homer says that deceptive Odysseus is "quick at every treachery under the sun—the man of twists and turns."[27] How intelligent, clever, and deceptive is Odysseus? How does he use language to get people to obey his will? Homer's epic poems depict Odysseus's strong intellect and cunning use of language. The *Iliad* and the *Odyssey* are the two epic poems attributed to Homer. Both were written nearly three thousand years ago. The *Iliad* takes place during the Trojan War, but the *Odyssey* is about Odysseus's difficult journey home after the war ends.

In the *Odyssey*, Homer describes how Odysseus wakes up after a shipwreck, finding himself naked on a strange island, his clothes torn off by the roaring sea and his bruised body covered with sea salt, sand, and seaweed. Odysseus must persuade the local inhabitants to help him, but he does not know if they are friendly or hostile to strangers. The only people nearby are young teenage girls doing laundry by the mouth of a river. At first he does not know who these girls are, not realizing that this is a princess named Nausicaa and her servants. How can he convince them to help a strange, filthy, naked man without terrifying them and causing them to run away? Elizabeth Vandiver explains how this incident demonstrates Odysseus's high intelligence and mastery of language:

> [Odysseus is] stark naked, his clothes have been torn off of him, he's bruised and battered, his hair is matted, he's covered with dried seaweed and salt and so on. And he hears the voices of the maidens and peeking out from the shrubbery, he sees that there's a bunch of young girls

out here. Now how is he to approach them without terrifying them? How can a naked, battered, bruised, wild-looking man come bursting out of the bushes and get these girls to stand still and listen to him long enough for him to persuade them that he's not going to hurt them? It's a very tricky situation to put it mildly . . .

There is an implicit threat of rape in this scene . . . In Greek literature and Greek mythology the seashore is a particularly dangerous area for young girls. There are many stories about girls being raped when they were at the seashore, when they were near the coast. Young girls in this society almost never would be out without male protectors of some sort or another . . . Also piracy was a problem in the ancient world. Obviously a woman on a seacoast would be vulnerable to being abducted by pirates for sexual purposes or to be sold into slavery . . .

So Odysseus has got to find some way to persuade Nausicaa that he won't hurt her, without offending her, without frightening her . . . He plucks a branch to cover his genitals and walks out of the bushes. The other girls scatter. They run away. Athena puts courage into Nausicaa's heart and she stands and waits for Odysseus to speak to her. His interaction with Nausicaa once again demonstrates his superb skill in rhetoric and his ability to fit his words to his audience . . .

[Odysseus begins by saying,] "I am at your knees, oh queen, but are you mortal or goddess? If indeed you are one of the gods who hold wide heaven, then I must find in you the nearest likeness to Artemis, the daughter of great Zeus, for beauty, figure, and stature . . ."

His mention of the specific goddess Artemis is very carefully chosen. Artemis is one of three goddesses who remain forever virgins. The other two are Athena, the goddess of wisdom and war, and Hestia, the goddess of the

> hearth. But Artemis is a far more militant virgin than the other two. There are many stories about the goddess Artemis inflicting terrible punishments on men who in any way seemed to trespass upon her chastity. One story of a man who saw Artemis naked inadvertently [while she was bathing in a forest]—he didn't mean to—but he saw Artemis naked, his punishment was to be turned into a stag and torn apart by his own hunting hounds while his mind remained human and he knew what was happening to him. In other words, if ever there was a goddess that no man in his right mind would even think about approaching sexually, that goddess is Artemis.
>
> So think of what Odysseus has just done. He has said to Nausicaa . . . I think you must be Artemis. Which carries with it the entire subtext of: since I think you must be Artemis I am in no way going to assault you, I am in no way going to hurt you, I am going to keep my distance, you are in power here. But by putting it that way, by saying I think you must be Artemis, he has avoided actually having to say I'm not going to rape you, because of course if he says that, he indicates that at least the thought was in his mind in some sense in a negative way. So he's reassured Nausicaa. He's also put in some pretty good flattery here. You look like Artemis . . . I've never seen anything so beautiful in my life.[28]

Of course, Odysseus is lying. He doesn't really think the young teenage princess Nausicaa is Artemis. Homer depicts Nausicaa as highly intelligent and very clever. She is not a pushover and can hold her own against Odysseus. During their conversation he reveals that he is a civilized and prestigious man, he says he realizes she is human, and he persuades her to go out of her way to help him. After Odysseus cleans his body in the river, his regal appearance further impresses Nausicaa and she secretly wants to marry him. That's quite a feat for a naked man covering his genitals with a branch, who washed up battered on the seashore. Language, charm, and flattery are powerful indeed.

The muscle of language is so dangerous because it can be used to flatter and manipulate or express sincerity and truth. The muscle of language can be a strong ally to peace and justice or deception and destruction. An expert liar and cunning manipulator, Odysseus uses language to deceive and destroy, making him one of the most dangerous men alive. Many people in ancient Greece thought lying was despicable. Achilles is an example of someone who detested lying. Classics scholar Bernard Knox tells us:

> "I hate that man like the very Gates of Death, who says one thing but hides another in his heart." These are the words of Achilles, the hero of the *Iliad* . . . He addressed them to Odysseus, who had come as leader of a delegation charged by Agamemnon and the Achaean chieftains to persuade Achilles to rejoin them in the attack on Troy. These are strange words with which to open an answer to what seems like a generous offer of compensation . . . but Achilles knows his man. Odysseus has told no lie, but he has concealed the truth . . .
>
> For Achilles a lie is something utterly abhorrent. But for Odysseus it is second nature, a point of pride . . . [Odysseus possesses] what Achilles so vehemently rejects—the intention to deceive. Odysseus has the talent necessary for the deceiver: he is a persuasive speaker.[29]

Although Odysseus is a three-dimensional complex character, he symbolizes why language is so dangerous. The *dangers of language* existed three thousand years ago in ancient Greece, and they still exist in the twenty-first century, because the potential hazards of language are part of the human condition. The current rise in racist ideologies and violent religious fanaticism, which use language to manipulate how people think, exploit their human vulnerabilities, and provide deceptive answers to very real problems, are among the many examples that show why Odysseus is a timeless metaphor for the reality that language is more powerful and dangerous than brute strength. When the old adage tells us, "The pen is mightier than the sword," it is not exaggerating.

When people quote this adage, they often think of the pen as a metaphor for journalism, writings that promote justice, and other forms of peaceful communication, but they usually don't interpret the pen as a metaphor for the harm language can cause. The pen can also promote hatred, deception, and dehumanization. The pen that incites hatred, advocates racism and sexism, rationalizes slavery and other unjust economic policies, reduces people's sense of dignity and worth, promotes greed and selfishness, encourages us to be apathetic rather than proactive in solving our global problems, defends environmental devastation, and suppresses the truth of our shared humanity is mightier in its ability to cause harm than the sword. In fact, those who kill with weapons often obey those who write with pens. The original saying, which is attributed to several people who lived over two thousand years ago, states, "The *word* is mightier than the sword." History has proven them to be correct, not only in terms of the capacity for words to do good, but also harm.

Former boxing champion Mike Tyson also explains why language is more powerful than brute strength in the twenty-first century. Although Tyson is describing the world today, his analysis could very well describe how Odysseus's brain overcame Giant Ajax's brawn:

> You hear the old guys say, "The toughest last longest." No, that's not true. This is not a tough guy world. This is a smart man's world. A tough guy is going to get hurt in this world. They're dinosaurs now, these tough psycho bad guys. They're not going to last now in the twenty-first century.[30]

If we look at how persuasive politicians and ambitious conquerors manipulated people in ancient history, we realize that this has always been a "smart man's world," at least as far back as the beginning of recorded history. The men (and women) who can use language to convince a hundred thousand people to kill for them, whether they lived three thousand years ago or today, are much more dangerous than the best trained killers in the world. Often, the best killers in the world are serving the will of the smart men who have mastered language and other skills.

Consider the vast amount of resources, time, and energy our society puts into protecting us from good killers. To protect us from good killers, our society spends billions of dollars on missiles and bombs, along with an army, air force, and navy. However, our society invests almost nothing toward protecting us from good talkers, who are far more dangerous than good killers. As Greek mythology shows us, good talkers have always been the most dangerous humans. But today good talkers, both male and female, are more dangerous than they have ever been, because they can cause nuclear war and environmental destruction on a global scale. The only way a society can protect itself from the dangers of good talkers is by becoming peace literate. Peace literacy gives people the kind of education that inoculates them from manipulation and the seductive lies that spread hatred, dehumanization, and irrational fear.

To protect ourselves from the deception and destruction possible through language, we must be trained in forms of peace literacy such as the art of living, the art of waging peace, and the art of listening. Just as training enables us to use language well, we must also train ourselves to not be fooled by language, which is why I discuss propaganda in my other books. When we learn how propaganda exploits our human vulnerabilities and tricks our conscience into supporting injustice, we become much more difficult to fool.

Just as a magician does not seem nearly as clever when we know how a magic trick is done, Odysseus does not seem nearly as smart when we know how his tricks attempt to fool us. To wield the weapon of nonviolence with maximum force as soldiers of peace, however, protecting ourselves from manipulation is not enough. We must also learn the skills that allow us to harness the vast power of language to serve truth, sincerity, peace, and justice.

Authentic Communication

Our society acknowledges that mastering language requires training. Although young children learn language naturally, we spend years teaching them proper grammar, how to read with a high level of comprehension, how to write well, and how to organize and communicate their thoughts. This helps them succeed at life. But our society does not yet recognize the importance of training ourselves to use language in service of truth, sincerity, peace, and justice. This helps humanity succeed as a whole. In a world where our technological capacity for destruction threatens our survival, using a force as powerful as language to serve truth, sincerity, peace, and justice is necessary for human survival. Today it is much easier to find information on how to use language to deceive, rather than how to use language to promote realistic peace.

Using language to serve truth, sincerity, peace, and justice is what I call *authentic communication*. This use of language is essential in the struggle against ignorance, deception, and injustice. Without authentic communication, we cannot effectively confront the root causes of our national and global problems. When we learn authentic communication and apply its practical power to our daily lives, everyone around us will benefit, we will benefit, and we will create small but significant ripples of peace and justice that can spread throughout our communities and around the world.

Today our political leaders usually emphasize economics, politics, and the use of military force, rather than better communication, when discussing how to solve our national and global problems. But Buddhist monk Thich Nhat Hanh explains why these problems cannot be solved unless we prioritize the improvement of communication:

> We live in a time when we have very sophisticated means for communication, but communication has become very difficult between individuals and groups of people. A father cannot talk to son. Mother cannot talk to daughter. Israelis cannot talk to Palestinians. And Hindus cannot talk to Muslims . . . Restoring communication is the basic work for peace, and our political and our spiritual leaders have to focus their energy on this matter.[31]

Rather than merely addressing surface symptoms, authentic communication allows us to identify and confront the root causes of our human problems. Authentic communication is something that all of us can learn and apply to our daily lives, and it begins with listening. *The first step for authentic communication is learning not only how to listen to others, but also to ourselves.* Listening to ourselves, which means becoming self-aware of our innermost thoughts, is just as important as listening to other people. One of the most useful ways we can listen to ourselves is by perceiving the underlying fires deep within us that cause the heat of our human aggression.

By perceiving the underlying fires beneath the heat of my own aggression, I can better understand why I am reacting aggressively to someone. Did something happen that caused me to feel disrespected? Or did something happen that reopened the old wounds of my childhood trauma? Am I reacting aggressively because I feel frustrated? Or is the heat of my aggression being caused by the fire of betrayal, humiliation, shame, insecurity, guilt, or fear? Am I feeling a bit aggressive today because of sleep deprivation or hunger? Did I wake up in a bad mood? Am I upset about something my boss said to me earlier in the day, and am I taking it out on a family member? Am I feeling aggressive because in the back of my mind I am worried about something?

Understanding the underlying fires that cause our own aggression empowers us in two ways. First, instead of being consumed by the intense heat of our aggression, which can cause us to react without thinking (and can cause us to take our aggression out on innocent people), we can identify and confront the root causes of our aggression. In other words, instead of dealing merely with surface symptoms, we can more effectively heal the underlying causes of our problems. Second, instead of just using a generic word such as "I am *angry*," I can use much more precise words to identify the source of my suffering. I can know that "I feel frustrated," or "I am reliving childhood trauma," or "I feel disrespected," or "I feel afraid."

Developing this level of self-awareness takes time. People often ask me if I meditate, but I am skeptical of some meditation practices because I see many people use them as a form of escapism. Instead of meditation, I practice the art of listening. However, it is important to keep in mind that there are very effective meditation techniques that have been around for thousands of years, but these techniques strongly resemble the art of listening, which no person invented and no religion can claim ownership of, because listening is as old as our species. What better purpose can meditation serve than to increase our awareness and understanding of ourselves, those around us, and the reality we inhabit together? That is what the art of listening achieves.

Just as the two steps for listening to others are empathy and concentration, these are also the two steps for listening to ourselves. When we turn our empathy and concentration inward, we can listen to ourselves with a level of awareness and understanding that is found in the best forms of traditional meditation. Concentration is necessary to listen to ourselves consistently, because it protects us from distractions, but why do we need empathy to listen to ourselves? One reason is that we cannot truly listen to ourselves unless we are honest with ourselves, and we cannot be completely honest with ourselves unless we have empathy for ourselves.

For example, if you make a mistake and say to yourself, "I am stupid" or "I am the biggest idiot in the world," that is actually not an honest assessment, because it is presenting a distorted view of reality and not taking into account a lot of key information. An honest assessment based on empathy would instead sound more like this: "I made this mistake because I was careless, and this is why I was careless, and this is what I am going to do to protect myself from being careless in the future, because I have the ability to grow and develop as a human being. And I will make mistakes occasionally, because I am human."

As a perfectionist who is extremely hard on myself, I have realized that having empathy for myself does not mean avoiding self-criticism, but *not destroying myself with self-criticism.* If we do not critique ourselves to some extent, we cannot grow and develop as human beings. Because my childhood trauma has given me a high capacity for rage that I tend to direct at myself, not destroying myself with self-criticism has been a huge struggle for me.

By directing our empathy inward, we can also feel compassion for ourselves when we are suffering from an underlying fire such as frustration, insecurity, or trauma. Feeling compassion for ourselves can be very difficult, especially if we have a damaged sense of self-worth and do not believe that we deserve our own compassion. Because of the way extreme childhood trauma has scarred my brain, my instinct is not to feel compassion for myself when I suffer or make a mistake, but to feel rage toward myself. My rage fills me with a strong urge to hit myself, cut myself, and mutilate my body. Sometimes in these rare moments I feel an intense desire to cut off one of my hands when I am enraged, and in those agonizing moments I desperately want to kill myself not because I am sad or hopeless, but because I hate myself. It's not that I want to commit suicide out of despair. Instead, I want to murder myself out of hatred.

The reason I am discussing these painful life experiences with you is that I understand how difficult it can be to feel compassion for yourself if childhood trauma has wounded your mind. But by working to direct my empathy inward, the fires of rage come less often for me, they are usually less severe, and I am better able to understand why they arise. Sometimes my rage returns with the full force of its wrath, urging me to self-destruct, and I am not sure if I will make it out alive. But somehow I survive the storm to live another day.

What has the art of listening taught me about rage? I have learned that rage wants to protect me so that I am never again abused as I was during my childhood, but the only way it knows how to protect me is by killing those around me. Rage wants to express my agony so that others can feel my trauma, so that my trauma does not feel so lonely anymore, but the only language rage speaks is violence. Rage wants to hurt me when I make mistakes because that is what it learned from my parents, because making mistakes puts me in severe distress and the only solution rage has for every problem is inflicting pain, because the only way rage knows how to help me is by hurting me. I no longer need rage to protect me, function as my form of expression, or try to help me, but rage is an old friend who wants to maintain at least a long-distance relationship just in case I need it someday, even though I know I won't.

Rage has been a painful friend to people at least as far back as the ancient world, where some writers understood how the agony of rage can be directed inward better than many people in the modern world do. In Sophocles's play *Ajax*, when Giant Ajax's self-worth is attacked and he feels betrayed because his comrades awarded Achilles's armor to Odysseus rather than him, Giant Ajax has a strong desire to murder his comrades and torture Odysseus. His rage is later turned inward when he kills himself by falling on his sword. In Sophocles's play *Oedipus the King*, when Oedipus finds out that his wife is actually his mother, he directs his rage inward by gouging out his eyes. In Euripides's play *Medea*, when Medea's husband replaces her with a younger wife, she murders her children, who are a part of her, as a way to seek revenge against her husband. Rage is an infected wound that wants to infect the world with its agony.

Peace literacy has given me a wide variety of skills that make me less reliant on rage. If it weren't for the art of listening and the ability it gives me to better deal with my rage, I would have died a violent death many years ago. How can we use the art of listening to deal with our own aggression? After using the art of listening to identify the underlying fire causing our aggression (for example, knowing that our aggression is being caused by the fire of fear), the second step is identifying the fuel that is feeding our fire. An example of this is asking yourself, "Why do I feel afraid?" The third step is calming the fire within us, and the fourth step is confronting the source of fuel.

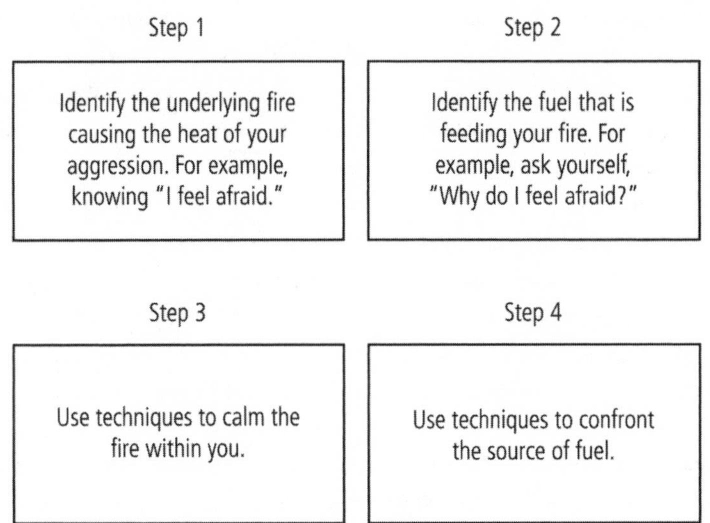

Figure 2.5: Dealing with Our Own Aggression

It might seem counterintuitive to calm the fire within us before confronting the source of fuel. But because our brain does not function well when we are in turmoil, if we can calm our fear, trauma, sense of feeling disrespected, or frustration even slightly, it can help our brain function better. By calming the fire within us as best we can before confronting the source of fuel, we can deal with a challenging situation much more effectively, because so many of our mental abilities function optimally when we are calm (in *The End of War* and *The Art of Waging Peace* I discuss the power of calm).

There are many techniques we can use to calm the fire within us, such as focusing on our breathing, having a friend we can confide in (just having someone to listen to us can help calm us down), exercising, or going for a walk. When I am in a conflict with someone and need an immediate way to remain calm, what works best for me is cultivating empathy. As long as I have empathy for someone I am in conflict with, I will not lose my temper, even if I become a little frustrated. If I lose empathy for the person, however, then a flood of rage might drown my ability to reason. That is why I have put so much effort into strengthening my muscle of empathy.

If we think the source of fuel feeding our fire is a person (such as a person disrespecting us), what techniques can we use to cultivate our empathy, improve our conflict resolution ability, and interact with the person more effectively? We can begin by seeing conflict as an opportunity, which is how martial arts and the military taught me to see conflict. How is conflict an opportunity that can benefit us?

Conflicts are manifestations of deeper underlying problems. Some of the deeper underlying problems that can cause conflict include misunderstanding, miscommunication, ignorance, and a person being in pain. In most cases, people are disrespectful because of these underlying problems, which are the actual sources of fuel that we should confront. So rather than attack a disrespectful person with insults we should instead confront the root causes of their disrespect by striving to clear up misunderstanding, miscommunication, ignorance, or using kindness to help relieve their pain. In *The Art of Waging Peace* I explain why the army taught me to always respond to disrespectful people in a respectful way.

Every conflict is an opportunity to gain greater clarity and understanding into these underlying problems, as if conflict were a microscope allowing us to see the viruses of misunderstanding, miscommunication, ignorance, or pain that have remained hidden until now. By gaining greater clarity and understanding into these underlying problems, we can heal the root causes of conflict.

Erich Fromm further explains how we can gain greater clarity and understanding by resolving conflict well:

> One other frequent error must be mentioned here. The illusion, namely, that love means necessarily the absence of conflict. Just as it is customary for people to believe that pain and sadness should be avoided under all circumstances, they believe that love means the absence of any conflict. And they find good reasons for this idea in the fact that the struggles around them seem only to be destructive interchanges which bring no good to either one of those concerned.
>
> But the reason for this lies in the fact that the "conflicts" of most people are actually attempts to avoid the *real* conflicts. They are disagreements on minor or superficial matters which by their very nature do not lend themselves to clarification or solution. Real conflicts between two people, those which do not serve to cover up or to project, but which are experienced on the deep level of inner reality to which they belong, are not destructive. They lead to clarification, they produce a catharsis from which both persons emerge with more knowledge and more strength.[32]

Interpersonal conflict arises naturally because human beings see the world from different angles. When we learn how to resolve conflict well, we can adjust our perspective and help other people adjust theirs. This leads to the kind of clarity, understanding, and sense of shared struggle that can bring people closer together. Resolving conflict poorly drives us apart, while resolving it well strengthens the bonds of solidarity. As Erich Fromm and many others have realized, love is not the absence of conflict, but the process of resolving conflict lovingly.

Also, every conflict gives us an opportunity to practice our skills in the art of listening, the art of waging peace, and the art of living. If we want to improve our skills, then we must practice. Resolving conflict well can be a valuable use of time that builds our skills and experience, because conflict in itself is not destructive. What causes so much harm is not really conflict, but *destructive conflict resolution*, where someone tries to resolve a conflict by punching you in the face. The vast majority of conflicts we are involved in will not end up in a fistfight if we are skilled at waging peace, and in *The Art of Waging Peace* I discuss the use of personal self-defense as a last resort.

If we think someone is the source of fuel feeding our fire, another way to cultivate our empathy and improve our conflict resolution ability is by giving the person the benefit of the doubt. Why should we do this? As I already mentioned, most conflicts (along with most acts of disrespect) are caused in some way by misunderstanding, miscommunication, ignorance, or people being in pain. By giving people the benefit of the doubt, I have often found that the primary source of fuel was not that particular person who seemed to be feeding my fire. Instead, the primary source of fuel was often misunderstanding and miscommunication. By giving people the benefit of the doubt and always seeking to clear up misunderstanding and miscommunication, we can confront this frequent source of fuel.

This begins the second step for authentic communication, which is speaking in a way that builds trust, respect, empathy, clarity, and understanding. Trust is vital for healthy connections between human beings, whether it is within a friendship, relationship, family, nation, or our global community. All people want to be around people they can trust.

Trust, respect, empathy, clarity, and understanding are ingredients that create healthy communities and strong democracies. These ingredients also enable the highest forms of cooperation. Giving people the benefit of the doubt is a way to harvest these ingredients. Rushing to judgment and assuming the worst is a way to destroy these ingredients.

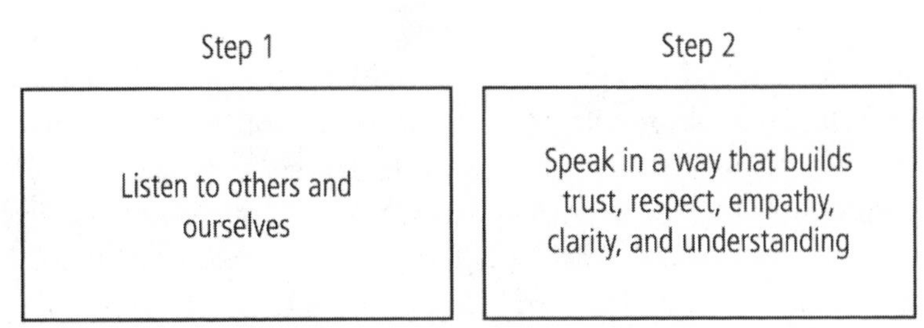

Figure 2.6: The Two Steps for Authentic Communication

Giving people the benefit of the doubt allows us to speak in a way that builds trust, respect, empathy, clarity, and understanding. Giving people the benefit of the doubt means withholding judgment until we can gather more information about the situation. When we assume the worst and jump to conclusions, we act from a position of ignorance and create unnecessary conflict, which can harm us and those around us. One way I give people the benefit of the doubt is by asking questions that strive to increase clarity and understanding.

This conflict resolution technique of giving people the benefit of the doubt and asking questions is something I learned in the army. If a soldier is late to work, there is a simple two-step process to deal with this situation. The first step is asking the person, "Why are you late? What happened?" This is a very useful way to approach a conflict, because maybe the person had a flat tire or family emergency. If he or she does not have a good reason for being late, the second step is asking, "What are you going to do to prevent this from happening again?" This second step empowers people to think critically. If they don't know how to prevent the problem from happening again, or their solution seems unlikely to work, we can help them by offering guidance. Where being late is concerned, many people in our society have never been taught the time-management skills that allow us to consistently show up early.*

* This simple two-step process is just one among many conflict resolution techniques. If a soldier was late repeatedly in my army unit, then disciplinary action would have to be taken. Also, a soldier arriving late because of an emergency should call someone in his or her chain of command, to provide accountability. When I joined the army in 2002, however, not everyone had cell phones.

I have also used this technique of asking questions when people want me to give them feedback on a project. For example, if people skilled at their craft ask me to give them constructive criticism on something they have created, how can I critique an aspect of their work? I can begin by asking, "Why did you do it this way?" If they don't have a good reason or I think there is another reason they should consider, I will ask, "Have you thought about doing it this way instead?" I ask these questions because when skilled people create something, they usually have very good reasons for doing things a certain way, which we are not aware of, and I don't want to arrogantly assume that I completely understand their decision-making process. If they don't have a good reason, then asking why they did something a certain way will reveal this. If they have a good reason, I may be able to suggest a more elegant and effective way to satisfy that reason. This technique of asking questions, which I first learned in the army, not only prevents unnecessary conflict, but also allows us to give people more insightful constructive criticism and better guidance.*

I also give people the benefit of the doubt when I do not know what kind of fire is causing the heat of their aggression. In fact, I may never find out what is causing their aggression, and because we live in a society where people are not trained to listen to their innermost thoughts, they might not even be self-aware of the fires causing them to act out aggressively. Nevertheless, I give people the benefit of the doubt by remembering that aggression is always caused by uncomfortable emotions. Even if I do not know whether people's aggression is being caused by fear, frustration, insecurity, childhood trauma, disrespect, a sense of emptiness in life, a threatened sense of self-worth, or humiliation, I can have empathy for their discomfort. Sometimes the most helpful questions we can ask people are simply, "Why are you

*I use this technique of asking questions when people are "skilled at their craft." If an English teacher is grading eighth-grade book reports or a coach is training high school football players, it can be unproductive to ask very inexperienced people, "Why did you do it this way?" Inexperience is often the answer. It can still be useful to ask questions when people are inexperienced, but it would be impractical for an English teacher to grade a middle school book report by addressing every mistake made from inexperience with the question, "Why did you do it this way?" Sometimes an English teacher simply needs to make red marks on the page, and sometimes a coach simply has to correct mistakes made from inexperience. Also, I don't always use this technique of asking questions when people are skilled at their craft. This is just one option I have among many, and the option I use depends on circumstances and my relationship with the person.

upset? What is bothering you? What can I do to help?"

Authentic communication, which is built on the art of listening, is important not only because it prevents unnecessary conflict, but also because time is ruthless. Because time's ruthless flow goes in only one direction, we cannot take back what we say. I know a middle school teacher who has her students bring toothpaste to class one day during the year. She has them squeeze out some toothpaste and then try to put it back in the tube. Time's ruthlessness is the reason why it is so difficult to put toothpaste back in the tube.

In a similar way, when we do not handle conflict respectfully and peacefully but instead say disrespectful and cruel things to people, we cannot take back our words. Because time is ruthless, it does not allow our words to return from where they came. Conflict that is not resolved well can destroy relationships, cause trauma, damage people's ability to trust, and even lead to murder. Again, knowing how to respectfully and peacefully resolve conflict is not about being politically correct, but dealing with the root causes of violence.

Knowing how to respectfully and peacefully resolve conflict also allows us to make good use of struggle and benefit from the passage of time. When we resolve conflict with authentic communication, we increase our clarity and understanding, and we improve our skill in the arts of listening, waging peace, and living. We also serve others, grow in wisdom, create ripples of peace and justice that can spread throughout our communities and around the world, and our struggles gain a positive purpose and fulfilling sense of meaning. Although we can use authentic communication to wage peace in our personal lives and local communities, soldiers of peace such as Gandhi, Martin Luther King Jr., Nelson Mandela, Wangari Maathai, and many others used authentic communication to wage peace on a large scale. Authentic communication promotes realistic peace in our local community, as well as our global community.

This chapter offers a brief introduction to authentic communication, which can take many years to master. When we strengthen the other muscles of our shared humanity such as reason, conscience, curiosity, and appreciation, we can further speak in ways that build trust, respect, empathy, clarity, and understanding (step 2 of authentic communication). To learn more about authentic communication, in *The Art of Waging Peace* I discuss truthful persuasion techniques that can transform how people think about controversial issues, in *The Cosmic Ocean* I discuss the importance of increasing the clarity of communication, and in the last book of this series I will discuss the role that humor can play in authentic communication.

Authentic communication is more powerful than deceptive communication, which Odysseus symbolizes, because his most dangerous forms of deception rarely work on people who are peace literate. On the other hand, authentic communication builds a level of respect and trust that all human beings crave, whether or not they are peace literate. Just as no one in human history has ever seriously said, "I hate it when people respect me," no one in human history has ever seriously said, "I hate being around people I can trust." All people want respect and trust,* which is what authentic communication creates, and what deceptive communication undermines. Deceptive communication can create the illusion of respect, but we cannot truly respect people if we are lying to and manipulating them.**

Someone might say, "I don't feel like respecting anyone, and I will continue to disrespect people as much as I want." However, a person with this intention is unable to change the human condition. It is a fact of the human condition that people respond best to respect, all human beings want to be listened to, empathy allows us to listen to people in the deepest way possible, and the feeling of being disrespected causes most human conflict. It is a fact of our world that so many of our personal, national, and global problems result from people lacking skills in the arts of listening, waging peace, and living. It is a fact of human survival that we need authentic communication to cooperatively navigate our ship the planet Earth through the ruthless sea of time.

If humanity is going to survive, we must use the powerful muscle of

* In *The Cosmic Ocean* I provide a full list of our human cravings. Respect and trust are part of our craving for nurturing relationships. Authentic communication strives to feed these cravings in healthy ways.

** In the last book of this series I will further discuss self-awareness and self-deception, and how some people can deceive themselves so much that they don't consciously realize they are deceiving others.

language to serve truth, sincerity, peace, and justice, rather than deception and destruction. We must also show people how to see through the tricks of Odysseus that hide our shared humanity, confuse our sense of justice, and conceal the road to peace. And we must offer people a higher vision of what it means to be human that is far more fulfilling than manipulating people for selfish interests. This vision of our highest human potential can be found in the star of truth and the lifestyle of love symbolized by Jesus, Buddha, and other peace heroes.

CHAPTER 3
The Star of Truth

Why Romanticizing the Past Endangers Humanity's Future

At West Point I began to think about a topic that was never discussed during my entire education from preschool through high school. That topic is the nature of truth. Because we have the technological capacity to drive ourselves and most life on Earth into extinction, believing illusions about reality endangers our survival, and gaining a deeper understanding of truth is humanity's only salvation. Despite this, today I hear some academics say there is no such thing as truth, there is no objective reality, and all truth is therefore relative.

I always find it strange when people say there is no objective reality and all truth is relative. The West Point honor code states, "A cadet will not lie, cheat, steal, or tolerate those who do." Imagine how absurd it would sound if a cadet caught stealing said, "Well you see, I didn't really steal this, because there is no objective reality and all truth is relative. Your truth may be that I stole this, but my truth is that I didn't really steal it. My truth is that all your possessions belong to me, and therefore it is not wrong for me to take things from you because my truth tells me that they were mine to begin with. In fact, my truth tells me that you are subhuman and your body belongs to me. I can do whatever I want to your body, because my truth tells me that you are inferior to me and your body is my possession."

Laws can be subjective (there was a time when state-sanctioned slavery made it legal to own people's bodies), but there are also scientific truths that transcend human laws. Imagine if a person wrongly imprisoned was found innocent due to DNA evidence, and a judge said, "We aren't going to let you out of prison, because DNA evidence means absolutely nothing since there is no such thing as objective reality, since there is no such thing as truth."*

I am not exaggerating or being facetious when I discuss the arguments people can make against the existence of truth. I have had some odd conversations with people over the years. Humans don't fully know what reality is, and the true nature of reality might be beyond our comprehension. Nevertheless, there are truths we can know about how our reality operates that allow us to make accurate predictions about the future, and therefore it is extremely important for us to know the truth.

For example, knowing the true causes of diseases (viruses are one of the possible causes) allows us to better predict how to reduce epidemics in the future than believing the myth that diseases are caused by angry Greek gods. For most of human history people did not know what viruses were. Without microscopes, how could they have known? Furthermore, knowing the truth of the laws of physics allows us to better predict how to create a safe airplane than having an inaccurate understanding of physics. Knowing the truth that smoking cigarettes is a risk factor for lung cancer and other illnesses allows us to predict that reducing smoking will improve human health.

In the early nineteenth century there was a popular myth that giving equal rights to black men and all women would destroy our society. This myth claimed they had inferior brains that could not handle the intellectual responsibility of voting, serving on a jury, shaping government policies, and other civic duties. But knowing the truth that women are not intellectually inferior to men and African Americans are not subhuman allowed equal rights activists to predict that our society would not fall apart if women and African Americans were given full equality. As I explained earlier in this book, it is a scientific fact that African Americans are not subhuman, and it is a scientific fact that women are not intellectually inferior to men.

I always try to give people the benefit of the doubt, which allows me

* DNA evidence is not an infallible method for establishing innocence or guilt, because inaccurate conclusions can result from human error and misinterpretation. Many people are working to improve the methods of examining DNA. An article by Matthew Shaer in the June 2016 issue of the *Atlantic* titled "The False Promise of DNA Testing" discusses this issue further. A quote in the article reads, "DNA is science. You can only blame the people who used it wrong."

to realize that some people are referring to interpersonal conflict when they say there is no such thing as truth. They are not referring to scientific truth. I saw a video of a popular speaker discussing how to communicate better, who said, "There is no truth. There's my truth, there's your truth, and everything is subjective."

But everything is not subjective when interpersonal conflict is concerned, and objective truth can in fact exist within interpersonal conflict. For example, if you and I have a conflict and I say, "I think our conflict is based on a misunderstanding, and I apologize if I disrespected you," I might be expressing an underlying truth about our conflict. Sometimes the objective reality is that a conflict is in fact based on a misunderstanding. Or if you and I have a conflict and I say, "I apologize for being so aggressive. I felt like you disrespected me so I overreacted, and now I realize that you did not intend to disrespect me. I misunderstood the situation and should not have reacted so angrily, and thank you for helping to clear this up," those insights can also be objectively true. If we have a conflict and I tell you, "I apologize for raising my voice, but I am having difficulty communicating right now because I feel so frustrated," I can be expressing an underlying truth about my psychological state.

Authentic communication is about perceiving and communicating deeper layers of truth and reality. For example, if you know that human aggression is caused by uncomfortable emotions such as fear, humiliation, insecurity, feeling disrespected, or betrayal, this deeper understanding of reality allows you to communicate more effectively and better predict how your actions will affect the future. If you humiliate and betray people, you will increase your chances of inflaming people's aggression, and if you treat people respectfully you will become better at reducing aggression and resolving conflict.

Gandhi said people can have a piece of the truth,[1] which means something very different from the myth that there is no such thing as truth. When someone refers to something as "their truth" this can actually mean "their *piece* of the truth," but this does not mean that everything is subjective. Instead, it means that if we put our pieces of truth together by listening to the perspective of others, we can gain greater clarity and understanding about reality and the root causes of our conflicts. As I discuss in *Peaceful Revolution*, a piece of the truth (when isolated from the rest of reality) can also be very dangerous, because a half-truth is often more dangerous than an outright lie, which is why war propaganda relies more on half-truths than outright lies.

For example, when I told my mother in 2009 that I was leaving the military and she shouted, "Are you out of your mind? Nobody is going to hire you. It's bad enough you look Asian, but you're also part black. Nobody is going to give a job to a black man who looks Asian," she was expressing her piece of the truth based on her and my father's life experiences.

If I had only believed in her piece of the truth, isolated from the rest of reality, I don't know where I would be today. I was having so many psychological problems in 2009 that I probably would have died if I stayed in the army. But I chose a path my mother did not think was possible by combining her piece of the truth with other pieces of the truth, such as the fact that some progress has happened and I have more opportunities today than my father did at my age. By combining the truth that some progress has happened with the truth that we can develop the skills needed to create a lot more progress and unravel the unjust systems that still exist in our world, I am able to maintain realistic hope while working hard on the mission of peace.

In this chapter we will discuss how truth is a metaphorical sword that allows us to attack ignorance and deception at their root, and why realistic peace cannot exist without truth. The sword of truth cuts through lies, illusions, and myths like a beam of light through darkness. By arming ourselves with truth, the masters of language lose the power to manipulate us. When people in Nazi Germany knew the truth, they could realize how deceptive and inaccurate Hitler's words were, despite his masterful speeches. But when they lacked the truth, they were easily deceived.

As I explain in *Peaceful Revolution*, some propagandists are unaware of the truth and genuinely believe their own propaganda, while some propagandists know the truth yet choose to become deceivers. Why does this happen? When people possess the sword of truth but lack strong muscles of empathy and conscience with which to wield it, they can become propagandists who serve injustice and hide the truth from people. But when our muscles of empathy and conscience are strong, we can become soldiers of peace who use the sword of truth to defeat injustice.

Truth is more powerful than Odysseus's manipulative mind and lavish lies, more powerful than all the propaganda in the world. But the sword of truth is useless if we do not learn how to find it and wield its power with maximum force. The sword of truth cannot protect humanity from deception and destruction if we do not embrace struggle and train ourselves to serve truth.

As humanity sails forward through the turbulent waters of time, stars in the constellation of peace such as struggle, training, and truth can safely guide our ship the planet Earth through the dangerous horizon of our fragile future. To navigate toward survival and prosperity we must embrace struggle, train ourselves in the arts of living, waging peace, and listening, and learn to wield the sword of truth. This sword allows us to defeat monsters such as ignorance and deception, which we will face during our journey forward through time. This sword is made from the starlight of truth, but to explore the nature of this metaphorical starlight, we must discuss the *myth of the golden age* and how it blocks the way to peace.

As I discussed in the first chapter, human beings have a strange relationship with time. Because our large brains can recognize and respond to time's ruthless flow in unique ways, this causes human beings to do odd things with time. As I already mentioned, one odd thing every culture does is attempt to prophesize the future, whether this involves looking for omens in the bloody organs of a sacrificial animal, consulting a fortune-teller, or using science to predict weather and natural disasters. The reason I call this behavior odd is that no other species does this. No other species tries to predict the future by going beyond what their senses can perceive in their current environment. No other species consults oracles, palm readers, or weather satellites.

A behavior even odder than our fascination with prophecy is our tendency to romanticize the past. Predicting the future can help us in many ways, but romanticizing the past harms our ability to create realistic peace and endangers our future. Many cultures romanticize the past, and this behavior is especially common in modern cultures. Romanticizing the past occurs when we not only believe in, but also long for a mythical past when people lived with little to no struggle, a time when human existence was not messy. To offer one example, I have met many Americans who romanticize the 1950s as a "golden age" in American history, a time when life was pure, clean, and without strife.

Romanticizing the past distorts the truth. The 1950s were certainly not a golden age for African Americans living under segregation and terrorism. This was an era when many black homes and churches were bombed by white supremacist groups. Synagogues were also bombed. Historian Clive Webb tells us, "Savage as the synagogue bombings were, the scale of assaults against African Americans was much higher. According to an investigation of six states by the ADL's [Anti-Defamation League's] southern office, fifty-nine black homes and establishments were bombed in 1950–51 alone."[2]

Obviously, the 1950s were not a golden age for African Americans, Jews, Latinos, Native Americans, women, or gay people. But they also were not a golden age for white people. White families have always had varying degrees of problems, and has there ever been such a thing as a family with no struggle? Many white families in the 1950s, like today, had alcoholic parents, child abuse, domestic violence, adultery, repressed rage, veterans suffering from war trauma, children not feeling loved, marriage problems, economic hardship, and people struggling to find purpose, meaning, and self-worth in their lives. The 1950s were also an era when most cars did not have seat belts, people were afraid of polio (the polio vaccine did not become widely available until the latter half of the 1950s), and poisonous lead was a common ingredient in gasoline and paint.

Romanticizing the past occurs when we neglect the problems in the past and neglect the progress in the present. American society is far from perfect today, but as I write these words in 2015 as someone who is half Korean, a quarter black, and a quarter white, this is the best year in American history to be multiethnic. Until 1967, just thirteen years before I was born in 1980, interracial marriage was illegal in many states. I would much rather look Asian and be part black in 2015 rather than in 1915, 1815, or even when I was growing up during the 1980s. I have far more rights than my ancestor Wyatt Chappell, who was born a slave in Alabama in 1835.

Furthermore, would most American women living in the twenty-first century rather live in 1915, an era when they lacked the right to vote, or in 1815, an era when they could not own property or go to college? For gay Americans, 2015 is the year when they have more rights than at any other point in American history. And, of course, all progress can be lost if enough people do not protect progress by embracing the struggle needed to create and maintain positive change, becoming highly skilled in waging peace, and learning to wield the sword of truth with maximum force.

The United States in 2015 is also much better for people with disabilities than it was in the 1950s. When people talk about the history of nonviolent movements, I rarely hear them mention the disability rights movement. In the 1950s people with disabilities, such as Ed Roberts who lived in California, could not even get a high school diploma. His mother had to petition the state department of education so that he could graduate from high school. In the documentary *Lives Worth Living*, which is about the disability rights movement, activist Judi Chamberlin describes the early life of Ed Roberts, who was born in 1939 and became a pioneer of the disability rights movement:

> Ed Roberts is a guy who had polio, and he had a mother who was a tenacious advocate. And so she lobbied for him to be able to go to high school with everyone else . . . They weren't going to let him graduate from high school because he hadn't fulfilled the physical education requirement. So she took it all the way up to the state department of education before he could get his high school diploma. And then he wanted to go to the University of California at Berkeley, and he was told, "Oh, we had another wheelchair guy in here one time and it didn't work out," so they weren't going to let him into college. They got Berkeley to agree to admit him, and the only way they would agree to admit him was if instead of housing him in the dorm, he was housed in the infirmary.[3]

In the 1950s people who could not walk were largely confined to their homes. They did not have access to public buildings due to the lack of wheelchair ramps, and sidewalks did not have "curb cuts," the angled surfaces that allow people to roll a wheelchair from the street onto a sidewalk. Curb cuts are something that most people today take for granted, not realizing that curb cuts exist around the country because a nonviolent movement struggled to make this happen. Ed Roberts explains:

> We secured the first curb cut in the country; it was at the corner of Bancroft and Telegraph Avenue [in Berkeley, California]. When we first talked to legislators about the issue, they told us, "Curb cuts, why do you need curb cuts? We never see people with disabilities out on the street. Who is going to use them?" They didn't understand that their reasoning was circular. When curb cuts were put in, they discovered that access for disabled people benefits many others as well. For instance, people pushing strollers use curb cuts, as do people on bikes and elderly people who can't lift their legs so high. So many people benefit from this accommodation. This is what the concept of universal design is all about.[4]

Can you imagine how people in 2015 would react if a person with a disability, such as a veteran paralyzed during the war in Afghanistan, was unable to go to college or access public buildings? People would see this as unjust. But in the 1950s people who were blind, deaf, unable to walk, or mentally ill did not have civil rights. In their book *More Than Ramps*, Lisa I. Iezzoni and Bonnie L. O'Day explain why disability rights became a civil rights issue:

> Design, or sometimes "redesign," to eliminate barriers and ensure access thus became central to ensuring civil rights for persons with disabilities. "Lack of access to buildings, programs, and transportation was more than an

> oversight. It was discrimination pure and simple, another kind of segregation" . . . Previous civil rights legislation barring discrimination based on race, ethnicity, and gender sought to ignore these characteristics, striving to judge people based on individual merit. But disability rights advocates recognized that they could not achieve their goal by an approach that more or less "ignored" disability. Instead, disability must first be acknowledged, then the path to civil rights cleared by tearing down barriers.[5]

The disability rights movement in the United States led to the Americans with Disabilities Act (ADA), which became American law in 1990 after a long and difficult struggle. The ADA has inspired 181 countries around the world to also pass disability rights laws. This is unprecedented in human history, because no society in the past ever had anything like the ADA. Disability rights laws are something that Americans should be proud of, yet this is an example of progress that most people I talk to are not even aware of, because they do not realize how bad things were in the past. In his article titled "How a Law to Protect Disabled Americans Became Imitated Around the World," journalist Joseph Shapiro tells us:

> The ADA was signed into law by President George H. W. Bush on July 26, 1990. The idea was that people with disabilities weren't expecting cures. Instead, they were demanding access. For wheelchair users that could mean curb cuts, a motorized lift so they could board a bus, a ramp into a building so they could get to work or school. It meant they could live where they wanted and socialize with friends—just like people without disabilities.
>
> Since 2000, 181 countries have passed disability civil rights laws inspired by the ADA, according to the Disability Rights Education and Defense Fund, a civil rights law and policy center.
>
> At the State Department conference [held in 2015

on disability rights], participants know some of the history of the American disability civil rights movement and about [Judy] Heumann, who is regarded as one of its heroes . . .

When Heumann was an infant in 1949, she got polio. When she was old enough to start her education, her New York City school rejected her. They told her a girl in a wheelchair would be a fire hazard, but her mother fought and Heumann was able to attend.

She went on to college and earned a degree in speech therapy to help children with disabilities. But when she tried to become a teacher, the New York City school system again told her the wheelchair would be a fire hazard.

A frustrated Heumann moved to California, where she became a leader in the new disability civil rights movement—ending the exclusion of people with disabilities . . .

Susan Sygall [is the] co-founder and head of Mobility International USA, one of the many American nonprofit groups that trains people with disabilities from around the world. Sygall's group, in Oregon, has taught 2,300 people with disabilities from around the world how to advocate for civil rights in their countries. When they come to Oregon, she says, they see how different life is for people with disabilities in America—and they then want to push for change in their own countries.

In the U.S., they see "the magic of the Americans with Disabilities Act," she says. "You can see that, yes, people with disabilities should and can ride the public buses. Yes, people with disabilities can and should be at high schools, at the universities. Yes, people with disabilities can be employed, can be leaders, can participate in recreation and sports, can basically have the same rights as everybody else."[6]

Life is not perfect for disabled Americans today, nor is the ADA a perfect law that has solved all the problems on the disability rights issue. Nevertheless, significant progress has been made. We cannot create a perfect world, but we can create further progress on any issue if we continue to sail toward the star of struggle. When we romanticize the past, we forget how bright the star of struggle has always been in the past.

Romanticizing the past is different from *nostalgia*, which occurs when we long for a specific experience from the past, because romanticizing the past oversimplifies complex societies and entire time periods. Before I offer other examples of people romanticizing the past as a golden age, we must discuss where the term *golden age* came from. It derived from the ancient Greeks. The Greek poet Hesiod, who was born around the eighth century BC, wrote that the gods first created a race of golden men to inhabit the earth. Hesiod explains:

> First of all the deathless gods who dwell on Olympus made a golden race of mortal men who lived in the time of Cronos when he was reigning in heaven. And they lived like gods without sorrow of heart, remote and free from toil and grief: miserable age rested not on them; but with legs and arms never failing they made merry with feasting beyond the reach of all evils. When they died, it was as though they were overcome with sleep, and they had all good things; for the fruitful earth unforced bare them fruit abundantly and without stint. They dwelt in ease and peace upon their lands with many good things, rich in flocks and loved by the blessed gods.[7]

After the superior race of golden men* died out, Hesiod says the Greek gods created a second inferior race of silver men followed by a third inferior

* Did Hesiod mean these golden men were metaphorically or literally made out of gold? We are not sure. In Plato's dialogue *Cratylus*, Socrates says Hesiod did not mean these golden men were literally made out of gold. The fact that Socrates has to say this suggests that some people in ancient Greece thought Hesiod was speaking literally.

race of bronze men, both of which were severely flawed and also died out. Then the Greek gods created a fourth race that was not as good as the golden men but better than the silver men and bronze men. Many of the people in the fourth race were part human and part divine. This was known as the Heroic Age, an era when gods often intermingled and reproduced with human beings. During the Heroic Age, heroes such as Heracles, Achilles, and Odysseus lived.

Hesiod believed that everyone in his era (the eighth and seventh centuries BC) was part of the iron race, a fifth race far inferior to the golden men of the remote past and the demigods of the Heroic Age (the time period around the thirteenth and twelfth centuries BC). The gods did not intermingle or reproduce with human beings of the iron race. To summarize, Hesiod described the five ages of humanity as the Golden Age, Silver Age, Bronze Age, Heroic Age (time period when Heracles, Achilles, and Odysseus lived), and Iron Age (time period when poets such as Hesiod and Homer lived).

People can romanticize the past to varying degrees. When I meet people who romanticize the 1950s, they don't romanticize it to the same extreme as Hesiod's story of golden men who never suffer, but they do view the 1950s as a time of purity and innocence. Homer, who lived around the same time as Hesiod, romanticized the Heroic Age slightly by depicting heroes from that time period as superior to himself and all people of the iron race. But Homer's *Iliad*, which is a story about heroes living during the Heroic Age, certainly does not romanticize the Heroic Age as innocent and pure. Instead, the *Iliad* offers vivid depictions of cruelty, rage, slavery, war trauma, and the suffering of civilians.

Homer romanticized the past slightly by depicting the heroes of the Heroic Age as much physically stronger than men of the iron race. In the *Iliad* a Greek soldier named Diomedes easily throws a boulder, which Homer says is so heavy that two men of the iron race would not even be able to lift it. The boulder hits the Trojan soldier Aeneas, whom the Romans believed was a forefather of Rome, causing him to pass out from pain. Diomedes is a young warrior who is not nearly as strong as Giant Ajax and might not even be as strong as stocky and muscular Odysseus. Homer describes the immense strength of Greek heroes such as Diomedes:

> Just as Diomedes hefted a boulder in his hands, a tremendous feat—no two men could hoist it, weak as men are now, but all on his own he raised it high with ease, flung it and struck Aeneas' thigh where the hipbone turns inside the pelvis, the joint they call the cup—it smashed the socket, snapped both tendons too and the jagged rock tore back the skin in shreds. The great fighter sank to his knees, bracing himself with one strong forearm planted against the earth, and the world went black as night before his eyes.[8]

When people romanticize the past slightly* as Homer did (without ignoring the cruelty, suffering, and injustice that existed in the past), this is not nearly as problematic as the more severe forms of romanticizing the past that are common today. In the first chapter I discussed how people romanticize nature, and in this chapter we must understand why so many people today romanticize the past and how this endangers human survival.

I first pondered the dangers of romanticizing the past when I was at West Point and one of my philosophy professors discussed how he wished he could live in ancient Athens during the fifth century BC. He said people in that society invented democracy and spent much of their time walking around discussing philosophy, being actively involved in politics, and exploring big questions. He said the fifth century BC in ancient Athens was the greatest time in human history to be alive.

I raised my hand and disagreed. I mentioned that in ancient Athens, a third of the population were slaves and women had no rights. I also mentioned that the ancient Athenians created an aggressive empire in the fifth century BC. During the Peloponnesian War that resulted, many Athenian

* An example of slight rather than extreme romanticizing is the way people refer to "the golden age of heavyweight boxing." This form of romanticizing is not being applied to a complex society or entire time period, but the much simpler category of a specific sport, where a few prominent boxers are used to define an entire era. This kind of slight romanticizing can oversimplify things a little bit, because if someone talks about a certain era as "the golden age of video games," they are usually only referring to the great games of that era, rather than the much larger number of mediocre and bad games that exist alongside the great ones.

men were killed in battle and around a third of the Athenian population died from plague.

Later on I thought about other problems in ancient Athens. Around a third of children died before age ten, and nobody, not even the richest Greeks, had access to antibiotics, modern dentistry and anesthesia, prescription glasses, or surgeons who could repair torn tendons, safely remove cataracts, and perform organ transplants. If someone living in the United States today is stabbed in the stomach, the person can be rushed to an emergency room. This was not possible in ancient Greece. In fact, modern medical technology is something many people today take for granted. During the American Revolutionary War, doctors performed surgery and amputated limbs without the use of anesthesia while patients were awake. Patients might be given something to bite on while their limb was being sawed off, and if they were lucky they would pass out from the pain.

The professor acknowledged my point about slavery in ancient Greece but seemed to dismiss the unjust treatment of women, which encouraged me to learn more about the history of women's rights on my own. I was surprised to learn that some men living in ancient Athens were more aware of the way women were unjustly treated than many modern men who romanticize ancient Athens. Euripides, a Greek playwright who lived in the fifth century BC, wrote a play about the mythological character Medea. In Greek mythology, Medea traveled with Jason and the Argonauts. She played a vital role by helping Jason obtain the Golden Fleece, which was the purpose of his journey.

Despite Medea's vital assistance to Jason in Greek mythology, women in ancient Athens had no rights, were seen as little better than slaves, and could be legally raped and beaten by their husbands. For the most part, Athenian women were expected to not voice their opinions in the presence of men, and they were also expected to spend most of their time in the home. The Greek playwright Aristophanes made fun of Euripides because his mother sold vegetables in the market, meaning that Euripides was from a lower class because his mother had to work outside of the home.

In several of his surviving plays, Euripides provides commentary on the status of women in ancient Greece. In his play *Medea*, Euripides shows

Medea taking revenge on her husband, Jason, because he replaces her with a younger bride. To describe the status of women in ancient Greek society, Euripides has his character Medea say:

> Of everything that is alive and has a mind, we women are the most wretched creatures. First of all, we have to buy a husband with a vast outlay of money—we have to take a master for our body . . . Divorce brings shame on a woman's reputation and we cannot refuse a husband his rights . . . I would rather stand three times in the battle line than bear one child."[9]

Commenting on this play, classics scholar Edith Hall says, "[Medea's speech] trenchantly exposes the jeopardy in which marriage placed women: besides the insulting dowry system, they were subject to legalized rape in marriage, a hypocritical double standard in divorce, and agonizing mortal danger in childbirth. This kind of speech outraged the Christian writer Origen, who criticized Euripides for inappropriately making women express argumentative opinions . . . It is indeed a remarkable feature of Euripidean tragedy that many of his best thinkers and talkers are women."[10]

At the end of the *Iliad*, the invading Greek army is on the verge of conquering Troy after the Greek warrior Achilles kills Hector, the greatest Trojan warrior. In his play *Hecuba*, Euripides describes what happens to the Trojan civilians conquered by the Greeks. In one scene he portrays Hector's mother, Hecuba, arguing against Odysseus for wanting to sacrifice her daughter. Hecuba is depicted as an intellectual equal to Odysseus, despite his cunning skill at manipulation.

In Euripides's play *The Trojan Women*, Hecuba finds out that she will become a slave to Odysseus. She regards him as the most evil man in the Greek army and says there is no fate worse than becoming his slave. Hecuba tells her fellow Trojan women: "The lot has assigned me as a slave to a foul man of trickery, an enemy of justice, a lawless monster who turns everything inside out and then back again with his double tongue, transforming men to hatred of what they once held dear. Weep for me, Trojan women. An evil fate has destroyed me. All is over for me, a wretched woman who has met with the most unhappy allocation of all."[11]

Homer and Euripides were both Greeks, yet they both portrayed the Trojans, their historic enemies, as nobler than the Greeks in several ways. This is quite remarkable. How often do you see American war films portray the enemy as nobler than the Americans? This is basically what Euripides did in his play *The Trojan Women*. The ancient Greeks, especially in the fifth century BC, prided themselves on being "civilized." They often dehumanized non-Greeks as being uncivilized barbarians. But in *The Trojan Women*, Hecuba calls her Greek conquerors barbaric by saying to them, "O you Greeks, you who have devised atrocities worthy of barbarians."[12]

Classics scholar S. A. Barlow says this statement from *The Trojan Women* "might be said to contain the heart of the play. It is supposedly civilized Greeks who are really the barbarians, and the barbarians who are the civilized ones—a slur on the values on which the Greeks had prided themselves for so long."[13] As history shows, dehumanizing people as barbarians caused the "civilized" Greeks to behave barbarically. In a similar way, dehumanizing Native Americans as savages caused the "civilized" Americans to behave savagely.

When we romanticize any era in the past as a golden age, as many people do today, we make that era much less fascinating. History is most compelling and instructive when it is complex, when it is filled with struggle and surprises. Professor Elizabeth Vandiver explains why ancient history is especially complex:

> It's very difficult to reconstruct the actual lives of ancient Athenian women or any other ancient women for that matter, since almost all our sources were written by men and presumably with men as the target audiences. And another problem, perhaps an even worse problem, is that many of the sources are prescriptive, rather than descriptive. That is, they are sources talking about how women should behave and how women should act, which is not by any means necessarily the same thing as

> describing how women do act. And the [Greek] tragedies themselves are both one of our most important and one of our most problematic resources for trying to figure out what the life of Athenian women was actually like.
>
> One of the most striking characteristics of Greek tragedies—I think anyone who has read any Greek tragedy would agree with this—is the presence of strong, powerful women in many of them. There's only one surviving tragedy, *Philoctetes* by Sophocles, that doesn't have a female character. The rest of them all include female characters. And some of the most memorable characters of Greek tragedy are women. Very frequently a woman is the protagonist, the main character of a tragedy, or an extremely important secondary character . . . All in all, the extant tragedies seem to indicate that the role of women in Athens and men's conception of women's essential personality and social functions were far more complex than has sometimes been thought.[14]

Another form of romanticizing the past is the myth of matriarchal prehistory, which is the belief that in the distant past all people lived in matriarchal societies where women ruled, people lived together peacefully, there were no taboos around sex, and life had little to no struggle or messiness. According to this myth, the matriarchies were overthrown by patriarchies, destroying the golden age that once existed.

As I mentioned earlier, one of the oddest things human beings can do with time is romanticize the past. This romanticizing can be slight, such as depicting Greek heroes as much stronger than us, or extreme, such as longing for a golden age when people lived with little to no struggle and human existence was not messy. What do I mean by the *messiness of human existence*? This messiness refers to the inevitable aspects of struggle that are part of being human. The messiness of human existence includes misunderstanding, conflict, our vulnerability to trauma, our search for trust, our shared human fallibility that causes us to make mistakes, and our shared human craving for purpose, meaning, and self-worth. When we distort the truth of the human condition by denying the messiness of human existence, we become naive about the challenges of living in a community and are more likely to romanticize the past.

Knowing that human beings often romanticize the past, we should be skeptical whenever we hear sweeping generalizations that sugarcoat any society in history, yet the myth of matriarchal prehistory makes sweeping generalizations that sugarcoat *all* societies in prehistory. In her book *The Myth of Matriarchal Prehistory: Why an Invented Past Won't Give Women a Future*, Cynthia Eller writes:

> As precedents go, the one offered by the myth of matriarchal prehistory is remarkable. It does not say that in the very distant past, there was a small group of people who were able for a short time to construct a society that gave women status and freedom and did not make war on other people or the natural world. Quite the contrary: according to feminist matriarchal myth, matriarchy was universal, it endured for all the millennia in which we were human, and was only supplanted very recently . . .
>
> A number of themes appear repeatedly in feminist descriptions of prehistoric matriarchal societies: peace, prosperity, harmony with nature, appropriate use of technology, sexual freedom (including reproductive freedom), and just and equitable roles for women and men . . . Some matriarchalists refer unapologetically to this era as a "utopia" or the "golden age." However, feminist matriarchalists are intent on bringing prehistoric peoples closer to themselves in imagination, so our ancestors are said to have had problems . . . but they did not have *our* problems, which are overwhelming . . .
>
> The myth of matriarchal prehistory is a universalizing story: once things were good, everywhere; now they are bad . . . Feminist matriarchalists portray women as

naturally good, kind, loving human beings . . . If this is what women are like, what should we expect from men? Mostly, it turns out, the opposite . . . Some feminist matriarchalists have described men as mutants whose "small and twisted Y chromosome" is "a genetic error" resulting from, perhaps, "disease or a radiation bombardment from the sun" . . . Some feminist matriarchalists try to provide—or at least allow for the existence of—positive male role models, the sort of men who might have lived and flourished in prehistoric times . . . According to most feminist matriarchalists, men are not beyond hope . . .

Foraging societies are often said by cultural anthropologists to be "egalitarian," so this looks like a hopeful place for feminist matriarchalists to begin [looking for contemporary societies similar to prehistoric matriarchal societies]. However, anthropologists mean something by the term egalitarianism that turns out, oddly enough, to be compatible with the most virulent misogyny and sexism. Egalitarian societies are defined by anthropologists as small groups which lack any elaborate political hierarchy. Individuals are free to come and go as they please; they have immediate access to resources and can exert influence over other individuals in their group. There are pecking orders in egalitarian societies, but they depend "more upon personal qualities and skills than upon inherited wealth or status at birth."

But among the "personal qualities" most frequently used to determine status in so-called egalitarian societies are "age, sex, and personal characteristics." Now age and sex are not earned. An individual's age changes, inexorably, and in this sense can be regarded as a kind of achieved status. But this is not so for sex, which is "ascribed for life." Thus arises the irony of speaking of societies which systematically discriminate against one sex in preference to the other as "egalitarian."

Such discrimination can be relatively minor, as it is among the Mbuti and San of Africa, where men are slightly more likely to participate in collective decision-making, but there are also many glaring examples of male authority, dominance, and disproportionate prestige in foraging societies. Even in societies that lack class systems or political leadership, one can find fathers giving away their daughters, husbands beating their wives or having legitimate control over them sexually, men raping women without penalty, and men claiming a monopoly on the most significant forms of ritual power . . .

If there is one broad pattern regarding women's status [in small tribes around the world today], it is that it is lower than men's, whatever the prevailing economy or women's specific place in it. Within this generalization, however, there is a staggering amount of variation, from vague nuances of differential personal autonomy or authority to unmistakable sexual slavery. If ethnographic reports are any indication, then women's status prehistorically was variable, not uniform; in some places it was probably very good, while in other places it was probably horrific . . .

Ethnographic analogies to contemporary groups with lifeways similar to those of prehistoric times (hunting and gathering or horticulture, practiced in small groups) show little sex egalitarianism and no matriarchy. Indeed, these societies always discriminate in some way between women and men, usually to women's detriment. Women may have powerful roles, but their power does not undermine or seriously challenge an overall system of male dominance in either these groups or ours, and there is no reason to believe that it would have in prehistoric societies either. If there are in fact societies where women's position is high and

> secure, these exceptions cannot lead us to believe that it was *this* pattern (rather than the more prevalent pattern of discrimination against women) which held in prehistory.[15]

Contrary to the myth that all human societies were once matriarchal, there is no known matriarchal society that has ever existed, where women as a group have higher status, authority, and influence than men.* There have been many *matrilineal* societies where one's ancestry is traced primarily through the mother rather than the father, but matrilineal does not mean matriarchal, and people often confuse these terms.

There are examples in European history where some queens had a lot of power, but this is an example of "class rights" rather than "women's rights." This power was bestowed because a queen was a member of the royal family, not because she was a woman. In medieval Europe, peasants (both male and female) often lacked basic human rights. There are also many examples where women in royal families were treated terribly. Today no British man has the legal right to publicly execute his wife, as King Henry VIII did to two of his wives.

When we believe the myth that all people in the distant past lived in matriarchies, we underestimate how revolutionary and unprecedented the women's rights movement of the nineteenth century truly was. This movement, which Elizabeth Cady Stanton, Susan B. Anthony, and many other female activists helped create, accomplished something new in history by spreading the revolutionary ideal of universal women's rights on a large scale. Frederick Douglass, an escaped slave who dedicated his life to ending slavery and promoting women's rights, said the women's rights movement was even more far-reaching and important than the movement to end slavery.

Historian Philip Foner tells us: "[Frederick Douglass] told the women at these [women's rights] meetings that he regarded their movement to be more important than the movement to end slavery, significant though that had been, because their struggle 'comprehends the liberation and elevation

* Some people have changed the definition of matriarchy to refer to men and women being fully equal, but as I will discuss later in this chapter, full women's equality in small tribes is elusive due to the divisions of labor that help these tribes manage community life and survive.

of one-half of the whole human family,' and 'if successful, it will be the most stupendous revolution the world has ever witnessed.'"[16]

The ideal of universal women's rights means women should have the same political, educational, and economic rights as men, and they should not be denied any occupations available to men.* For example, in the Iroquois Confederacy women had some political power (such as the ability to choose chiefs). But these women could not become chiefs and also lacked the universal right to vote. Although women in the Iroquois Confederacy (and many indigenous societies) had more status than women in ancient Athens, women in practically all indigenous societies lacked the freedom to *fully* pursue occupations and lifestyles traditionally reserved for men, such as being warriors. If anyone today said women should not be allowed to attend West Point or join the military, that person would be called a sexist.

We should not judge indigenous societies by modern standards, because morality depends on choice. Thousands of years ago indigenous people living in Europe hunted wooly mammoths, using their bones and ivory to construct shelters and wearing their fur to stay warm during a harsh ice age. Today many people think that killing African elephants and using their ivory, along with wearing any kind of fur, is immoral. This is because we have so many other options today for construction materials and clothing fabrics. Indigenous Europeans wearing the skin of an endangered animal during the ice age was not the same as a modern person wearing the skin of an endangered leopard, because we have so many options they did not have.

In a similar way, if a doctor three hundred years ago amputated someone's infected leg without using anesthesia, that was not immoral, because this was the doctor's best option. But if a doctor today with access to antibiotics and anesthesia cuts off someone's infected leg without first trying to heal the infection or reduce the person's pain, that is certainly immoral, because a modern doctor has more options than a doctor living three

* There are some occupations, such as playing in the NFL, where women are denied a professional career due to physical requirements. However, over 99.9 percent of American men are not athletic enough to play in the NFL. According to the ideal of universal women's rights, having separate sports leagues (tennis, soccer, basketball, boxing, etc.) for men and women, due to their different physiques, is not considered sexist.

hundred years ago. Indigenous societies had divisions of labor based on gender, which were sometimes strict and sometimes more flexible, because it seemed to assist their survival. In modern society our survival does not depend on divisions of labor based on gender.

The fact that people in the distant past had so few options should make us skeptical when someone sugarcoats any ancient or prehistoric society as a romanticized utopia. I have heard many people say that indigenous tribes in the past lived in "Eden" or "paradise." We certainly have modern problems they didn't have, but they also had problems we don't have. Progress does not remove all problems but instead causes life's challenges to change shape and size, since struggle is a feature of reality that always remains in some form.

Strangulated hernia is just one problem among many that would not exist in Eden or paradise, but exists in indigenous tribes. Born in 1875, medical doctor Albert Schweitzer described the problem of strangulated hernia, which afflicted many indigenous Africans in the region where he built his hospital. Schweitzer said:

> [The Africans] also suffer much oftener than white people from strangulated hernia, in which the intestine becomes constricted and blocked, so that it can no longer empty itself. It then becomes enormously inflated by the gases which form, and this causes terrible pain. Then after several days of torture, death takes place, unless the intestine can be got back through the rupture into the abdomen. Our ancestors were well acquainted with this terrible method of dying, but we no longer see it in Europe because every case is operated upon as soon as ever it is recognized. "Let not the sun go down upon your—strangulated hernia," is the maxim continually impressed upon medical students. But in Africa this terrible death is quite common. There are few Africans who have not as boys seen some man rolling in the sand of his hut and howling with agony till death came to release him. So now, the

> moment a man feels that his rupture is a strangulated one—rupture is far rarer among women—he begs his friends to put him in a canoe and bring him to me.
>
> How can I describe my feelings when a poor fellow is brought to me in this condition? I am the only person within hundreds of miles who can help him . . . We must all die. But that I can save him from days of torture, that is what I feel as my great and ever new privilege. Pain is a more terrible lord of mankind than even death himself. So, when the poor, moaning creature comes, I lay my hand on his forehead and say to him: "Don't be afraid! In an hour's time you shall be put to sleep, and when you wake you won't feel any more pain."[17]

There are four reasons why people romanticize the past, and all four reasons endanger human survival in a different way.* The first reason is the desire to cover up a sense of guilt. This is why some people in the American South romanticize the era of slavery by saying slaves were not treated badly and most slaves were happy being slaves. This is also why American western expansion has been romanticized in a way that downplays the massacre of Native Americans.

Many countries romanticize their past in a way that sugarcoats past atrocities they committed. This form of romanticizing is dangerous because it prevents us from understanding on a deep and empathetic level why injustice happens and learning from these mistakes. Because technology has given us the capacity to destroy ourselves, it has never been more important for human beings to develop the ability to acknowledge and learn from our mistakes. This ability is an essential part of the art of living, the art of waging peace, and the art of listening.

The second reason people romanticize the past is to build up a damaged

* These four reasons address why people romanticize societies and entire time periods in the past. These four reasons do not address the slight romanticizing of special slices of life, such as "the golden age of baseball."

sense of self-worth. Women have been degraded so much throughout history that it is understandable why the myth of matriarchal prehistory can be so appealing. When our self-worth is damaged by an oppressive system, we can respond by romanticizing the past in a way that elevates our worth and diminishes the worth of those we perceive as our oppressors.

In his biography *Malcolm X: A Life of Reinvention*, Manning Marable describes how African American preacher Wallace Fard, who founded the Nation of Islam, influenced Malcolm Little (also known as Malcolm X) and many other African Americans with the myth of a golden age that existed before white people inhabited the earth:

> By 1931, news of his controversial addresses attracted hundreds of blacks, many desperately seeking a message of hope as the country sank into depression . . . The most controversial dimension of Fard's preaching concerned Euro-Americans. Since black Americans [according to Fard] were both Asiatics and Earth's Original People, what were whites? The reason that both Marcus Garvey and Noble Drew Ali had failed, Fard taught, was that neither had fully grasped the true nature of whites: as Malcolm Little was to learn, they were "devils."
>
> To explain this, Fard presented his parable, Yacub's History, centered on the genetic plot of an evil "Big Head" scientist named Yacub, who lived thousands of years ago. A member of the exalted tribe of Shabazz, Yacub nevertheless used his scientific skills to produce genetic mutations that culminated in the creation of the white race. Although the naturally crafty and violent whites were banished to the caves of Caucasus, they ultimately achieved control over the entire earth. The Original People, Fard taught, subsequently "went to sleep" mentally and spiritually. The task of the Nation of Islam was to bring into consciousness the "lost-found" Asiatic black man from his centuries-long slumber.

> The demonizing of the white race, the glorification of blacks, and the bombastic blend of orthodox Islam, Moorish science, and numerology were a seductive message to unemployed and disillusioned African Americans.[18]

When we build our self-worth on a sense of gender, racial, or national superiority, whether it is a matriarchal myth that depicts women as superior to men or Fard's myth that portrays African Americans as superior to whites, we create an "us versus them" dichotomy that denies our shared humanity. As I will discuss later in this chapter, the myth that men are naturally destructive can also create a self-fulfilling prophecy that encourages men to be more aggressive, and neglects the countless men who embraced compassion as a way of life, such as Buddha, Lao-tzu, Jesus, Saint Francis of Assisi, Henry David Thoreau, Leo Tolstoy, Mahatma Gandhi, Martin Luther King Jr., Albert Schweitzer, Nelson Mandela, Archbishop Desmond Tutu, Khan Abdul Ghaffar Khan, Cesar Chavez, Thich Nhat Hanh, and Archbishop Oscar Romero, just to mention a few.

As a child I struggled a lot with my racial identity. Although I am half Korean, a quarter black, and a quarter white, I felt like an outcast because I did not fully belong to any of these racial groups. In my other books I discuss how the pain of feeling like a racial outcast fueled my journey to understand the many ways our shared humanity transcends race, nationality, and religion.

Because I embarked on this journey to understand and embrace our shared humanity, today when I read the wisdom of the ancient Greeks I feel a sense of pride in humanity, even though I am not Greek, because I am human and they were human. Today when I learn about the wisdom of indigenous peoples I also feel a sense of pride in humanity, because all of us descended from indigenous tribes who lived in the distant past, and no matter what tribe today expresses this wisdom, I am human and they are human. The wisdom of ancient Chinese and Indian philosophers causes me to think, "Their wisdom is a testament to human greatness." No matter what culture people come from, the wisdom they express is a tribute not only to themselves, but also to the glory and greatness of humanity and the grandeur of life.

It took me years to become deeply literate in our shared humanity, and every book in this series reveals the truth of our shared humanity. Internalizing this truth in our daily lives can certainly be a struggle, but if more people do not embrace this struggle, then we will not be able to solve our most serious national and global problems. Embracing our shared humanity does not mean completely ignoring our differences, but it does mean not having to reduce the worth of others to increase our own sense of worth. Self-worth based on our shared humanity does not have to say women are better than men, blacks are better than whites, Europeans are better than non-Europeans, or any country is the "best country in the world." Seeing our shared humanity emanate from all people and myself makes me feel larger and more fulfilled than limiting my identity ever did.

Despite living in overtly racist conditions that most people today cannot imagine, Malcolm X went from viewing white people as "devils" to embracing our shared humanity. One month before his death, he said, "I believe in recognizing every human being as a human being, neither white, black, brown nor red. When you are dealing with humanity as one family, there's no question of integration or intermarriage. It's just one human being marrying another human being, or one human being living around and with another human being."[19]

The third reason people romanticize the past is that they are cynical about the possibility of progress, which creates the illusion that there is no such thing as progress.* Just because struggle will always exist does not mean progress does not exist. Cynicism toward progress is a defense mechanism that protects us from disappointment. Cynicism also allows us to rationalize our inaction with the belief that nothing will ever change for the better, so what is the point of striving to improve our world to the best of our ability? In *Peaceful Revolution* I discuss the difference between cynicism and skepticism, and why skepticism is important for discerning the truth and protecting ourselves from manipulation.

* Cynicism can have many definitions. In this chapter I am focusing on cynicism toward progress, which primarily acts as a defense mechanism against disappointment and a justification for complacency and apathy. People can also be cynical toward human nature, hope, and ideals. In *Peaceful Revolution* I discuss how to combat these forms of cynicism.

Cynicism exists along a broad spectrum, because people can experience cynicism in large or small amounts. In large doses, cynicism can make a person apathetic, lethargic about life, and completely inactive in creating the change our world needs most. In small doses, cynicism can cause an activist to pessimistically preach to the choir and spread an "us versus them" message that stereotypes those on the other side of the issue, rather than reaching beyond the choir and offering constructive solutions.

Because cynicism is so dangerous to nonviolent movements and to progress, it is also dangerous to humanity. Embracing realistic hope rather than cynicism means not only acknowledging the reality of progress but also the possibility of *regress*. If we believe the myth that "time heals all wounds" and do not wage peace with a sense of urgency, the forces of injustice can turn back the progress that has been made, making our world far more unjust in the future than it is today.

The fourth reason people romanticize the past is that they are longing for a time and place immune to time's ruthlessness, a time and place without struggle and the messiness of human existence. But humanity will not overcome the serious problems that threaten our survival unless we embrace the star of struggle and train ourselves to make the most of struggle. The reasons people romanticize the past—guilt, self-worth, the numbness of cynicism (I will discuss how trauma can cause cynicism in the last book of this series), and responding to time's ruthlessness—encourage me to have even more empathy for humanity. We are remarkable creatures worthy of awe, not only in our glory and greatness, but also in our vulnerability. There is also a fifth *possible* reason that people in the future may romanticize the past, which I will discuss below.

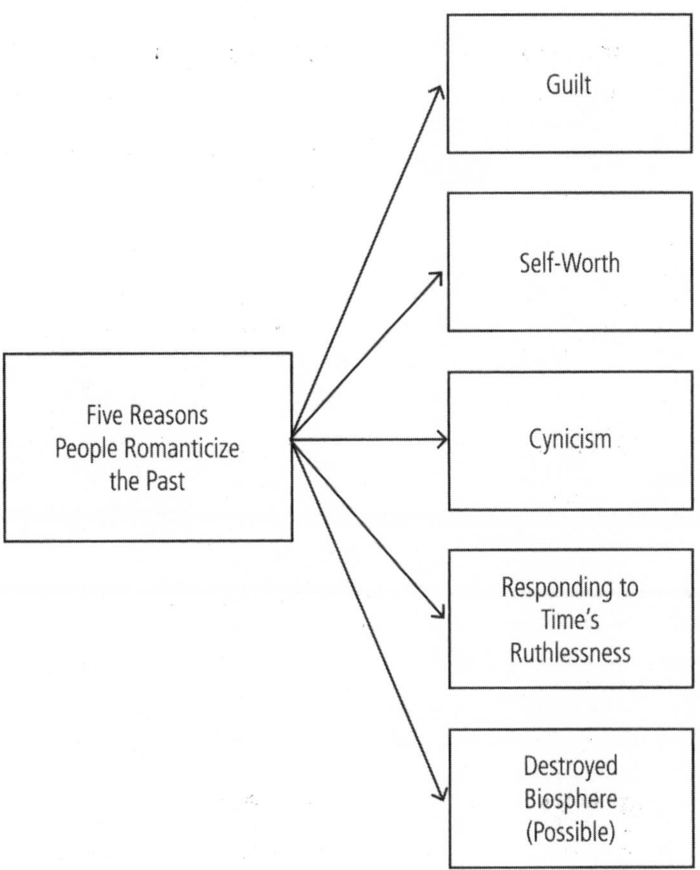

Figure 3.1: Five Reasons People Romanticize the Past

If we do not wage peace to solve our global problems, people in the future may have a fifth reason to romanticize the past. The fifth reason could be that if we destroy our delicate biosphere, people in the future would romanticize the past because life truly was relatively idyllic when I wrote these words in 2015, as compared to a world where our atmosphere and oceans could no longer sustain complex life. One reason I have realistic hope that we can create a brighter future is that we have the sword of truth. If we want to ensure that humanity prevails, we must first ensure that truth prevails.*

The Peace Hero Ideal

As I discussed in chapter 2, why must we learn the art of living? Why aren't we born with all the skills and wisdom necessary to live well? The reason is that our brains are so complex. An oak tree knows how to be an oak tree. It doesn't need a mentor or role model to guide it. A caterpillar knows how to turn into a butterfly and thrive in the world. It doesn't have to attend school or be instructed by its parents. But human beings, more than any other species on the planet, must learn to be what we are. We must learn to be human.

This is why children in every culture need role models and mentors to guide them, such as parents, teachers, community members, or even religious icons such as Jesus and Buddha. This is why people in every culture need an ideal to strive toward, an ideal that represents our highest human potential.

In our culture, this ideal is known as the "hero." In ancient Greece, heroes were not moral, but exceptional. The Greek heroes included Achilles, Odysseus, Heracles, and many others. Achilles was the mightiest warrior alive, Odysseus was a brilliant tactician and talented speaker as well as a powerful warrior, and Heracles was the strongest man in the world who endured extraordinary suffering.

Unlike the ancient Greek heroes, the "peace hero" is not admired for being physically exceptional, but morally exceptional. Peace heroes such as

* To address a counterpoint that might come up, what about people living in war-torn countries? Is it beneficial for them to romanticize the past? A person living in a war-torn country can desperately want the war to end without romanticizing the past, because the problems that cause a war usually existed long before the war erupted. For example, a Jewish person living in Europe during World War II could desperately want the war to end without romanticizing Europe's past as being free from anti-Semitism. Prior to World War II, anti-Semitism was rampant in many parts of Europe, not just Germany. As I explained earlier, nostalgia is different from romanticizing the past, and there are some very poetic scenes in the *Iliad* where people are nostalgic about certain aspects of life before the war began. I will discuss nostalgia as a form of transcendence in the last book of this series.

Buddha, Lao-tzu, Amos, Jesus, Lucretia Mott, Lydia Maria Child, Sojourner Truth, Mahatma Gandhi, Khan Abdul Ghaffar Khan, Helen Keller, Martin Luther King Jr., Wangari Matthai, Cesar Chavez, Nelson Mandela, Dorothy Stang, Archbishop Oscar Romero, and many others were not exceptional killers like Achilles or exceptionally strong like Heracles, but exceptionally moral in the ways humanity must emulate if we are going to survive during our fragile future. Peace heroes cannot propel heavy boulders with the might of the Greek hero Diomedes, but they can propel truth with enough force to shatter ignorance, deception, and injustice.

One of the early peace heroes was Socrates. Socrates, similar to later peace heroes such as Gandhi, Albert Schweitzer, Saint Francis of Assisi, General Smedley Butler, and Leo Tolstoy, had served in the military. Socrates went from being courageous on the battlefield to courageously challenging injustice in his society, replacing the weapons of war with the weapon of truth.

In his book *Socrates Against Athens*, historian James A. Colaiaco tells us: "[Socrates] is challenging his fellow Athenians to rise to a new moral conception of the heroic . . . Socrates carried out his mission without fear of death. But he contradicted the traditional notion of the hero . . . For him, vengeance is unjust, and honor is won only in the pursuit of moral virtue, even at the expense of violating the values of the community. The new hero that Socrates represented was not one who excelled on the battlefield or one who surrendered his life unthinkingly to the polis [city-state], but one who remained steadfast in his commitment to justice."[20]

The peace hero, which is the new hero that Socrates represented, has five characteristics. The first characteristic all peace heroes have in common is that they reject vengeance. Could you imagine Jesus, Buddha, Martin Luther King Jr., Nelson Mandela, or Malala Yousafzai embracing vengeance? If they did, they would not be the people we admire. Instead of embracing vengeance, the second characteristic all peace heroes have in common is that they raise up justice.[21] I will further discuss justice in the next chapter.

The third characteristic all peace heroes have in common is that they recognize our interconnectedness, allowing them to understand on a deep level how their work is built on the efforts of countless others. This is one reason why peace heroes do not see themselves as heroes, but as people trying to reflect a peaceful ideal.

By recognizing our interconnectedness, people who reflect the peace hero ideal are often embarrassed when anyone praises them as heroes. Paradoxically, one sign of a true peace hero is not seeing oneself as a hero. Frederick Douglass, who dedicated his life to ending slavery and furthering women's rights, said, "We never feel more ashamed of our humble efforts in the cause of emancipation than when we contrast them with the silent, unobserved and unapplauded efforts of those women through whose constant and persevering endeavors this annual [anti-slavery] exhibition is given to the American public."[22]

The vast majority of people who reflect the peace hero ideal are not famous. Commenting on these unsung heroes of peace and justice, Albert Schweitzer said, "The sum of these [actions from people who aren't famous], however, is a thousand times stronger than the acts of those who receive wide public recognition. The latter, compared to the former, are like the foam on the waves of a deep ocean."[23]

The fourth characteristic of the peace hero ideal is respecting and serving the well-being of others. The attitude of service requires the attitude of respect. Nobel Peace Prize laureate Wangari Maathai, who dedicated her life to environmental protection, democratic progress, and women's rights, explains the ideal of service, which is the opposite of selfishness:

> One dimension of service that I feel strongly about is the principle of servant leadership. In *The Challenge for Africa*, I explored examples of individuals who helped their communities by dedicating themselves to assisting the development of all its members, no matter their social or economic status. Such leadership was, of course, evident in the ministry of prophets and saints. Jesus, for one, modeled how to serve. He offered himself and his message to those on the margins of his society: the poor, the outcasts, women, even beggars. Jesus' ministry was the opposite of self-service: it did not create victims of predatory

leadership that exploits the vulnerability of its followers.

Selfless service is the basis for much of what we admire in those we see as exemplars of what is best in humanity—people who represent a model of not only self-empowerment but also of how to motivate others to act for the common good. These models are found in the realm of politics (among individuals such as Nelson Mandela, Julius Nyerere of Tanzania, and the leaders of Kenya's fighters for independence, the best known of whom is Dedan Kimathi Waciuri); in campaigns for civil and human rights (Mahatma Gandhi, Rev. Martin Luther King, Jr., and earlier champions who fought against slavery and colonialism); and among those who championed the dignity of the poor and dispossessed (Dorothy Day of the *Catholic Worker*, Mother Teresa of Calcutta, and the Brazilian environmentalist and union leader Chico Mendes, who was slain in 1988).

I also see such a dedication in Archbishop Oscar Romero of El Salvador, who was assassinated in 1980 for speaking out on behalf of the victims of the civil war in his country; Father Jerzy Popieluszko, who was kidnapped and killed in 1984, because of his support for the Polish trade union Solidarity; and the American nun Dorothy Stang, who was murdered in Brazil in 2005 while defending the rights of the landless and the protection of rain forest. I am inspired by my fellow Nobel laureate Aung San Suu Kyi of Burma for continuing to stand up for what is just, even when the most fundamental human rights have been denied to her. Because of the force of their example, sometimes at the cost of their own lives, all of these individuals have allowed other ordinary people to stand with them and accomplish extraordinary deeds.

In moments when we feel challenged, we would do well to remember such heroes and others like them, who

> have made a commitment to service, and the struggles they endured—many of them motivated by their faith tradition.[24]

The fifth characteristic of the peace hero ideal is redefining worth and honor. When Greek warriors in the *Iliad* or Japanese samurai fought for honor, they were really fighting for their sense of worth. In many past cultures, honor was seen as a sense of self-worth based on what others said and thought about us. To insult people's honor meant insulting their self-worth. Because human beings crave a sense of worthiness, countless people throughout history have been willing to risk their lives to defend their sense of self-worth. Countless cultures around the world have also conditioned men to use violence to defend their self-worth.

In many cultures such as ancient Greece, people based their self-worth on external symbols of honor, such as possessions. The more material wealth Achilles accumulated from conquering, the greater his honor, the greater his sense of self-worth. Surprisingly, one of the first characters in the annals of literature, mythology, and history to challenge the value system represented by Greek heroes such as Achilles was Achilles himself.

In the *Iliad*, two of the motivators that compel Greek warriors to fight are honor (self-worth) and glory (everlasting fame that allows them to transcend time). When King Agamemnon disrespects Achilles by insulting his self-worth in front of the Greek army, Achilles refuses to fight the Trojans anymore. Since he is the best Greek warrior, the Greeks suffer heavy losses due to his absence.

Agamemnon insulted Achilles's honor by taking away one of his possessions, a beautiful female slave named Briseus. She had been a free woman, but during the Trojan War she was enslaved and given to Achilles as a trophy to award his superior ability as a warrior. When Agamemnon takes her away, this insult to Achilles's honor (self-worth) would be similar to a rich man in our society feeling his self-worth was attacked after losing a possession that symbolized his status, such as a luxury car, mansion, or prestigious job title.

Just as the ancient Greeks based their self-worth on external status symbols, it is not uncommon for a man in our society to feel his self-worth increase when he is married to a young and beautiful "trophy wife." Women can also base their self-worth on external status symbols. Like ancient Greek heroes, many men and women in our society display expensive material possessions as status symbols that increase their sense of self-worth. Also, many modern hunters display animal heads as trophies, or get their picture taken with animals they have killed (which they show off to their friends), to symbolize their worth as a hunter.

Our society tends to judge people's worth based on external status symbols, which can include the amount of money they make, what kind of car they drive, and the size of their house. Martin Luther King Jr. said, "We are prone to judge success by the index of our salaries or the size of our automobiles, rather than by the quality of our service and relationship to humanity."[25] Human beings cannot survive without using tools, so it is natural for us to be fascinated with objects. People do not become materialistic simply because they own and use objects. Instead, the problem of materialism results when our cravings for purpose, meaning, and self-worth get wrapped up in the excessive accumulation of objects.

Why is Achilles so enraged at Agamemnon? Achilles not only feels humiliated because his self-worth has been attacked, but he also feels betrayed after risking his life so many times for Agamemnon, whom Achilles sees as a bad leader. In *The Art of Waging Peace* I discuss how West Point taught me that the most effective leaders practice what they preach and lead by example. Achilles describes how Agamemnon does not lead by example: "Agamemnon . . . always skulking behind the lines, safe in his fast ships—and he would take it all [that I fought for], he'd parcel out some scraps but keep the lion's share."[26]

Achilles is also enraged because Agamemnon took away a woman Achilles seemed to genuinely love. Achilles is a complex character. Although he won Briseus as a trophy, he seems to genuinely care about her. Despite being a slave, Briseus believes that Achilles is going to make her his "lawful, wedded wife."[27] Describing his love for Briseus, Achilles says, "Any decent man, a man with sense, loves his own, cares for his own as deeply as I, I loved that woman with all my heart, though I won her like a trophy with my spear."[28]

Agamemnon sends Odysseus, Phoenix (a father figure to Achilles who helped raise him), and Giant Ajax to persuade Achilles to return to battle. Odysseus explains that Agamemnon will return Briseus to Achilles and give him immense material wealth that will restore and greatly increase his honor. But Achilles responds in a shocking way. He challenges the value system of his society by saying he no longer cares about honor and glory. Not even Odysseus can persuade him to return to battle.

Elizabeth Vandiver describes how Achilles rejects values such as honor (which is called *timê* in ancient Greek, pronounced *tee-may*) and glory (which is called *kleos* in ancient Greek):

> Achilles replies to Odysseus in an absolutely astonishing speech that really seems to undercut the entire basis of his society. Odysseus has after all appealed to timê (honor) with this offer of recompense from Agamemnon. [Odysseus] said you lost the timê of Briseus, but look at how much more you'll be given back. Not just will Briseus be restored to you, untouched, unharmed . . . but you will get all these other things as well. There will be absolutely no question in anyone's mind that you are the greatest, most honored warrior of all of us.
>
> How does Achilles respond to that? Well he responds in effect by saying that he simply does not care anymore about any of this . . . Achilles in effect says that he no longer is concerned with timê, he no longer cares about timê, it no longer has anything to say to him. In effect, he says that if timê can be taken away irrationally at a leader's whim, then it has no value. Why fight for something so unstable? Why fight for something that Agamemnon can remove from him at a whim at a moment's notice? The fact that Agamemnon is now giving it back is at this juncture pointless for Achilles. The point is that it could be taken away arbitrarily, so the fact that it can be given back arbitrarily doesn't really help anymore. He is no longer interested in timê . . .

> Odysseus has tried the standard appeal to timê and to kleos (glory) . . . As for kleos, [Achilles basically says] well I don't care about that, I would just as soon live a long life and die at home in bed and never mind kleos. In effect, in short, Achilles has said I reject the entire basis of our society, I reject the entire warrior ethos in which we have all been brought up, I reject everything that the rest of you think is important.[29]

Unlike the traditional Greek hero, but like many peace heroes, Achilles rejects a sense of self-worth based on the accumulation of material wealth, and he also rejects a sense of glory based on the pursuit of everlasting fame. Nevertheless, I would certainly not call Achilles a peace hero, because not only does he embrace vengeance, but he later returns to embracing fame-based glory before and after the death of his closest comrade, Patroclus. And unlike Jesus and other peace heroes, Achilles not only behaves very selfishly at times, but he also has a high capacity for berserker rage that causes him to behave in psychotic ways.

Just as Achilles questions the values of his society, the samurai protagonists in Akira Kurosawa's films *Seven Samurai*, *Yojimbo*, and *Sanjuro* also serve as examples of warriors who do not seek self-worth through the accumulation of material wealth or glory through the pursuit of everlasting fame. Instead, these protagonists demonstrate selfless service, which Kurosawa contrasts with the far more numerous samurai who are focused on external status. Unlike Achilles, who can behave very selfishly at times, Kurosawa's samurai heroes are unselfish.

As I explain in *The Cosmic Ocean*, human beings crave self-worth. Knowing that people desperately want to feel worthy increases my empathy for all of humanity. People can feed their craving for self-worth in a variety of ways, and some ways are healthier than others. The excessive accumulation of material wealth is an unstable foundation for self-worth, and people can base their self-worth on material wealth to different degrees. In *The Cosmic Ocean* I show that a more stable and fulfilling foundation for self-worth can be gained through finding healthy sources of purpose and meaning in our lives, having good friendships and relationships, achieving a sense of belonging based on our shared humanity, overcoming challenge, increasing our understanding, strengthening the muscles of our shared humanity, healing our psychological wounds, and striving to achieve our full human potential.

To summarize, the following diagram shows the five characteristics of the peace hero ideal:

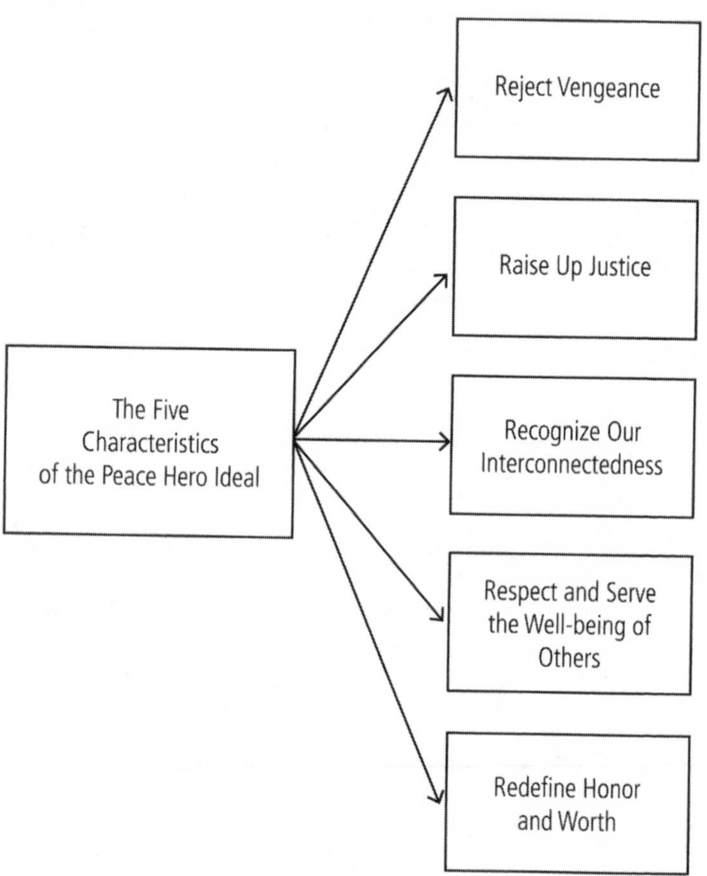

Figure 3.2: The Five Characteristics of the Peace Hero Ideal

How do peace heroes redefine honor and worth? If humanity is going to survive during our fragile future, we must promote a higher form of honor, a *higher form of self-worth*, based not on the excessive accumulation of material wealth or the reduction of living beings into trophies.

This higher form of honor, which I learned at West Point, is based on integrity and the pursuit of truth. At West Point I was taught that I should base my self-worth on my integrity, the quality of my character, and my service to truth. This higher form of honor cannot be arbitrarily taken away from us by other people, as Agamemnon did to Achilles. At West Point I learned that the only person who can take this higher form of honor away from me is me, if I betray my integrity, character, and responsibility to truth.

At West Point I learned that integrity means being honest not only with others, but also with myself. If I am not truthful with myself, then I cannot learn from my mistakes, grow as a human being, and achieve my full potential. If I am not truthful with myself, then I will try to deceive my conscience by rationalizing my unjust behavior, rather than striving to behave more ethically by correcting my unjust behavior.

The inability to be truthful with ourselves (by listening deeply to ourselves) or truthful with others is a personality trait associated with narcissism and even many sociopaths. Being truthful with ourselves and others is essential for the well-being of every community, whether it is a local community or our global human community (in *The Art of Waging Peace* I discuss the importance of balancing truth with tact). At West Point I learned that when we have integrity, we *live courageously* and improve the health of our relationships, family, and any community we interact with. Every person with integrity matters, because sometimes just one person with integrity can disrupt the machinery of injustice. The film *Twelve Angry Men* is an example of how just one person with integrity can make a positive difference.

West Point's honor code teaches cadets to not lie, steal, cheat, or tolerate those who do. If a person internalizes the highest ideals of the West Point honor code, he or she will also live courageously with integrity. In the television series *Star Trek: The Next Generation*, Starfleet Academy is based on

West Point and the other service academies. In one episode (which has been shown in some classes at the service academies), Captain Jean-Luc Picard finds out that a cadet at Starfleet Academy has violated the honor code. Captain Picard tells him: "The first duty of every Starfleet officer is to the truth, whether it's scientific truth, or historical truth, or personal truth."[30]

Personal truth is another way of saying integrity. As soldiers of peace we must serve the ideal of truth, because if we do not sail toward the star of scientific truth, historical truth, and personal truth, humanity will not be able to survive the dangers of our fragile future. Liberty, justice, and peace are powerful ideals, but they cannot exist without the ideal of truth. Truth is the ideal that brings liberty, justice, and peace to life. It is the ideal that makes all of our other ideals possible.

The women's rights movement and civil rights movement worked to create just laws based on truth. These movements also challenged unjust laws based on untruth. Since it is a scientific truth that women are not intellectually inferior to men, women's rights activists viewed laws that discriminate against women as unjust. Since it is a scientific truth that African Americans are not subhuman, civil rights activists viewed laws that discriminate against African Americans as unjust.

Civil disobedience is the act of challenging an unjust law because a person obeys a higher law based on truth. Civil disobedience occurs when someone publicly disobeys an unjust law such as racial segregation and then willingly accepts the penalty.* By willingly accepting the penalty, such as imprisonment, a person practicing civil disobedience tries to make the unjust law a public issue. If the person practicing civil disobedience is truly on the side of truth and justice, the defiant act will prick people's conscience more and more as time passes, changing unjust laws in the long term. There are many examples in history where this has happened.

Socrates practiced civil disobedience when he willingly accepted his

* Willingly accepting the penalty does not mean that people engaged in civil disobedience do not defend themselves in court. Instead, willingly accepting the penalty means that they do not run from being arrested or try to illegally escape from prison. There were many examples during the civil rights movement where lawyers worked to get civil rights activists out of prison, but they used the legal process. Socrates also used the legal process when he defended his mission during his trial.

execution after being put on trial in ancient Athens. He also reflected the peace hero ideal when he did not seek vengeance against his executioners.

By accepting the penalty of execution, Socrates protected the rule of law. The rule of law is important, especially in the modern world, because there are many just laws, such as laws against murder, rape, slavery, stealing, discrimination against women, child molestation, human sacrifice, bribery, blackmail, fraud, and cruelty to animals, just to name a few. Although Socrates's friends offered to help him escape from prison so that he could avoid being executed, he became an example of civil disobedience by refusing to escape. His act of civil disobedience in service of truth and justice, combined with his heroic courage when facing death, is why Socrates became one of the most influential peace heroes in human history.

When the announcement was made at his trial that he would be executed, Socrates cited his military experience and said the following to everyone gathered at the court:

> In a court of law, just as in warfare, neither I nor any other ought to use his wits to escape death by any means. In battle it is often obvious that you could escape being killed by giving up your arms and throwing yourself upon the mercy of your pursuers; and in every kind of danger there are plenty of devices for avoiding death if you are unscrupulous enough to stop at nothing. But I suggest, gentlemen, that the difficulty is not so much to escape death; the real difficulty is to escape from wickedness, which is far more fleet of foot. In this present instance I, the slow old man, have been overtaken by the slower of the two, but my accusers, who are clever and quick, have been overtaken by the faster: by iniquity. When I leave this court I shall go away condemned by you to death, but they will go away convicted by Truth herself of depravity and injustice. And they accept their sentence even as I accept mine. No doubt it was bound to be so, and I think that the result is fair enough . . .

> You have brought about my death in the belief that through it you will be delivered from submitting the conduct of your lives to criticism; but I say that the result will be just the opposite. You will have more critics, whom up till now I have restrained without your knowing it; and being younger they will be harsher to you and will cause you more annoyance. If you expect to stop denunciation of your wrong way of life by putting people to death, there is something amiss with your reasoning . . .
>
> For my own part I bear no grudge at all against those who condemned me and accused me, although it was not with this kind intention that they did so, but because they thought that they were hurting me; and that is culpable of them. However, I ask them to grant me one favour. When my sons grow up, gentlemen, if you think that they are putting money or anything else before goodness, take your revenge by plaguing them as I plagued you; and if they fancy themselves for no reason, you must scold them just as I scolded you, for neglecting the important things and thinking that they are good for something when they are good for nothing. If you do this, I shall have had justice at your hands—I *and* my children.
>
> Well, now it is time to be off, I to die and you to live; but which of us has the happier prospect is unknown to anyone but God.[31]

A female character named Antigone might have inspired Socrates to practice civil disobedience against the Athenian government.* Antigone was the protagonist in a famous play titled *Antigone*, written by the Athenian

* Although it is possible that the play *Antigone* influenced Socrates, it is also possible that Sophocles and Socrates were both influenced by a discussion in ancient Athens about loyalty to divine law versus state law. And although the theme of divine law having supremacy over state law is presented in *Antigone*, many Athenians might have perceived *Antigone* as being a play more about state loyalty versus family loyalty.

playwright Sophocles. When *Antigone* was first performed in ancient Athens around 441 BC,* Socrates was in his late twenties. He was executed at about age seventy.

Antigone is a female character who resembles Socrates in several ways. She defies an unjust law, in the form of her uncle's edict that she cannot bury her brother. Her uncle is King Creon of Thebes. She also bases her defiance on a higher law, which people have called truth, natural law, or divine law. Some people have also called this God's law. According to Gandhi's conception of religion, *truth is God*.[32] Antigone, like Socrates, also has every intention of accepting the penalty for her defiance. Elizabeth Vandiver explains:

> [Antigone] is directly and intentionally defying the head of her household. She is a citizen who is defying lawful authority. She is a woman who is defying male authority . . . Now her reason for this three-fold act of defiance is that she thinks Creon did not have the right to make the edict that he made. She thinks that his edict was unjust and she says quite clearly that she holds herself bound by the gods' laws, not by Creon's laws. When Creon asks her if she knew of the edict telling her she must not bury her brother, she says of course I knew about it, it had been announced publicly. He then asks her, so you then dared to disobey anyway?
>
> And this is what Antigone says: "Yes, it was not Zeus that made that proclamation, nor did justice which lives with those below enact such laws as that for mankind. I did not believe your proclamation had such power to enable one who will someday die to override God's ordinances, unwritten and secure. [Divine laws] are not of today and yesterday. They live forever. None knows when they first were."

* The exact year of the play's first performance is disputed, but it was performed around 441 BC.

> So she quite clearly states that she finds herself bound by higher laws, by the laws of the gods, rather than by Creon's laws . . . One way of reading *Antigone* can be to see it as the first drama on the topic of civil disobedience. Because what we really have here in *Antigone* is a discussion of what we now call civil disobedience. Creon thinks that the law must be obeyed, whether an individual agrees with it or not. Antigone thinks that her individual understanding of the gods' laws supersedes human laws, and that is the essence of civil disobedience.
>
> If you think about the great civil rights movement of the 1950s and 1960s, many of those who opposed that said the laws may be unjust but they are the laws so you should obey them. And of course the great activists of the civil rights movement, Martin Luther King and the others said no, the laws are unjust and therefore we must break them openly, intentionally, and take the legal penalties for so doing. That's the essence of civil disobedience. That's what Antigone does. She breaks the law and she has every intention of taking the penalty for breaking the law.[33]

In his book *Socrates Against Athens*,* James Colaiaco describes how Socrates, who had a revolutionary impact on human history that resulted in many of the freedoms and rights we have today, was likely influenced by the character Antigone:

> No Athenian anticipated that the tragic conflict portrayed on stage in Sophocles' *Antigone* foreshadowed the drama of the trial of Socrates. Life imitated art . . . Socrates took a stand similar to that of Sophocles' female

* In *Socrates Against Athens*, James Colaiaco discusses the flaws in I. F. Stone's theory that the execution of Socrates could be seen as justified because he was a threat to democracy. One reason I. F. Stone's theory is so flawed is because he romanticized and oversimplified ancient Athens.

protagonist. Produced in 441 B.C., when Athens' power was at its zenith, *Antigone* was performed throughout the Peloponnesian War and was familiar to most citizens . . . The conflict between Socrates and Athens, like that between Antigone and Creon, King of Thebes, was a conflict between principles . . . *Antigone* illustrates that the question of an individual conscientiously violating a state law was openly debated in the time of Socrates . . . For Socrates, the higher law of God was the basis for resistance to state commands that violate conscience. Civil disobedience, the deliberate, conscientious breaking of a law of the state, has an ancient history. It assumes a distinction between civil law and morality . . .

Over the centuries, several philosophers, from Socrates to Aquinas to John Locke, have maintained that state laws contrary to the higher law of God or natural moral law are invalid. John Milton refused to obey the censorship laws of seventeenth-century England. Quakers in colonial America refused to pay taxes for military purposes because they were morally opposed to war. The American Founding Fathers brought forth a new nation on the basis of the natural right to disobey unjust authority. Thomas Jefferson acknowledged a higher law when he endorsed the epigram: "Disobedience to tyrants is obedience to God." The nineteenth-century American abolitionists defied fugitive slave laws on the grounds that slavery was opposed to the law of God . . . Like Socrates, [Martin Luther] King demonstrated a respect for the rule of law and, at the same time, in his famous *Letter from Birmingham Jail*, declared his readiness to defy unjust laws on the basis of God and conscience . . . In defending his resistance to the state on the basis of a superior obligation to obey God, Socrates, like Antigone, provided a philosophical justification for civil disobedience.[34]

Although laws are often subjective, what prevents civil disobedience from turning laws into something that are *completely* subjective? Civil disobedience is only effective in the long term if it serves truth. For example, if I stand in front of a voting booth in order to prevent women from voting, claiming that I am obeying a higher law that women should not be allowed to vote and then willingly accept the legal penalty for my actions, is that civil disobedience? The truth is that women are not intellectually inferior to men, so I have no foundation on the basis of truth (which we can also call "higher law") to prevent women from voting. If I am allowed to vote because I am a man, there is no scientific foundation to support denying this right to women. On the other hand, there is a scientific foundation for preventing five-year-old children from voting, because they are not intellectually equal to adults.

When civil disobedience serves truth and justice, it can surprise us. In 2012 I attended an event where fifteen people who had been arrested for protesting a missile launch at Vandenberg Air Force Base discussed their reasons for breaking the law. One man who spent several years in the Marine Corps said he protested the missile launch because of something that happened to him in basic training. Some of the peace activists who stereotype the military were expecting to hear a horror story about the Marine Corps, but he said something surprising. He said that when he attended basic training shortly after the Vietnam War, he had an unusual drill sergeant. One day he and the other recruits asked the drill sergeant what they should do if their unit committed an atrocity similar to the My Lai massacre (where American soldiers massacred several hundred unarmed Vietnamese civilians during the Vietnam War).

His drill sergeant told the recruits that they must stop the massacre. The recruits asked the drill sergeant what would happen if they tried to stop it, and he said, "One of two things will probably happen. You will either be shot on the spot, or you will be court-martialed. But it doesn't matter, because you always have to do the right thing." Then the man arrested for civil disobedience told the audience, "I got arrested for protesting the missile launch because my drill sergeant told me to always do the right thing."

People often stereotype the military, but I gained a greater understanding of integrity at West Point than I did during my entire education from preschool through high school, where I never heard integrity discussed a single time. Honor (self-worth) based on external status symbols, along with the higher form of honor (higher form of self-worth) based on our integrity, the quality of our character, and our service to truth, exist as a broad spectrum, and people can be at different points along this spectrum. Peace heroes redefine honor and worth by serving as examples of the higher form of honor, encouraging all of us to make progress along this spectrum toward self-worth based on integrity, quality of character, and service to truth.

Integrity means much more than simply not cheating in school, because integrity is an essential part of the art of listening, the art of waging peace, and the art of living that promotes healthy relationships, families, communities, workplaces, and democracies. If integrity were emphasized in our education system, this would not mean that every single person would be honest, but this would create more honest people, give children more examples of what it meant to live with integrity, and create a strong social norm that people should have integrity (which would make it easier to hold people accountable for lacking integrity).

Emphasizing integrity in our education system would also help people to challenge injustice. By basing their self-worth on internal qualities they can control, rather than external status symbols that can arbitrarily be taken away from them, peace heroes gain the fortitude needed to overcome ridicule and danger in service of justice. We must remember that when peace heroes throughout history challenged injustice, they often faced ridicule and danger because they also challenged their culture.

Today I hear many people talk about culture as if it is always good and something we should never question, but all long-standing societal injustices have been a part of culture. Slavery was once a deeply ingrained feature of cultures around the world. The oppression of women was also a cultural phenomenon. In countless societies, animal sacrifice was both a religious and cultural practice. When European monarchs ruled societies with nearly absolute power, this was also a cultural tradition. Today many people justify bullfighting and other forms of animal cruelty as part of their culture. Segregation in the American South was a part of culture. When a person has difficulty rationalizing an injustice, the rationalization of last resort is "Well, it's just a part of our culture."

Peace heroes who challenge long-standing societal injustices are viewed by many as disrespecting culture, because these injustices are always a part of culture. However, peace heroes gain the moral authority needed to improve their culture by embracing the three elements of universal respect, which are listening, speaking to people's potential, and not being hypocritical. In *The Art of Waging Peace* I discuss how peace heroes have increased support for their various causes by connecting new ideas to cherished cultural ideals. Culture best serves humanity when it is fluid rather than static and free to grow toward our highest ideals, including the peace hero ideal. We must never let culture stand in the way of justice, but improve culture so that it serves justice.

Will Veritas Prevail Before It's Too Late?

A soldier of peace is someone who strives to reflect the peace hero ideal as much as possible, to make the peace hero ideal a way of life. A soldier of peace is a servant of empathy, reason, and truth. If honor to a soldier of peace means integrity, what does glory mean to a soldier of peace? As I mentioned in the first chapter, glory is the ability to transcend time, and there are more fulfilling ways than fame to transcend time. In the last book of this series, I will discuss the many ways we can transcend time.

There is also a form of truth that transcends time. I call this *timeless truth*. When the old adage says, "There is nothing new under the sun,"[35] I interpret this as another way of saying "timeless truth" or "eternal truth." Einstein made revolutionary discoveries about the laws of physics, but he did not invent these laws. Instead, he saw what others could not see. The laws of physics that Einstein discovered seemed new only to humanity; they were not new to reality. These laws are timeless, because they do not age as mortals do.

According to philosopher Friedrich Nietzsche, the highest form of originality is the ability to see something new in the old, which can also mean the ability to perceive timeless truth in places where others cannot see it. Nietzsche said, "Original—Not that one is the first to see something new, but that one sees *as new* what is old, long familiar, seen and overlooked by everybody, is what distinguishes truly original minds."[36]

Timeless truth, which shines from the underlying essence of reality, has no expiration date that we are aware of. As I said in chapter 1, time is a thief that steals everything it touches, keeps everything it steals, and destroys everything it keeps. However, timeless truth is a feature of reality that time cannot touch, steal, keep, and destroy. As far as we know, the only way for the deepest truths of our universe to end would be if time itself along with our universe ended.* The flow of time has the power to change the color of our hair and the texture of our skin, but it does not have the power to change the truths that transcend time.

In Greek mythology, the goddess Veritas symbolizes truth. Like timeless truth, she is eternal and cannot be killed. According to an Aesop's fable that I will share below, the immortal goddess Veritas** prevails in the race against deception, even when deception has a successful start. In other words, deception can start out convincingly disguised as truth, but timeless truth builds momentum gradually and persistently, reveals the illusion beneath this disguise, and eventually wins the race against deception in the long term.

To offer just one example where truth won the race against untruth, the Roman Catholic Church censored Galileo when he said the planets revolved around the sun and tried to keep his ideas hidden from humanity, but he had timeless truth on his side. We now know that the timeless truth Galileo asserted applies not only to our solar system, but also throughout our entire universe, since the laws of physics make it impossible for a star and collection of planets to revolve around a single planet. History offers numerous examples in which the agents of untruth had far more money and military might than the agents of truth, but timeless truth eventually revealed

* There could also be timeless truths that transcend our universe, since our universe only encompasses what we can perceive with our limited senses.

** The only surviving version of this Aesop's fable is in Latin, and the name Veritas is the Latin name for truth (Aletheia in Greek).

itself, gradually grew in power, and overcame those who spread deception and illusion. This is because timeless truth, reality, or what Gandhi called God, is more powerful in the long term than the deceptions and illusions our mortal minds create.

To become literate in the nature of reality, we must gain a deep understanding of the timeless truths that govern reality, which are the same truths that govern our survival. The four stars in the constellation of peace symbolize some of the timeless truths we must understand to survive and prosper as a species. Aesop depicts the power of truth (Veritas) in a fable about Prometheus, an immortal Titan who gave the gift of fire to humanity. In this fable, Aesop describes how truth prevails against deception:

> Prometheus, the titan of forethought and clever counsel, was a divine potter that was assigned the task of molding mankind out of clay. One day, he decided to dedicate his skill to sculpting the form of the spirit Veritas—Truth—so that he would be able to instill men with virtue. As he toiled, he was called away from his workshop by a sudden summons from [Zeus] the King of the Gods.
>
> Dolus—Trickery—had recently become one of Prometheus' apprentices, and was left in charge of the workshop in the titan's absence. Dolus used his time in the workshop to create a figure with the same size and possessing the same features as Veritas with his crafty, sly hands. When he was almost finished with his sculpture, which was truly almost identical to Prometheus' work, he ran out of clay to use for her feet. The divine potter returned, and Dolus scurried to his seat, trembling with fear that his master should discover what he had done and punish him.
>
> Prometheus was startled by the similarities between the two clay figures and decided he would take credit for both as a testament to his own skill. He put both statues in the kiln, and after they had been fired, he breathed life

> into them. Veritas walked with measured, steady steps, while her twin was immobile, stuck in her tracks. The imitation Veritas, a forgery and product of deception and artifice, acquired the name Mendacium—Falsehood.
>
> Falsehood has no feet: now and again something that is false can start off successfully, but with time, Truth will always prevail.[37]

All societal injustices are based on simple myths. If we do not challenge these myths, we cannot defeat injustice. For example, the American slavery system was based on the myth that African Americans are subhuman and born to be slaves. During the nineteenth century in America, laws that prevented women from voting and owning property were based on the myth that women are intellectually inferior to men. Human sacrifice was based on the myth that killing people in religious ceremonies would prevent catastrophes and win divine favors.

In addition, opposition to disability rights was based on the myth that people with disabilities do not have lives worth living. In the documentary *Lives Worth Living*, activist Ann Ford says, "There was a belief that if you had a disability you didn't have any desire to live a life, you didn't have the goals and the dreams that somebody non-disabled had."[38] Unjust systems that abuse and kill animals are based on several myths, including the myth that animals do not experience complex emotions and are like machines (in the last book of this series, I will discuss the many myths that sustain our abuse of animals).

The myths that sustain injustice are always dangerous. The myth that human activity is not the leading cause of modern climate change threatens most life on our planet. The myth that men are naturally violent (I debunk this myth in my other books) creates a self-fulfilling prophecy by framing masculinity as the expression of violent aggression, and neglects the countless men who have reflected the five characteristics of the peace hero ideal. In my other books I explain how the unjust system of modern war is based on the myth that human beings are naturally violent, the myth that war is inevitable, and the myth that war in the twenty-first century makes us safe.

Unjust economic policies are based on a variety of myths that must be challenged, such as the myth of trickle-down theory. When economic models do not reflect how reality actually works, they can cause a lot of harm, which is why the study of economics should be part of literacy in the nature of reality.

Describing how the dangerous myths that sustain injustice wear a disguise of righteousness, Martin Luther King Jr. said, "It seems to be a fact of life that human beings cannot continue to do wrong without eventually reaching out for some rationalization to clothe their acts in the garments of righteousness. And so, with the growth of slavery, men had to convince themselves that a system which was so economically profitable was morally justifiable. The attempt to give moral sanction to a profitable system gave birth to the doctrine of white supremacy."[39]

To sustain unjust systems, human beings must justify injustice. We must rationalize wrong. In *Peaceful Revolution* I describe the process of "mental gymnastics" that allows people to deceive their conscience. Even Adolf Hitler had to rationalize his wrongdoing. In his autobiography *Mein Kampf*, Hitler said, "Today I believe that I am acting in accordance with the will of the Almighty Creator: by defending myself against the Jew, I am fighting for the work of the Lord."[40]

It is because unjust systems require the justification of injustice and the rationalization of wrong, that the masters of language who serve deception and destruction are so dangerous. By using words to justify injustice and rationalize wrong, people like Odysseus can manipulate large numbers of followers to serve and even die for an unjust system disguised as justice. If we do not challenge the myths that sustain unjust systems, humanity cannot make progress and solve our global problems. As I will discuss in the next chapter, all of our efforts to wage peace, every strategy and tactic, must be directed at shattering these myths.

When underlying myths are debunked, only then can an unjust system begin to be remade in the image of justice. Because the light of truth is needed to cast out the ignorance, deception, and illusions that sustain injustice, truth is humanity's only salvation. Women's rights activist Ida B. Wells tells us, "The way to right wrongs is to turn the light of truth upon them."[41]

Communicating truth does not mean merely throwing facts at people, which is often ineffective. To communicate truth effectively, we must frame truth in a way that appeals to a variety of worldviews. We must also make truth accessible, understandable, and inspiring. In *The Art of Waging Peace* I explain how we can do this, and I also discuss why simply being a truth teller is not enough to overcome the significant challenges threatening our world. To wield the weapon of nonviolence with maximum force, we must be *skilled* truth tellers.

When we strengthen our muscle of language it becomes authentic communication, a higher expression of language. And when the muscle of language reaches the height of its strength, it becomes skilled truth telling.

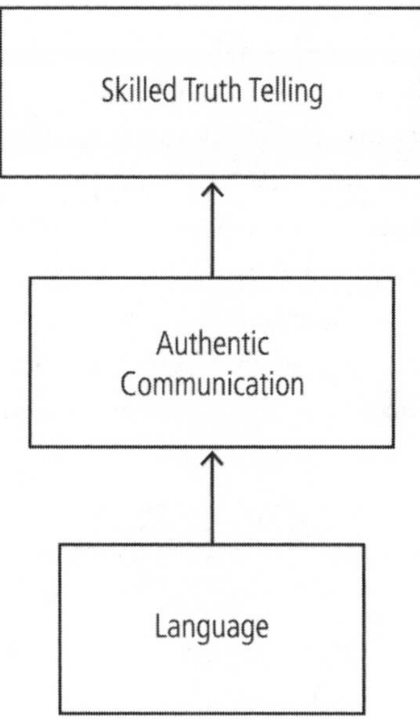

Figure 3.3: The Muscle of Language

Unlike skilled truth telling, violence cannot heal the root causes of our problems, because violence cannot defeat the underlying myths that sustain injustice. Martin Luther King Jr. said, "Through violence you may murder the liar, but you cannot murder the lie, nor establish the truth."[42] Violence can kill a racist, but not racism. Violence can kill a sexist, but not sexism. The sword of truth is the only weapon that can defeat the underlying myths that sustain these and other injustices.

We can use the sword of truth to slay ideas based on untruth, but those ideas do not always stay dead. For example, people today can resurrect the untruth that our planet is flat. However, when people in modern America resurrect that old idea, the untruth becomes a metaphorical zombie. If I gave a lecture at a college tomorrow and said, "Today I want to talk about why the world is actually flat," or "Today I want to talk about why we need to sacrifice human beings to the gods to stop drought," or "Today I want to talk about why the Irish are subhuman and I should not go to prison for murdering an Irish person," or "Today I want to talk about why we need to bring back state-sanctioned slavery and deny American women the right to vote, own property, and go to college," those old ideas would resemble metaphorical zombies by appearing frightening, unnatural, and dangerous to almost everyone in the class.* Just as a zombie cannot easily blend in with the living, a *zombie idea* that is the resurrection of an old untruth cannot easily blend in with modern social norms based on truth.

Some Americans today actually believe that the world is flat, state-sanctioned slavery should be brought back, and women should not be allowed to vote, own property, and go to college, but these people are in the minority. We must protect ourselves from dangerous untruths by having a strong education system that can imprison inaccurate ideas with the chains of truth,

* Although the old *zombie ideas* that we should sacrifice humans to the gods, bring back state-sanctioned slavery, and deny American women the right to vote, own property, and go to college would appear frightening, unnatural, and dangerous to most people in a twenty-first century American classroom, the old zombie idea that the world is flat might seem more silly and amusing rather than frightening and dangerous. However, when we understand the importance of scientific literacy for solving our national and global problems, we can realize why the world being flat is a zombie idea that is quite dangerous. Scientific literacy falls underneath literacy in the nature of reality.

and we must have just laws that protect us from those who want to act on untruth by enslaving others, oppressing women, or sacrificing human beings. Peace literacy, not censorship or violence, is our best protection against the root causes of untruth, deception, manipulation, and injustice.

Furthermore, we must realize that many popular ideas today, which most people do not yet realize are based on untruth, will become zombie ideas in the future. Where the old zombie ideas that would sound absurd in a classroom today are concerned, we must be vigilant rather than complacent, because if our education system and society do not protect the truths our ancestors worked so hard to reveal, old zombie ideas could infect a large segment of the population and even spread to a point that they become the new norm. The novel *I Am Legend* shows that when the world is overrun with zombies,* the living are seen as monsters. We must not allow that to happen to the world of ideas.

Throughout history truth has prevailed, but now more than ever, truth requires the help of soldiers of peace who reflect the five characteristics of the peace hero ideal. Veritas is so powerful that she transcends time itself, but she cannot protect our fragile future without soldiers of peace as her allies. In a world where humanity has the technological ability to destroy itself, we urgently need soldiers of peace armed with the sword of truth to combat the myths and deception that promote destruction. Many generals in history have callously treated soldiers in war as expendable, but there is no such thing as an expendable soldier of peace in the struggle to serve Veritas and reflect the peace hero ideal. In a world filled with myths and deception, every person with integrity is needed, and all of us can become soldiers of peace in the battle to protect human survival and the well-being of our world.

A question we must ask today is not *will truth prevail?* but *will truth prevail before it's too late?* Since time is a ruthless sea that has no compassion for humanity, will enough people learn the timeless truths that humanity

* Some people debate whether the creatures in *I Am Legend* are zombies, vampires, or "zombie vampires." They have elements of both (with the film showing more zombie characteristics and the novel showing more vampire characteristics) and might be a unique kind of creature. The novel is very different from the film and supports my point more than the film does.

needs to survive before our urgent global problems doom us to extinction? Will enough people wield the sword of truth to combat the myths that sustain injustice before it's too late? We must answer these questions with our actions. As humanity sails the turbulent waters of time, we must answer these questions by embracing struggle, training ourselves to achieve our highest potential, protecting our ship the planet Earth with the sword of truth, and using the starlight of strategy to guide us through the darkness of our fragile and unknown future.

CHAPTER 4

The Star of Strategy

Romantic Illusions of Violence

Waging peace gave me a strategy for living that rage could not give me. Because of my extreme childhood trauma and mixed racial background, I have faced difficult obstacles in my life that I could not have overcome without strategy. There is so much that we cannot control in life, and strategy allows us to make the most of what little we can control. Waging peace is a higher evolution of strategic thinking that has allowed me to improve my quality of life, make a positive difference in the lives of those around me, contribute toward creating realistic peace, and not self-destruct in a violent rampage. To understand why the strategy of waging peace can help our country and planet even more than it has helped me, we must explore the metaphors of nonviolence.

Because reality is so complex, we can use a variety of metaphors to better understand any aspect of reality. When metaphors are used properly, they make our complex reality appear simple, accessible, and understandable without oversimplifying complexity. Martin Luther King Jr. called nonviolence "the sword that heals," I call it "the sword of truth," and Gandhi called it "the sword of love." Each metaphor allows us to see reality from a different angle, revealing timeless truths that exist as features on the landscape of reality.

What are some other names for nonviolence? In addition to "the sword of love," Gandhi also called the weapon of nonviolence by the name *satyagraha*, which basically means truth-force. I often use the term *waging peace* to describe nonviolence, because waging peace sounds like a verb. The term *nonviolence* has many misconceptions, such as the myth that nonviolence is passive and weak, but the term *waging peace* immediately clears up these misconceptions. Waging peace sounds active rather than passive, communicating the idea that peace is action, peace is a process, peace involves struggle. As someone who has suffered from a high capacity for rage, I have found that waging peace is even more potent and powerful than rage, but in a constructive rather than destructive way.

To understand waging peace, we must understand not just the stars of struggle, training, and truth. We must also understand the star of strategy. What is strategy? Because of time, motion is a fundamental feature of reality. We often use the word "change" to describe the motion of reality. Strategy is our ability to channel this motion, this change, in a direction we want so that we can achieve *maximum intended impact.*

Where waging peace is concerned, strategy allows us to become cocreators in our unfolding universe so that we can shape our future in a way that serves our survival and prosperity. Because time is ruthless and has no mercy if we do not effectively solve our problems, strategy is essential for maximizing the effectiveness of our efforts.

Time has been a central theme throughout this book, and the four stars in the constellation of peace (that represent four features of reality we must understand to create realistic peace) all relate to different aspects of time. Chapter 1 discussed how struggle is an inevitable consequence of the passage of time. Chapter 2 discussed how we can make good use of time by training ourselves to become fully human and using our life experiences to grow in wisdom. Chapter 3 discussed how timeless truth transcends time. And this chapter discusses how strategy allows us to channel the motion of time (also known as "change") to achieve maximum intended impact.

I have heard some peace activists reject the importance of strategy, because they associate it entirely with war. Furthermore, most people outside of the peace movement do not immediately think of strategy when they hear the word "peace," because they see peace activism as naive. But in this chapter we will discuss how waging peace is a higher evolution in strategic thinking.

My understanding of strategy was shaped by my experiences at West Point, along with the image of the West Point crest. Greek mythology has two primary war deities, one male and one female. The ancient Greeks depicted the war god Ares as a homicidal maniac filled with bloodlust, while they depicted the war goddess Athena as a paragon of wisdom. Thousands of years later, Athena is a symbol that endures. Her helmet is the central feature on the West Point crest.

America's oldest engineering college, West Point was founded in 1802 to train military officers to serve in the corps of engineers, and its current crest (also called the "coat of arms") was adopted over a century ago. According to the West Point public affairs office, "The coat of arms and motto were adopted in 1898. Col. Charles W. Larned, professor of drawing, headed a committee to design a coat of arms for the Academy . . . The committee began with the creation of an emblem that consisted of a sword, a universal symbol of war, and the helmet of Pallas Athena. Athena, a fully armed mythological goddess, is associated with the arts of war, and her helmet signifies wisdom and learning. The emblem is attached to a shield, bearing the arms of the United States, and on the shield's crest is a bald eagle, the national symbol. The eagle's claws hold 13 arrows representing the 13 original states and oak and olive branches, traditional symbols of peace."[1]

The ancient Greeks tended to loathe bloodthirsty Ares, while wise Athena was widely worshipped as both the patron goddess of Sparta and Athens, with the latter city being named after her. A fascinating aspect of Greek mythology is that the female war deity Athena is much more powerful than the male war deity Ares, even though warfare in the ancient world was the domain of men, largely due to their greater upper body strength during an era of warfare when size and strength mattered a lot. As I explained in chapter 2, the Romans had superior training and tactics that allowed them to overcome physically larger opponents. In a similar way, Athena, a symbol of strategy, is able to overpower Ares, a symbol of brute force, even though he is a large male.

When Ares makes the foolish mistake of attacking Athena in the *Iliad*, Homer depicts Athena, a female figure, as being much more powerful than the physically massive male figure Ares:

> [Ares] stabbed at [Athena's] battle-shield of storm . . . not even Zeus's lightning bolt can break its front. Bloody Ares lunged at it now with giant lance and Athena backed away, her powerful hand hefting a boulder off the plain, black, jagged, a ton weight that men in the old days planted there to mark off plowland—[Athena] hurled that boundary-stone at Ares, struck his neck, loosed his limbs, and down he crashed and out over seven acres sprawled the enormous god and his mane dragged in the dust, his armor clashed around him.
>
> Athena laughed aloud, glorying over him, winging insults: "Colossal fool—it never even occurred to you, not even now when you matched your strength with mine, just how much greater I claim to be than you . . ."
>
> Triumphant Athena turned her shining eyes away and Aphrodite daughter of Zeus took Ares's hand and led him off the field, racked with groans, barely able to gather back his strength."[2]

According to Homer, Athena is probably more powerful than every Greek deity except her father Zeus, the king of the gods. And according to Hesiod, who wrote around the same time as Homer, Athena is just as strong as Zeus. Hesiod said Athena is "equal to her father [Zeus] in strength and in wise understanding."[3] Considering the severe oppression of women in ancient Athens and the widespread Greek belief that women were subhuman, it seems shocking that the goddess Athena along with women in Greek tragedy are depicted as highly intelligent and powerful characters. This is one of the most intriguing paradoxes in history.*

War and hunting are widely considered the two traditional domains of men, which is why it is so surprising that in Greek mythology, women symbolize both of these domains. In addition to Athena as a symbol of war, Artemis is a female deity, often depicted wielding a bow and arrow, who symbolizes hunting. In Greek mythology, female deities not only symbolize war and hunting, but they also symbolize truth, peace, justice, and good order. Later in this chapter we will discuss the goddesses that symbolize peace, justice, and good order. We will also discuss why the metaphor of a goddess helps us better understand the true nature of justice.

To understand why strategy is necessary to promote truth, peace, justice, and good order, we must first recognize that the universe gives us only three options for solving any human problem. The first option is *do nothing.* The second option is *use a violent method.* The third option is *use a method that is not violent.*** Can you think of any option other than those three? That is all the universe gives us. That is all we have to work with, but within those three options are infinite possibilities.

* Cynthia Eller (in her book *The Myth of Matriarchal Prehistory*) and Elizabeth Vandiver cite Athena as one among many examples where a goddess worshipping culture does not provide greater rights for women. Athenian men worshipped the goddess Athena, yet Athenian women were severely oppressed. Paradoxically, there are many goddess-worshipping cultures where women have less status than men, and many cultures have war goddesses, even though war has been a traditional male domain.

** Options that are not violent can include warning aggression (also known as posturing), which I discuss in *The End of War* and *The Cosmic Ocean*, the three forms of deflection, which I discuss in *The Art of Waging Peace*, and waging peace, which I discuss in all of my books. "Not violence" is a broad category that includes nonviolence (waging peace), the three forms of deflection, and warning aggression. One reason I prefer the term waging peace is because the term nonviolence is often incorrectly used interchangeably with "not violence," whereas waging peace is a term that intuitively communicates that it means more than just the absence of violence. Options that are "not violent" can be harmful, since "not violent" and "peaceful" are not synonymous. In *The Cosmic Ocean* I offer a precise definition of violence and discuss why we should not overuse the word "violence."

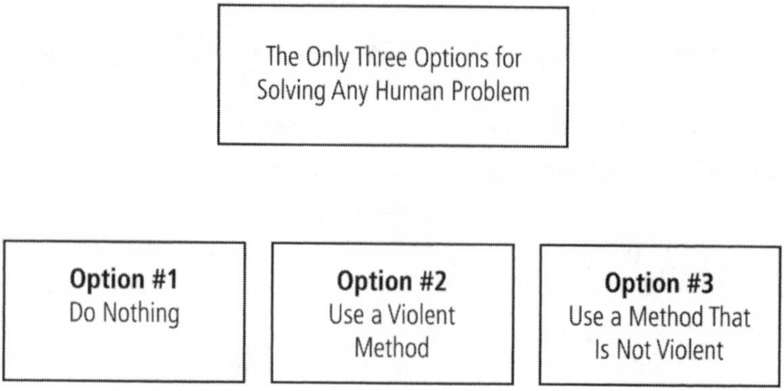

The Only Three Options for Solving Any Human Problem		
Option #1 Do Nothing	**Option #2** Use a Violent Method	**Option #3** Use a Method That Is Not Violent

Figure 4.1: The Only Three Options for Solving Any Human Problem

Is there a fourth option, a combination of using violence and not using violence? When solving a problem, any amount of violence makes a method appear violent. For example, if you and a coworker try to resolve a conflict by dialoguing, and during this discussion your coworker punches you in the face, you will naturally perceive the person's method as violent, even though he or she actually used a combination of nonviolence (dialogue) and violence (punching).

This is because human beings perceive the use of violence in peaceful conflict resolution like we perceive poison in water. If someone puts just one drop of poison in your glass of water, you will perceive the poison as tainting all the water and won't want to drink it. In a similar way, if someone punches you while using peaceful conflict resolution techniques, just one drop of violence will taint all the water of peaceful conflict resolution, causing you to perceive the person's method as violent.

On an international level, if a foreign country pursues negotiating options with your country while violently attacking you (which was the relationship between Sparta and Athens during much of the Peloponnesian War), you would probably not say, "They are using a combination of not using violence and using violence." Instead, the natural reaction would be, "They are attacking us. They are using a violent method, which taints the nature of negotiations." This is why we have only three options for solving any human problem: do nothing, use a violent method, or use a method that is not violent. We can first do nothing, then attempt a method that does not use violence, and then pursue a violent method, but we cannot simultaneously pursue a method that is violent and not violent, just as we cannot simultaneously do nothing and pursue a violent method.

If we have a problem we can solve and we choose the first option by doing nothing, how likely are we to solve the problem? The likelihood is very low.* If we instead become proactive by embracing struggle, we have a much higher probability of solving the problem. As a result, the only real options the universe gives us for solving our human problems are using a violent method or a method that is not violent. This raises a critical question: which method is more effective for solving our human problems? A violent method? Or a method that is not violent? To answer this question, we must discuss how the principles of military strategy apply to waging peace.

Military strategy teaches us to not confront opponents where they are strongest, but to instead confront them where they are weakest. When Martin Luther King Jr. and the civil rights movement opposed segregation and other racist government policies, where was the U.S. government strongest? Its greatest strength then and now is the use of violence. Today the U.S. government controls the army, navy, air force, marines, special forces, National Guard, FBI, CIA, and extensive police forces. If you fight the U.S. government with violence on its own soil, where it has "home-field advantage," it will crush you. In addition, during the civil rights era of the 1950s and 1960s, white people not only had deadlier weapons, a lot more money, and a much better trained military than black people, but they also significantly outnumbered the minority black population.

King was a student of history who knew that when the Native Americans protected their freedom, families, and way of life by using violence against the U.S. government, the U.S. government responded by escalating

* Sometimes inaction is action if there is intent and strategy behind the inaction, rather than complacency and apathy behind the inaction. In his book *The Gift of Fear*, Gavin de Becker discusses why ignoring threats is sometimes the best strategy, showing how inaction that is not passive and naive but well-reasoned, intentional, and based on good strategy is a kind of action.

its violent policies against them. King saw the weakness of using violence against a militarily stronger opponent, yet he admired the bravery of the Native Americans, along with the "courageous efforts" of violent rebels such as Nat Turner and Denmark Vesey. When King was asked during an interview whether he approved of Hungary's violent 1956 rebellion, he replied, "*I admire freedom fighters wherever they are* [emphasis added], but I still believe that nonviolence is the strongest approach . . . Organized nonviolent resistance is the most powerful weapon that oppressed people can use in breaking loose from the bondage of oppression."[4]

Gandhi and King both believed that violence could be used as a last resort for personal self-defense. But they saw how violence can be an ineffective way to solve large-scale social problems, such as overthrowing an oppressive system, because it violates a basic principle of military strategy—*do not attack opponents* (e.g., oppressive systems) *where they are strongest and you are weakest.* The following excerpt from King's book *Where Do We Go from Here?*, published in 1967 a year before his death, shows his strategic brilliance:

> As we have seen, the first public expression of disenchantment with nonviolence arose around the question of "self-defense." In a sense this is a false issue, for the right to defend one's home and one's person when attacked has been guaranteed through the ages by common law. In a nonviolent demonstration, however, self-defense must be approached from another perspective . . .
>
> It is dangerous to organize a movement around self-defense. The line of demarcation between defensive violence and aggressive violence is very thin. The minute a program of violence is enunciated, even for self-defense, the atmosphere is filled with talk of violence, and the words falling on unsophisticated ears may be interpreted as an invitation to aggression.
>
> One of the main questions that the Negro must confront in his pursuit of freedom is that of effectiveness.

What is the most effective way to achieve the desired goal? If a method is not effective, no matter how much steam it releases, it is an expression of weakness, not of strength. Now the plain, inexorable fact is that any attempt of the American Negro to overthrow his oppressor with violence will not work. We do not need President Johnson to tell us this by reminding Negro rioters that they are outnumbered ten to one. The courageous efforts of our own insurrectionist brothers, such as Denmark Vesey and Nat Turner, should be eternal reminders to us that violent rebellion is doomed from the start. In violent warfare one must be prepared to face the fact that there will be casualties by the thousands. Anyone leading a violent rebellion must be willing to make an honest assessment regarding the possible casualties to a minority population confronting a well-armed, wealthy majority with a fanatical right wing that would delight in exterminating thousands of black men, women and children . . .

The futility of violence in the struggle for racial justice has been tragically etched in all the recent Negro riots. There is something painfully sad about a riot. One sees screaming youngsters and angry adults fighting hopelessly and aimlessly against impossible odds. Deep down within them you perceive a desire for self-destruction, a suicidal longing. Occasionally Negroes contend that the 1965 Watts riot and the other riots in various cities represented effective civil rights action. But those who express this view always end up with stumbling words when asked what concrete gains have been won as a result. At best the riots have produced a little additional antipoverty money, allotted by frightened government officials, and a few water sprinklers to cool the children of the ghettos. It is something like improving the food in a prison while the people remain securely incarcerated behind bars. Nowhere have

> the riots won any concrete improvements such as have the organized protest demonstrations . . .
>
> When one tries to pin down advocates of violence as to what acts would be effective, the answers are blatantly illogical. Sometimes they talk of overthrowing racist state and local governments. They fail to see that no internal revolution has ever succeeded in overthrowing a government by violence unless the government had already lost the allegiance and effective control of its armed forces. Anyone in his right mind knows that this will not happen in the United States. In a violent racial situation, the power structure has the local police, the state troopers, the national guard and finally the army to call on, all of which are predominantly white.
>
> Furthermore, few if any violent revolutions have been successful unless the violent minority had the sympathy and support of the nonresisting majority. Castro may have had only a few Cubans actually fighting with him, but he would never have overthrown the Batista regime unless he had had the sympathy of the vast majority of the Cuban people. It is perfectly clear that a violent revolution on the part of American blacks would find no sympathy and support from the white population and very little from the majority of the Negroes themselves.
>
> *This is no time for romantic illusions* [emphasis added] and empty philosophical debates about freedom. This is a time for action. What is needed is a strategy for change, a tactical program that will bring the Negro into the mainstream of American life as quickly as possible. [5]

King realized that our society is filled with various "romantic illusions." Some of the most dangerous romantic illusions I hear are the ones that concern violence. Our society is flooded with media depictions of violence, but those depictions (which often romanticize violence) mostly serve to distort our understanding of the true nature of violence. Ironically, the more violence we consume from the media, the less educated we tend to become about violence.

I hear many people say that nonviolence is naive. However, our society's understanding of violence is so distorted by Hollywood illusions where an action hero kills a hundred bad guys with ease, that our society's view of violence is far more naive. This naiveté is expressed in many ways. For example, I often hear people say that the U.S. government was afraid of Malcolm X and other black nationalists because they had guns, which allowed African Americans to intimidate the U.S. government into treating them more respectfully and creating equal rights. According to this myth, the reason why the U.S. government supported Martin Luther King Jr. and other peaceful civil rights activists was because it was so terrified of Malcolm X. But if we look at American history, we can see why this was not true.

From its very origins, the fledgling U.S. government had the audacity to fight the British Empire, which was arguably the most powerful empire in the world at that time. After the American Revolution, the U.S. government was not afraid to wage war against large Native American populations, even though these people controlled their own territory, gained access to rifles, and had more relative military might than the African American population of the 1950s and 1960s.* Nor was the U.S. government afraid to wage war against rebelling Southern states, killing many white Americans during the Civil War. In addition, during World War II the U.S. government was not afraid to fight Nazi Germany (which had one of the best militaries in world history) or the Japanese Empire (which was a regional superpower that also had a very strong military). And during the Korean War, the U.S. government was not afraid to fight the North Koreans and Chinese (who had tanks, military aircraft, and many more soldiers than the U.S.

* I am referring to the relative military might of Native Americans to the U.S. government in the nineteenth century, as compared to the relative military might of African Americans to the U.S. government in the twentieth century. In the nineteenth century the U.S. government was not a military superpower (it was not as strong as the European empires), and Native Americans had their own territory. In the twentieth century the U.S. government created the most powerful military in human history, and African Americans were some of the biggest underdogs in human history.

government). Nor was the U.S. government afraid to invade Vietnam or Iraq, even though these countries had large armies containing hundreds of thousands of soldiers.

After World War II the U.S. government created the most powerful military in human history. Since World War II until now (I am writing this in the year 2015), the only times the U.S. government* has ever shown any serious fear of waging war is when an adversary possesses a nuclear weapon or when the war might upset the American population and create civil unrest. This is not a political statement. This is the reality of American military history.

There were certainly people in the federal government, as well as state and local governments, who did not want African Americans to become violent (these governments are not monolithic), but the belief that the U.S. government as a whole was afraid of African Americans with guns, and that people with meager rifles could scare the U.S. government into submission, when the British Empire, Confederate states, and Nazi Germany could not scare the U.S. government into submission, is inaccurate. Many of these African Americans, including Malcolm X, did not even have any military training. What is Malcolm X, armed with a gun but having no military training, going to do against an army of tanks and highly trained killers? World history shows that governments possessing a lot of tanks, bombs, military aircraft, and well-trained soldiers don't have much fear of guns.

When white people saw peaceful African Americans being viciously attacked on television during the civil rights era, it upset much of the white population. But if those African Americans had waged war against white Americans, killing white women and children in the process, very few white people would have been upset if extreme violent measures had been taken against African Americans in the name of "security." If you doubt this, remember that when the Japanese government attacked Pearl Harbor (a military rather than civilian target), the U.S. government put over a hundred thousand Japanese Americans in prison camps, even though many were U.S.

* When I say "U.S. government" in this context, I am referring to the majority of U.S. government officials, who seem quite fearless when waging war is concerned, perhaps because they don't have to fight in war.

citizens. Many Japanese Americans died from illnesses in those prison camps.

So imagine how the U.S. government and white supremacists would have responded if African Americans across the country, rather than attacking a military target, started massacring white women and children. Martin Luther King Jr. believed that the response would have been genocide. Contrary to some of the myths about Malcolm X that I have heard, he also saw the danger of waging open war against white Americans when he supported a policy of self-defense (to compensate for the many instances where American laws did not protect African Americans) rather than aggression, and at the end of his life he was leaning more toward nonviolence rather than violence.

The myth that Malcolm X symbolized violence depicts him as a caricature rather than as a complex and evolving human being. Seeing him as a complex and evolving person rather than as a caricature, Martin Luther King Jr. said the following about the assassination of Malcolm X: "I think it is even more unfortunate that this great tragedy occurred at a time when Malcolm X was reevaluating his own philosophical presuppositions and moving toward a greater understanding of the nonviolent movement and toward more tolerance of white people generally."[6]

Nat Turner was an African American slave who led a rebellion in 1831 that killed white women and children in Virginia. His rebellion shows that, historically, white Americans have responded to black people killing whites not by giving black people their freedom, but by further abusing them. Historically, when white people feared black people they responded by escalating racism, not by decreasing racism and creating equal rights. In their book *Five Thousand Years of Slavery*, Marjorie Gann and Janet Willen tell us:

> The bloodiest slave revolt in United States history happened in Virginia in 1831. Nat Turner and six other slaves killed five whites at the plantation where he was enslaved . . . Turner gained followers as he went from plantation to plantation, until approximately sixty of them had killed about sixty whites, mostly women and children. The state's militia captured most of the slaves, but Turner hid

> out for sixty-eight days before he was caught and hanged.
>
> The rebellion so terrorized whites that they went on rampages throughout the South to uncover other plots of rebellion, and to intimidate blacks so they would never again rise up in revolt. Free blacks as well as slaves were at the mercy of whites [as an unknown number of blacks in Virginia were murdered by white mobs] . . . For another two weeks the outrages continued, with beatings, searches, and arrests. The authorities had to keep a group of blacks in jail to protect them from the white mob until the capture of Nat Turner helped to quell the whites' rage.
>
> Once again, rebellion resulted in stricter laws. In Virginia, blacks could no longer hold religious meetings at night unless they had written permission from their masters or overseers. New laws prohibited the teaching of reading and writing to slaves. In 1834, the state banned free blacks from entering Virginia, in case they stirred up trouble.[7]

In *The Art of Waging Peace* I discuss how laws are an essential method for "deflecting" violence, yet African Americans were often excluded from the protection that laws offered. In his book *This Nonviolent Stuff'll Get You Killed*, Charles E. Cobb Jr. discusses how African Americans armed with guns tried to provide the kind of protection that law enforcement officials were unwilling to provide. Throughout the South, many African Americans protected their homes simply by using guns to scare hostile whites away. Despite this defensive use of guns (which in most cases actually consisted of "warning aggression," a topic I discuss in my other books), Cobb explains one reason why African Americans were afraid of initiating violent attacks against whites:

> To say that Reconstruction failed does not adequately describe what actually happened in the South after the Civil War. Reconstruction did not fail; it was destroyed,

> crushed by more than a decade of savage campaigns of violence carried out both by the local governments that had largely remained intact and by vigilante terrorists. Lynchings and other forms of mob violence were the instruments of Reconstruction's brutal death. The overwhelming violence against blacks during this period goes a long way toward explaining why, even though guns were common in twentieth-century black southern communities, there were few black paramilitary units and they rarely attacked or fought back with arms against white-supremacist authority, even in areas like the Mississippi Delta, central Alabama, or southwest Georgia, where blacks were an overwhelming majority of the population. The memories of Reconstruction and its violent demise dictated caution. Overt displays of force, organization, and resistance by the black community might once again trigger an instantaneous and overwhelming reaction from white-supremacist power and its foot soldiers—who were everywhere in the South—with little prospect of federal intervention.[8]

I have heard some people say that if African Americans become violent by killing whites, then they will be able to intimidate the white population into respecting them and leaving them alone. But this myth does not reflect reality. The depiction of African Americans as violent and dangerous harms rather than helps the black population. The stereotype that African American men are naturally violent dates back to slavery, and history shows that this stereotype makes it more likely that violence will be inflicted on all black people. Psychologists Joel Wong and Alison E. Schwing explain: "The assumption that African American males are criminals dates back to slavery. One stereotype emerging from that time and perpetuated today is the view of the African American male as a violent brute . . . This stereotype could be reflected in a number of stressful, racism-related experiences of African American boys or young men. For example, when a white person refuses to ride an elevator with a young black man."[9]

Dehumanization makes it much easier to kill people, and our behavior can make it much easier for people to dehumanize us. People often dehumanize others by saying, "They are violent, barbaric, irrational, and dangerous." But nobody ever dehumanizes a group by saying, "They are respectful, disciplined, rational, and good listeners." When we are agents of destruction we reinforce the negative stereotype that dehumanization creates for us. When we use nonviolence and reflect the peace hero ideal, we shatter this stereotype.

Martin Luther King Jr. was a strategic genius who realized that when oppressed people in the modern world use violence, this tends to reinforce negative stereotypes about them, which makes it easier for people to dehumanize and kill them, while oppressed people who use nonviolence are able to break stereotypes and *rehumanize* themselves. This is why King said the weapon of nonviolence "ennobles the man who wields it."[10]

When oppressed people use the weapon of nonviolence, they also break the stereotype that they are submissive, cowardly, undisciplined, and unintelligent (which was another common stereotype of African Americans). In this way, nonviolence allowed African Americans to refute the stereotype that they are violent brutes, along with the stereotype that they are submissive cowards. King further explained how the weapon of nonviolence has a rehumanizing effect on those who wield it: "The Negro's method of nonviolent direct action is not only suitable as a remedy for injustice; its very nature is such that it challenges the myth of [racial] inferiority. Even the most reluctant are forced to recognize that no inferior people could choose and successfully pursue a course involving such extensive sacrifice, bravery and skill."[11]

There are other examples where our society has romantic illusions of violence. During my lectures people have said that if Hitler had not taken guns away from German Jews, they could have overthrown him and prevented World War II. But is this true? Could the innocent German Jews killed in the Holocaust have used rifles to overthrow Hitler?

From a military strategic perspective, this would have been virtually impossible. How do we know this? As military history shows, the combined military might of the United States, Soviet Union, Britain, Canada, Australia, and numerous other allied countries could barely stop Hitler.

General Patton's vast numbers of tanks, millions of Soviet soldiers pouring across the Eastern Front to attack Germany, British and American bombing campaigns of German cities, and tens of millions of allied troops—many armed with weapons far deadlier than rifles—could barely stop Hitler.

The idea that German Jews killed in the Holocaust, many of whom had no military training, could have overthrown the Nazi government is not realistic from a military strategic perspective, especially since they would have been fighting on German soil where Hitler had home-field advantage. Nonviolence is often considered naive, but isn't the idea of poorly armed civilians overthrowing Hitler at the height of his power on his own territory far more naive? At West Point I learned that if Hitler had not invaded the Soviet Union, the Allies probably would have lost World War II, since Hitler had to commit most of his units and resources to fighting the Soviets, and millions of Soviet soldiers died trying to stop Hitler. Between 1939 and 1945 the Soviets manufactured 158,218 aircraft, 516,648 artillery, and 105,251 tanks and SPGs (self-propelled guns).[12]

Hitler disarmed German Jews, who comprised less than one percent of the German population, but not because he was seriously concerned that such a tiny group would overthrow or stop him, but because he wanted to make it as easy as possible to kill them. Who are the people who rule a country? The people who have the allegiance of the military and police forces.* Even in a representative democracy, voting simply determines who will have the allegiance of the military and police forces. There was no way that German Jews in the late 1930s were going to overthrow the entire Nazi regime by gaining the allegiance of the Nazi-controlled military and police.

* This is true in all countries, even the ones that don't have a military (such as Costa Rica). If I fly to Costa Rica, force my way into the president's office, and try to rule the country, who are the police going to arrest, me or the elected president? The elected officials in Costa Rica have the allegiance of the police, and therefore they rule the country with the consent of the people. In 1940 the German military and police as institutions were loyal to Hitler and the Nazi regime. It is a myth that just killing Hitler in 1940 would have ended World War II, because the Nazi regime had a chain of command filled with true believers in the Nazi cause. This is why the plot that nearly succeeded in the assasination of Hitler in 1944 also included a plan to arrest top officials in the Nazi chain of command and gain control of the reserve army. Ancient Rome had a civil war because the allegiance of the military became split. Julius Caesar won this civil war because he had a better army than his opponents.

At the same time when Germany was loosening gun laws for non-Jewish Germans, it passed a law in 1938 that prohibited Jews "from acquiring, possessing, and carrying firearms and ammunition, as well as truncheons or stabbing weapons."[13] Does this mean Hitler was afraid that people with truncheons (e.g., clubs, bats, and batons) and large knives would overthrow him, or that he instead wanted to ruthlessly reduce all forms of resistance as much as possible? Some people say that organized violent resistance on behalf of German Jews could not have overthrown Hitler or prevented World War II, but could have prevented the concentration camp killings. This claim is partially true, but also misleading.

In 1937 there were around 70 million people living in Germany, and only about 214,000 of them were Jews. In 1933 there were about 522,000 Jews living in Germany, which was still less than one percent of the German population (several hundred thousand Jews fled Germany between 1933 and 1937).[14] If the Nazi regime had faced an armed uprising from such a tiny percentage of the population, would Hitler (a person not afraid to wage war against mighty European empires and the Soviet Union) have backed down and let these violent resisters live, or would he have instead used extreme violent force and the home-field advantage of controlling Germany to kill these people and their families in their neighborhoods? Hitler, who used propaganda to depict himself as a protector of innocent life, tried to hide the concentration camp killings from most of the German population. But as researchers Erica Chenoweth and Maria Stephan show, dictators are often able to gain wide public support for the massacre of violent rebels by claiming the need to provide "security" and "safety."

The U.S. Holocaust Memorial Museum describes how Jews living outside of Germany (where Hitler did not have home-field advantage) used violent resistance, but were unable to stop the Nazi war machine and save most Jews from the concentration camps. I have met people who talk about World War II like it is an action movie or video game. Just as a hero in an action movie or video game can kill hundreds of enemies with ease, I have met people who imagine that a small number of heroes armed with guns could have beaten the Nazis, when in reality it took a massive allied military force that outnumbered the German military to beat the Nazis. Even in places where Jews had guns and home-field advantage, these courageous fighters still couldn't prevent the Holocaust. The U.S. Holocaust Memorial Museum explains:

> Jewish civilians offered armed resistance in over 100 ghettos in occupied Poland and the Soviet Union. In April–May 1943, Jews in the Warsaw ghetto rose in armed revolt after rumors that the Germans would deport the remaining ghetto inhabitants to the Treblinka killing center. As German SS and police units entered the ghetto, members of the Jewish Fighting Organization (Zydowska Organizacja Bojowa; ZOB) and other Jewish groups attacked German tanks with Molotov cocktails, hand grenades, and a handful of small arms. Although the Germans, shocked by the ferocity of resistance, were able to end the major fighting within a few days, it took the vastly superior German forces nearly a month before they were able to completely pacify the ghetto and deport virtually all of the remaining inhabitants. For months after the end of the Warsaw ghetto uprising, individual Jewish resisters continued to hide in the ruins of the ghetto, which SS and police units patrolled to prevent attacks on German personnel.
>
> During the same year, ghetto inhabitants rose against the Germans in Vilna (Vilnius), Bialystok, and a number of other ghettos. Many ghetto fighters took up arms in the knowledge that the majority of ghetto inhabitants had already been deported to the killing centers; and also in the knowledge that their resistance even now could not save from destruction the remaining Jews who could not fight. But they fought for the sake of Jewish honor and to avenge the slaughter of so many Jews.[15]

In 1940 Gandhi wrote a letter to Hitler. The letter's content demonstrates that Gandhi had a deep understanding of strategy, which was not distorted by naively romantic illusions of violence. Gandhi was in a unique position, because he was resisting the evil system of British colonialism. He saw World War II not as an oversimplistic battle of good versus evil, but as the evil systems of Nazi and Japanese imperialism clashing against the evil system of European colonialism.

Gandhi's strategic brilliance is shown in his ability to be prophetic. He realized that the Nazis were masters of violence, but he suspected that their overconfidence would cause them to wage war against the most powerful nations in the world. In 1940, shortly after World War II began, Gandhi realized that a rival nation would eventually improve on the Nazi's mastery of violence and beat them with their own weapon. Gandhi's letter tried to appeal to Hitler's humanity while expressing deep strategic insights about the limitations of violence, to which Hitler never responded. Gandhi wrote:

> Your own writings and pronouncements and those of your friends and admirers leave no room for doubt that many of your acts are monstrous and unbecoming of human dignity, especially in the estimation of men like me who believe in universal friendliness. Such are your humiliation of Czechoslovakia, the rape of Poland and the swallowing of Denmark. I am aware that your view of life regards such spoliations as virtuous acts. But we have been taught from childhood to regard them as acts degrading humanity. Hence we cannot possibly wish success to your arms.
>
> But ours is a unique position. We resist British Imperialism no less than Nazism . . . One-fifth of the human race has been brought under the British heel by means that will not bear scrutiny . . . Ours is an unarmed revolt against the British rule . . . We have been trying for the past half a century to throw off the British rule. The movement of [Indian] independence has been never so strong as now . . . We have attained a very fair measure of success through non-violent effort. We were groping for the right means to combat the most organized violence in the world which the British power represents. You have challenged

> it. It remains to be seen which is the better organized, the German or the British.
>
> We know what the British heel means for us and the non-European races of the world. But we would never wish to end the British rule with German aid . . . *If not the British, some other power will certainly improve upon your method and beat you with your own weapon* [emphasis added]. You are leaving no legacy to your people of which they would feel proud.[16]

There are many myths about Gandhi, such as the myth that he always rejected all uses of violence. In *The Art of Waging Peace* I discuss how Gandhi served in the military as a medic and had the rank of sergeant major, was awarded the War Medal by the British Empire, worked as a military recruiter, and supported Poland's violent resistance against Nazi Germany. Gandhi believed that if a person or country is *truly* using violence in self-defense as a last resort against a much stronger opponent, then the use of violence is not immoral, even though it may be extremely ineffective. Gandhi used the term *almost nonviolence* to describe the application of violence as a last resort against a much stronger opponent, because this form of violence is *almost as moral as nonviolence.* If a woman uses violence as a last resort to defend herself against a rapist, Gandhi would not call this immoral. In 1940 he said:

> If Poland has that measure of uttermost bravery and an equal measure of selflessness, history will forget that she defended herself with violence. Her violence will be counted almost as nonviolence . . . If a man fights with his sword single handed against a horde of dacoits [robbers] armed to the teeth, I should say he is fighting almost nonviolently. Haven't I said to our women that, if in defence of their honour they used their nails and teeth and even a dagger, I should regard their conduct nonviolent? . . . Supposing a mouse in fighting a cat tried to resist the cat with his sharp beak, would you call that mouse violent?

> In the same way, for the Poles to stand valiantly against the German hordes vastly superior in numbers, military equipment and strength, was almost nonviolence.[17]

In *The Art of Waging Peace* I discuss when it might be necessary to use violence instead of nonviolence in personal self-defense situations, but when should oppressed people use violence instead of nonviolence to defeat an oppressive system? I have five simple questions that can help us understand when we might want to consider using violence to confront oppression.

The first question is, do you own your own navy or air force? Since the United States and British Empire during World War II possessed large navies and air forces, defeating the Nazis militarily would be very difficult, but it was feasible.

The second question is, do you have a better-trained military or more soldiers than the oppressive system? In chapter 2 we discussed how training helps us succeed at any human endeavor, and that training is the great equalizer. Oppressed people almost always have a less well-trained military, less money, less resources, and less destructive weapons than the oppressive system. When this is the case, oppressed people can partially compensate for these deficiencies if their army is much larger than the oppressive system's army.

The third question is, are you getting financial or military support from another powerful country? When oppressed people successfully use violence to resist an opponent with a stronger military, they often have the support of another powerful country. To mention a few examples, the Americans were supported by the French and Spanish empires during the American Revolution, the Vietnamese were supported by China and the Soviet Union during the Vietnam War, and the Afghans were supported by the United States during the Soviet occupation of Afghanistan. In ancient history, the Messenian slaves who revolted against their Spartan slave masters had the help of the powerful Greek city-state Thebes. If you want to use violence against an oppressive system, is another powerful country sending you antiaircraft missiles, military advisors, or millions of dollars to buy weapons and ammunition?

The fourth question is, do you have home-field advantage? If a group of people had violently risen up against Hitler on German soil in 1938,

Hitler would have had home-field advantage, because he controlled the local police forces and national infrastructure. It would have been much more difficult for Hitler's opponents to hide in Berlin than in Stalingrad or Paris. Also, waging war in a faraway land can become extremely expensive and strategically ineffective, because you must transport supplies and soldiers to a distant place where they do not know the area nearly as well as the population native to that land.

In *The Art of War*, written around twenty-five hundred years ago, Sun Tzu explains how waging war in a faraway land can harm a country financially: "When a country is impoverished by military operations, it is because of transporting supplies to a distant place. Transport supplies to a distant place, and the populace will be impoverished. Those who are near the army sell at high prices. Because of high prices, the wealth of the common people is exhausted. When resources are exhausted, then levies are made under pressure. When power and resources are exhausted, then the homeland is drained. The common people are deprived of seventy percent of their budget, while the government's expenses for equipment amount to sixty percent of its budget."[18]

The fifth question is, does the majority of the local population not oppose your cause? As Martin Luther King Jr. explained, a large percentage of the Cuban population sympathized with Fidel Castro and Che Guevara's war against the corrupt Batista regime. If oppressed people want to use violence to defeat a militarily weak oppressor that has not lost effective control of its armed forces, such as the Cuban government during the 1950s, they should be able to answer yes to at least one of these five questions. But if oppressed people want to use violence to defeat a military superpower, such as an empire, they should be able to answer yes to several of these five questions. I am not aware of any example in history where oppressed people* violently overthrew their oppressor without being able to answer yes to at least one of these five questions.

* I am referring to oppressed people who don't have the means to overthrow an oppressive government via a coup d'état.

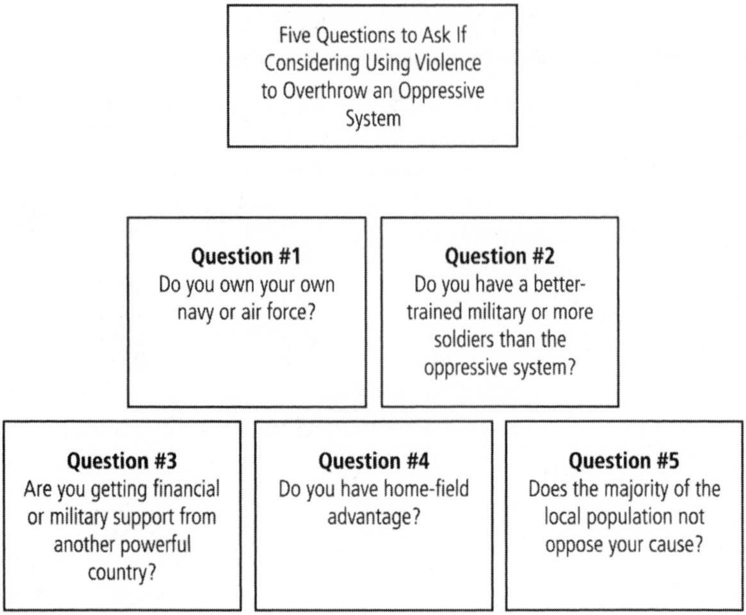

Five Questions to Ask If Considering Using Violence to Overthrow an Oppressive System

Question #1
Do you own your own navy or air force?

Question #2
Do you have a better-trained military or more soldiers than the oppressive system?

Question #3
Are you getting financial or military support from another powerful country?

Question #4
Do you have home-field advantage?

Question #5
Does the majority of the local population not oppose your cause?

Figure 4.2: Five Questions to Ask If Considering Using Violence to Overthrow an Oppressive System

When the Americans defeated the British Empire during the American Revolutionary War, they could answer yes to question 1 (they had a weak navy, but the French and Spanish empires helped them with powerful navies), question 3 (they had support from France, Spain, and other nations), question 4 (they had home-field advantage), and question 5 (the majority of the population did not oppose their cause). That's four out of five, but even answering yes to all but one of these questions does not guarantee victory. It simply increases the probability of victory, since war is unpredictable.

Regarding the American Revolutionary War, some historians estimate that only a third of Americans supported the revolution, a third opposed it, and a third was indifferent. Historian Robert Calhoon says that about 40 to 45 percent of Americans supported the revolution, and only about 15 to 20 percent opposed it, with nearly half of the American population not wanting to be involved in the struggle.[19] It is difficult to precisely assess opinions in that time period, but if one-third of Americans supported the revolution and a third was indifferent, that means two-thirds did not oppose it. In 1940 the majority of Germans would have opposed an attempt to overthrow the Nazi regime.

During the civil rights era of the 1950s and 1960s, African Americans could not answer yes to any of these five questions. Not one. African Americans did not even have home-field advantage, because they did not possess a large territory or control any government or police force at the state or national level. And African Americans were confronting the U.S. government, which did not have a weak military, or merely a strong military, but the most powerful military in human history. When I hear people say that African Americans during the civil rights era could have used violence to gain their freedom and human rights, this shows how naive our society's understanding of violence truly is. African Americans were such an enormous underdog that the civil rights movement is easily one of the greatest David versus Goliath struggles in human history.

By the late 1960s the majority of Americans did not oppose full racial integration and equality, so by that point African Americans could answer yes to question five, but attitudes changed dramatically on this issue because of nonviolent action. In 1950 the majority of Americans opposed full racial integration and equality, and if African Americans had attempted to use aggressive warfare in the early 1950s to overthrow oppression, this would have increased opposition against them, because propaganda would have depicted them not as freedom fighters but as violent brutes endangering peace and security. Even today, when people believe the stereotype that African Americans are violent and dangerous, they are less likely to view African Americans in an empathetic way and are more likely to be prejudiced.

During my lectures people have referenced the American Civil War, saying that if slavery could be defeated with violence, why couldn't segregation be defeated with violence? This is comparing apples and oranges, because slavery was defeated with violence because the North, which had a more powerful military than the South, conquered its adversary. The Union soldiers also outnumbered the Confederate soldiers nearly two to one. In the early twentieth century, there was no militarily powerful government anywhere in the world willing to wage war on behalf of African Americans (later in this chapter I will discuss how the civil rights movement eventually convinced the federal government to protect civil rights with armed troops). During the American Civil War, the North was also determined to prevent the European empires from militarily supporting the South. If the South had received significant military aid from the European empires, it might have won the war.

When a national government not occupied by a foreign power just has a good military, it can conquer many adversaries. A national government, because it has so many advantages that oppressed people do not, such as territorial control, possession of national resources and infrastructure, the ability to create currency, and the capacity to recruit, train, and arm a large number of soldiers, only needs to answer yes to question 2 (having a better-trained military or more soldiers) to win a war. Having a well-trained military played a critical role in the ability of the Romans to create a large empire.

Where the use of violence is concerned, oppressed people are at a severe disadvantage when compared to national governments. Gandhi and Martin Luther King Jr. realized that nonviolence is a powerful weapon that allows oppressed people to overcome this severe disadvantage. Gandhi and King used the word "weapon" because they saw nonviolence as the next evolution in warfare, a higher evolution of strategy, that allows us to fight injustice with much better results than the use of violence.* To revisit a quote that I used at the beginning of this book, King said, "Nonviolence is a powerful and just weapon. It is a weapon unique in history, which cuts without wounding and ennobles the man who wields it. It is a sword that heals."[20]

Where India was concerned, Gandhi could have answered yes to question 2 (the Indians greatly outnumbered the British), question 4 (the Indians had home-field advantage), and question 5 (the majority of Indians did not oppose Indian independence). That's three out of five, yet Gandhi chose nonviolence because he was not naive, and nonviolence is not naive.

* So far in this chapter I have discussed the use of violence against people. In the last book of this series I will discuss the limitations of "property destruction" in the struggle for justice.

A strategic genius, Gandhi knew that for oppressed people, nonviolence is a more powerful weapon than violence, *even if oppressed people can answer yes to all five questions.*

Since Gandhi's death, the groundbreaking research of Erica Chenoweth and Maria Stephan, conveyed in their book *Why Civil Resistance Works*, has shown that nonviolence is more likely than violence to defeat a militarily superior adversary. Again, Gandhi's strategic brilliance allowed him to be prophetic. Erica Chenoweth explains: "From 1900 to 2006, nonviolent campaigns worldwide were twice as likely to succeed outright as violent insurgencies. And there's more. This trend has been increasing over time, so that in the last fifty years, nonviolent campaigns are becoming increasingly successful and common, whereas violent insurgencies are becoming increasingly rare and unsuccessful. This is true even in those extremely brutal authoritarian conditions where I expected nonviolent resistance to fail."[21]

Another romantic illusion of violence is the naive belief that overwhelming military force can solve our current global problems. This romantic illusion causes people to believe that we can defeat twenty-first century terrorism the same way we won World War II, by conquering and holding territory. At West Point I learned that technology forces warfare to evolve. The reason soldiers today no longer ride horses into battle, use bows and arrows, and wield spears is because of the gun. The reason people no longer fight in massive trenches, as they did during World War I, is because the tank and airplane were greatly improved and mass-produced. But there is a technological innovation that has changed warfare more than the gun, tank, or airplane. That technological innovation is mass media.

Today most people's understanding of violence is naive, because they do not realize how much the Internet, the newest incarnation of mass media, has changed warfare. The most powerful weapon that ISIS has is the Internet, which has allowed ISIS to recruit people from all over the world. For most of human history, people from across the world had to send a military over land or sea to attack you, but the Internet allows people from across the world to convince your fellow citizens to attack you.

To be effective as a terrorist group, ISIS needs two things to happen. It needs to dehumanize the people it kills, and it also needs Western countries to dehumanize Muslims. When Western countries dehumanize Muslims, this further alienates Muslim populations and increases recruitment for ISIS. ISIS commits horrible atrocities against Westerners because it wants us to overreact by stereotyping, dehumanizing, and alienating Muslims.

Every time Western countries stereotype, dehumanize, and alienate Muslims, they are doing exactly what ISIS wants. A basic principle of military strategy is that we should not do what our opponents want. In order for ISIS's plan to work, it needs to dehumanize its enemies, but perhaps more importantly, it needs Americans and Europeans to dehumanize Muslims.

Modern terrorism cannot be compared to Nazi Germany, because the Nazis were not able to use the Internet as a weapon. Trying to fight modern terrorism the way we fought the Nazis, when today the Internet and other forms of mass media have dramatically changed twenty-first century warfare, would be like trying to fight the Nazis by using horses, spears, bows and arrows. Fifteen of the nineteen hijackers during the September 11 attacks were from Saudi Arabia, one of the United States' closest allies. ISIS seems to have better mastered the weapon of the Internet than Al Qaida, because ISIS is more adept at convincing American and European citizens to kill their fellow citizens.

Because technology has changed warfare in the twenty-first century and allowed modern terrorist groups to wage a digital military campaign, it is naive to believe that we can defeat terrorism by conquering and holding territory, which has become an archaic and counterproductive form of warfare. During the era of the Internet revolution, it is naive to believe that we can use violence to defeat the ideologies that sustain terrorism. Modern terrorist groups such as ISIS (and whatever group comes after ISIS) use the latest technology to reach people across national boundaries, and with the Internet they can recruit people from all over the world, including people on American and European soil. And they only have to recruit a tiny amount of Americans and Europeans, initiate a single attack, and kill a few people to cause the huge overreactions that they want from their opponents. Let us not react in ways that ISIS wants.

Rage is a kind of language that I spent many years learning. As I have worked to heal my rage, I have developed a level of empathy, understanding, and purpose that has made me grateful for my rage. Because I have such a high capacity for rage, I understand how seductive the language of rage can be, and I realize that many people commit violence not because they believe it is strategically effective, but because they simply want to express their rage and share their trauma. If I did not have waging peace as an alternative to my mother tongue of rage, I do not think that I would be able to control my desire to murder people.

Many people believe the romantic illusion that rage is a sign of strength, when it is actually a sign of agony. We are only as good as our options, and peace literacy gives people healthy options for healing their agony and expressing their pain in more productive ways. Peace literacy gave me the option of communicating through waging peace, which is a language far more potent and powerful than rage. Rage releases a lot of steam, but it is not an effective way to solve the root causes of our problems. As Martin Luther King Jr. said when I quoted him earlier, "If a method is not effective, no matter how much steam it releases, it is an expression of weakness, not of strength."[22]

Romantic Illusions versus Realistic Peace

It is unfortunate that our society sees the fundamental nature of war as violence, when the fundamental nature of war is actually deception. Perhaps if we realized that deception permeates every aspect of war, including the political speeches that advocate war, we would be less easily fooled by war propaganda. In *The Art of War*, Sun Tzu discusses some of the ways warfare is based on deception: "All warfare is based on deception. Hence, when able to attack, we must seem unable; when using our forces, we must seem inactive; when we are near, we must make the enemy believe we are far away; when far away, we must make him believe we are near."[23]

Unlike the deception of waging war, in many ways waging peace is the art of truth-telling. The underlying purpose of the women's rights movement was to expose the truth about women's equality, and the underlying purpose of the civil rights movement was to expose the truth that African Americans are human beings. Where waging peace is concerned, every strategy and tactic must be aimed at dismantling the myths that sustain injustice.

Odysseus is a useful metaphor for deception, because he is mortal. The myths and deceptions that sustain unjust systems are also mortal like Odysseus. On the other hand, timeless truth, symbolized by the immortal goddess Veritas, is eternal. Since the birth of humanity it has always been true that women are not less than human and no race was designed for slavery, but myths and deceptions conceal these truths. Unlike timeless truth, which can be concealed but never destroyed, the lifespan of a lie can be cut short by the sword of truth.

In Greek mythology, stories about Athena show how war is connected to deception. The war goddess Athena's favorite mortal is Odysseus, an expert at deception. Although she is a virgin and Odysseus is not her son, Athena behaves like a protective mother who helps her favorite mortal at the expense of others. When Odysseus competes in a footrace in the *Iliad*, Athena trips one of the runners so that Odysseus can win. Enraged, the runner says that Athena is "always beside Odysseus—just like the man's mother, rushing to put his rivals in the dust."[24]

The play *Ajax*, written by Sophocles in the fifth century BC, depicts what happens after the Greek army awards Achilles's armor to Odysseus rather than Giant Ajax. In the play, Athena not only favors Odysseus, but she goes out of her way to humiliate Giant Ajax, causing his suicide. Just as Sun Tzu realized that war favors deception and strategy over size and strength, the war goddess Athena favors cunning Odysseus over Giant Ajax.

To make our complex reality understandable during this confusing era in human history, and to create realistic peace, we need new metaphors. Athena can serve as one of these new metaphors. How is waging peace connected to strategy? Waging peace is a higher evolution of strategy, a higher evolution of Athena, that is allied with her half-sister Veritas, the immortal goddess of truth, rather than the mortal deceiver Odysseus. This higher evolution of Athena is needed to heal the root causes of our problems and protect our fragile future. This higher evolution of Athena is needed now more than ever, because romantic illusions of violence cannot solve the problems that threaten our national and global security.

The 2009 U.S. Army Sustainability Report lists several threats to national security, which include severe income disparity, poverty, and climate change. The U.S. Army Sustainability Report states: "The Army is facing several global challenges to sustainability that create a volatile security environment with an increased potential for conflict . . . Globalization's increased interdependence and connectivity has led to greater disparities in wealth, which foster conditions that can lead to conflict . . . Population growth and poverty; the poor in fast-growing urban areas are especially vulnerable to antigovernment and radical ideologies . . . Climate change and natural disasters strain already limited resources, increasing the potential for humanitarian crises and population migrations."[25]

When the U.S. Army says that "greater disparities in wealth . . . poverty . . . and climate change" are dangerous, these were among the same concerns expressed by the Occupy movement. When the U.S. Army and Occupy movement agree on something, I think we should pay attention. Without the higher evolution of strategy, the higher evolution of Athena, that is found in waging peace, we cannot protect ourselves from national security threats such as severe income disparity, poverty, and climate change. None of these problems can be solved by waging war. In addition, none of these problems, which affect people around the world, can be solved by a single country. That is reality. During the twenty-first century, protecting our national security requires us to develop the peace literacy skills necessary to work together as a global community. During the twenty-first century, protecting our national security also requires us to develop the peace literacy skills necessary to create a new vision of global security.

In the four chapters of this book, I discuss four kinds of romantic illusions that impair our understanding of realistic peace, encourage naiveté, and threaten human survival. During an era when we have the technological capacity to destroy ourselves, human survival depends on our ability to understand and promote realistic peace:

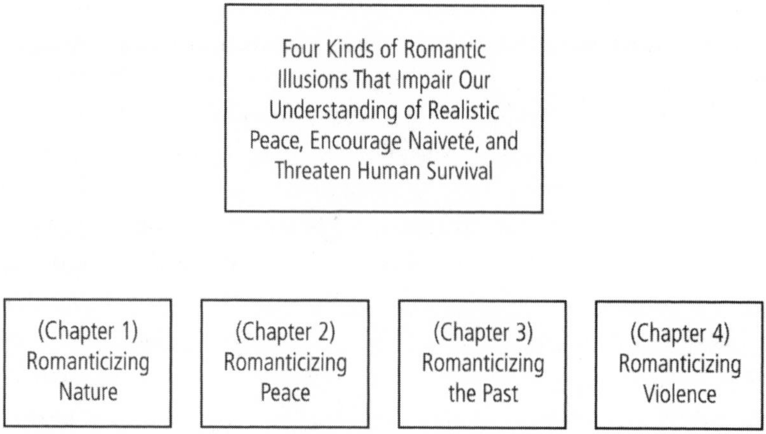

Four Kinds of Romantic Illusions That Impair Our Understanding of Realistic Peace, Encourage Naiveté, and Threaten Human Survival

(Chapter 1) Romanticizing Nature	(Chapter 2) Romanticizing Peace	(Chapter 3) Romanticizing the Past	(Chapter 4) Romanticizing Violence

Figure 4.3: Four Kinds of Romantic Illusions That Harm Realistic Peace

Romantic illusions of peace are just as dangerous as romantic illusions of violence. I have met people who romanticize peace as being more powerful than it really is. Some of these people have told me things such as, "Peace is so powerful that you just have to believe in peace, deep in your heart, and the power of that belief will overcome all evil. If enough people simply believe in peace, then we will have peace throughout our world." In chapter 2 I quoted Gandhi discussing the dangerous idea that peace is simply a mere belief. Contrary to the romantic illusion that peace is a mere belief, realistic peace requires training, skills, deep understanding, a strong muscle of empathy, committed effort, cooperation, truth, and so much more.

A sword has no power unless it has someone to wield it. Without the hands of a human, a sword is lifeless. In a similar way, peace only comes to life when we wage peace. The weapon of nonviolence is only as powerful as the character and skills of those who wield it. Contrary to the romantic illusion that peace can be created and sustained by belief alone, the peace we create is not invincible, but can be destroyed if we do not behave as good stewards who actively protect and nurture peace. Like the vulnerable garden of democracy, peace is also a vulnerable garden that will wilt and die if we are apathetic rather than vigilant.

Romantic illusions of violence are especially seductive in our society. If I had not gone to West Point, I don't think I would understand the strategic limitations of violence that allow me to see through these romantic illusions. But in the twenty-first century, even going to West Point is not enough. If I had not studied and understood the strategic brilliance of Gandhi and Martin Luther King Jr., I would not have learned why nonviolence is a higher evolution of strategy needed for human survival during our fragile future.

Violence has its uses (which I explain in *The Art of Waging Peace*), but it is unpredictable and can easily backfire. On a strategic level, however, violence cannot solve any of the global problems that threaten our delicate biosphere. Violence cannot change the belief systems that cause environmental destruction, nor can violence heal the root causes of extremism and fanaticism. Violence can attack slavery, but it cannot defeat racism. Violence can attack symptoms, but it cannot defeat the ignorance, misunderstandings, and deception that cause these symptoms. As Martin Luther King Jr. said, violence can kill the liar, but it cannot kill the lies that sustain unjust systems.

If humanity solves its current global problems and survives long into our fragile future, I think people a thousand years from now will look back on us the way we look back on European doctors who practiced medieval medicine a thousand years ago. Just as European doctors in the eleventh century did not have literacy in modern medicine, which would have empowered them to see the underlying conditions and microorganisms that cause illness, many people today do not have literacy in our shared humanity, the art of living, the art of waging peace, the art of listening, or the nature of reality, which empowers us to see the underlying conditions and myths that cause so many of our human problems. And just as European doctors in the eleventh century often used treatments that caused more harm than good, many people today support government policies for dealing with extremism and fanaticism that make these problems worse.

Waging peace to solve our global problems is such a tremendous struggle that humanity might not survive. Time is ruthless and there is no law of nature that says humanity must survive forever, so we must admit the possibility of human extinction. As we discussed earlier, the universe has given us only three options for solving any human problem. Do nothing. Use a violent method. Or use a method that is not violent. Doing nothing and using violence, as options, cannot kill the lies that keep humanity trapped in a cycle of illusion, division, and destruction.

Waging peace is the best option the universe has given us for solving the root causes of our problems. That is what we have to work with. I am not dissatisfied with what the universe has given us, because I see the vast potential and infinite possibilities that we can unlock when we become peace literate. Even though we face global problems that threaten human survival, I have a large amount of realistic hope, because I know the power that we can unleash when we embrace struggle, train ourselves to become fully human, wield the sword of truth, and choose the higher evolution of strategy that is waging peace.

Lady Justice

Peace is more than just the absence of war. Peace is also the presence of many ingredients. To understand the many ingredients in the meal of peace—the nourishment our species needs to prevent its extinction—we must first discuss the nature of ideas.

As my mentor Jo Ann Deck learned from Philip Wood, the owner of the publishing company she worked for, *ideas are the highest form of technology*. The Romans primarily saw peace as the absence of war that results from military conquest, and PEACE GIVEN TO THE WORLD was a common inscription on the medals awarded to Roman soldiers.[26] But some Romans began to grasp a new technology, in the form of the new idea that peace is more than just the absence of war.

The Roman senator and historian Tacitus grasped this new idea when he put some surprising words in the mouth of a Briton "barbarian" who was rebelling against Roman rule. In the following quote, Tacitus has the Briton say that the Romans make a desert and call it peace: "But there is no nation beyond us; nothing but waves and rocks, and the still more hostile Romans, whose arrogance we cannot escape by obsequiousness and submission. These plunderers of the world, after exhausting the land by their devastations, are rifling the ocean: stimulated by avarice . . . To ravage, to slaughter, to usurp under false titles, they call empire; and *where they make a desert, they call it peace* [emphasis added]."[27]

Tacitus seemed to grasp the new idea that peace, in the form of military conquest, destruction, and oppression, is not peace at all, but a metaphorical desert.* To offer another example of changing attitudes toward peace, the ancient Greek historian Plutarch tells a story about Ariston, a Spartan king in the sixth century BC who seemed to grasp the new idea that waging peace was a higher evolution of strategy, a better technology of ideas, than waging war. Plutarch tells us:

> When someone commended the maxim of Cleomenes, who, on being asked what a good king ought to do, said, "To do good to his friends and evil to his enemies," Ariston said, "How much better, my good sir, to do good to our friends, and to make friends of our enemies?" This, which is universally conceded to be one of Socrates' maxims, is also referred to Ariston.[28]

Why did these new ideas not become the norm in ancient Greece and Rome? One reason is that the ancient world did not have the *social and ideological infrastructure* necessary to support these new ideas on a broad scale. In a similar way, if you had the ability to travel back in time with your smartphone to ancient Greece, you would not be able to use your phone to its full potential, because back then there was no infrastructure in the form of the Internet, GPS satellites, or wireless grid to support this technology. Even without this infrastructure, you could still use many features on your smartphone, such as the camera, calculator, voice recorder, mp3 player, movie player, and many of the apps, but you could not recharge your phone because there was no electric grid in ancient Greece (again no infrastructure) to power your phone.

* Tacitus was still a man of his time. It is likely that he believed in imperialism, which is why it is so surprising that he expressed this viewpoint in his writing.

Why did people who lived over two thousand years ago, such as Socrates, Jesus, Lao-tzu, Buddha, and many others, express the ideals of waging peace, but the first multinational nonviolent movements that opposed unjust systems, such as the movements to abolish state-sanctioned slavery and establish universal women's rights, not happen until the eighteenth and nineteenth centuries? Where the technology of waging peace is concerned, we need a social and ideological infrastructure that allows us to unlock the full potential of this technology of ideas, and that infrastructure did not become strong enough to enable multinational nonviolent movements until the eighteenth and nineteenth centuries. Just as the technological infrastructure that enables the full capabilities of a smartphone did not exist in ancient Greece and Rome, the social and ideological infrastructure that enables the full capabilities of waging peace also did not exist back then.

This social and ideological infrastructure includes a sufficient flow of information between people and communities, ideals such as universal human rights, and mass communication tools such as pamphlets (on which Thomas Paine relied), the telegraph and international newspapers (on which Gandhi relied), television (on which Martin Luther King Jr. relied), and the Internet (on which modern movements rely). The ancient Greeks and Romans were missing many components of our modern social and ideological infrastructure, such as journalists, news outlets, printing presses that can cheaply mass-produce books that challenge how people think, cameras that can capture images of injustice, and ideals such as freedom of speech, freedom of the press, and universal human rights.

In their book *Why Civil Resistance Works*, Erica Chenoweth and Maria Stephan discuss how nonviolence, since 1900, has been able to defeat many dictators who try to suppress this social and ideological infrastructure in their countries. It is impossible for any modern dictator to completely outlaw camera technology, and democratic ideals have become so popular around the world that many dictators today try to create the illusion they are somewhat democratic through rigged elections, propaganda, or some other means.

Peace literacy is the next essential step in the evolution of humanity's social and ideological infrastructure. As more people in our society and around the world become peace literate, we will unlock practical solutions to our national and global problems that so many people today cannot see, and we will be able to harness the full power of waging peace. In the twenty-first century, peace literacy is a new component of our social and ideological infrastructure that is necessary to enable human survival and prosperity during our fragile future. In a similar way, in the eighteenth century the ideal of universal human rights was a new component of the social and ideological infrastructure that enabled the anti-slavery and women's rights movements.

Where did the ideal of universal human rights come from? The widespread idea that all human beings, even if they are women or enslaved, have the same inalienable rights as the richest kings, resulted from the European Enlightenment that took place around the seventeenth and eighteenth centuries. This new idea helped form the social and ideological infrastructure that powered the movements to abolish slavery and give women equal rights.

The American Revolution occurred when American landowners asserted their inalienable human rights and rebelled against the British monarchy. Decades after the landowners and their rebel army won the American Revolutionary War with the help of European allies, however, most Americans still did not have basic human rights. In her book *The History of Human Rights*, Micheline Ishay tells us:

> [During the Enlightenment] freedom of religion* and opinion, and property rights broke the back of feudal

* Regarding Micheline Ishay's mention of "freedom of religion" as an Enlightenment ideal, I have heard people say that freedom of religion already existed in the Middle East, India, and ancient Greece before the European Enlightenment. Although these cultures had some elements that we associate with freedom of religion, our modern understanding of freedom of religion, which derived from the Enlightenment, goes beyond what existed in those cultures. For example, ancient Greek religion was less dogmatic about belief (allowing people to worship a variety of gods) but more dogmatic about rituals (e.g., the need for the city-state to conduct animal sacrifice, celebrate religious festivals, etc.). Socrates was executed partly because his views and actions were seen as sacrilegious. Furthermore, freedom of religion also includes the freedom to question and criticize religion (religious reformers rely on this). In parts of the medieval Middle East where Christians and Jews could worship openly, how many governments would have tolerated people who publicly challenged the teachings of the Koran and popular religious leaders? In India, the caste system put religious restrictions on the lowest caste. Prior to the Enlightenment, Genghis Khan might have been the first person to create something close to what we now consider freedom of religion.

> regimes and transformed humankind's prospects for realizing human rights. Despite the Enlightenment's critical contribution to the development of the modern human rights agenda, the revolutions of the mid-seventeenth and eighteenth centuries remained incomplete. Many individuals were still considered ineligible to be entrusted with all the freedoms invoked by the English, American, and French declarations of rights. Propertyless male citizens and all women were considered secondary or passive citizens and denied voting rights and political participation; women's legal status continued to be subjugated to the authority of their husbands; with rare exceptions, slavery persisted; the rights of indigenous populations within European colonies were violated; in many places, homosexuality was still regarded as a criminal act; the civil rights of Jews continued to be denied even in revolutionary countries.[29]

After the landowners asserted their human rights, this encouraged poor whites, blacks, and women to wonder, "If the landowners have the same inalienable rights as the monarchs, why don't we have the same inalienable rights as the landowners?" Lucretia Mott, Elizabeth Cady Stanton, Susan B. Anthony, and Frederick Douglass, who all worked to abolish state-sanctioned slavery and promote women's rights, cited the American Revolution as an inspiration for their work. The American Revolution gave them hope that even more ambitious revolutions, such as the revolution to end state-sanctioned slavery and the revolution to establish universal women's rights, were possible.

In her book *The Political Thought of Elizabeth Cady Stanton*, Sue Davis explains: "Granting equal legal and political rights to women, Cady Stanton often contended, would fulfill the promise of the [American] Revolution. Withholding those rights would not only obstruct the progress of society but also confirm that America in the mid-nineteenth century had failed to live up to the principles on which the nation was founded. She presented women's degraded position as cruelly inconsistent with the liberal principles of natural rights and equality that ran through the Declaration of Independence."[30]

However, the Europeans did not invent the new idea of universal human rights, just as Isaac Newton and Albert Einstein did not invent the laws of physics. The ideal of universal human rights is based on the truth that medieval monarchs were not chosen by God to be kings, Africans* were not born to be slaves, and women are not intellectually inferior to men. Saying that kings are human and fallible rather than divine, Africans are human beings, and women have the intellectual capacity needed to attend college and participate in democracy contains as much scientific truth as saying the Earth and other planets in our solar system revolve around the sun.

In this way, new ideas are new expressions of timeless truth, rather than the creation of something out of thin air. When new ideas express truth, they reveal deeper and deeper layers of our hidden reality. Just as Nietzsche realized that original thought involves seeing what others do not notice, Gandhi realized that humanity did not invent truth or the principles of nonviolence, but discovered what was there all along. Gandhi said, "Truth and non-violence are as old as the hills."[31]

Later in this chapter I will discuss how over two thousand years ago, the ancient Chinese expressed ideals similar to those of the European Enlightenment. Also, the principles of nonviolence can be found among the wisdom of indigenous peoples, although this wisdom can become suppressed when societies expand into populations numbering in the hundreds of thousands or millions, which creates social stratification and other issues that small indigenous tribes don't have to deal with.

The European Enlightenment made significant contributions to our social and ideological infrastructure, but it did not go far enough. Today our social and ideological infrastructure requires peace literacy so that the ideal of universal human rights and the power of waging peace can achieve their full potential. This infrastructure grows stronger as more people become

* As I mention in my other books, many races have been enslaved, including many groups of Europeans. But during and after the Enlightenment, slavery became associated mostly with Africans.

literate in our shared humanity, the art of living, the art of waging peace, the art of listening, and the nature of reality. This infrastructure also grows stronger as more people embrace struggle rather than submit to apathy, acquire training that empowers them to become fully human, serve truth rather than illusion, and choose the higher evolution of strategy that is waging peace.

This book shows how the overarching metaphors throughout this book series tie together. To journey through the turbulent waters of time on the cosmic ocean toward survival and prosperity (which I also call "the road to peace"), the muscles of our shared humanity must be strong so that we can overcome adversity (which I discuss in *Peaceful Revolution*), we must wield the infinite shield and the sword that heals so that we can defeat monsters such as ignorance and deception (which I discuss in *The Art of Waging Peace*), we must nourish ourselves with healthy ways of feeding our craving for purpose, meaning, nurturing relationships, explanations, expression, inspiration, belonging, self-worth, challenge, and transcendence (which I discuss in *The Cosmic Ocean*), and we must be guided by the constellation of peace so that we do not stray down a path of apathy and self-destruction (which I discuss in *Soldiers of Peace*). In the last book of this series, *The Transcendent Mystery*, I will discuss how the road to peace can take us to a place beyond words where the muscle of language cannot reach.

The metaphor that we are journeying together on the road to peace allows us to see an angle of reality, while the metaphor that we are sailing the sea of time as a global family allows us to see another angle of reality. To strengthen our social and ideological infrastructure, we must add many new ideas to our understanding of reality, such as the truth that human survival requires us to replace the archaic ideal of universal human rights with the updated ideal of *universal human rights and responsibilities.*

In 1940 Gandhi replied to science-fiction author H. G. Wells's attempt to write a declaration of human rights. Gandhi was assassinated in 1948, but he would probably have been very critical of the Universal Declaration of Human Rights, which was created in 1948 and ratified in 1949, because it does not mention the word "responsibility" once. Gandhi realized that rights require a sense of responsibility, because rights are easily taken away if we are complacent. In *Peaceful Revolution* I discuss how the muscle of appreciation creates the psychological foundation for stewardship, a healthy form of responsibility.*

In a telegram response to H. G. Wells, Gandhi said: "Have carefully read your five articles. You will permit me to say you are on the wrong track. I feel sure that I can draw up a better charter of rights than you have drawn up. But of what good will it be? Who will become its guardian? . . . I suggest the right way. Begin with a charter of Duties of Man and I promise the rights will follow as spring follows winter."[32]

The Universal Declaration of Human Rights, like the European Enlightenment, was a step in the right direction, but it did not go far enough. Viktor Frankl also realized that all rights, such as the right to freedom, require a sense of responsibility. The more freedom we gain, the greater our sense of responsibility must become. Today our species is free to drive itself toward extinction, and therefore shouldn't our sense of responsibility to each other and our planet be the greatest it has ever been in human history? Freedom without a sense of responsibility can lead to immature and reckless behavior that threatens the foundations of our freedom. Because we have the technological capacity to destroy ourselves, freedom without a sense of responsibility threatens our survival.

In his book *Man's Search for Meaning*, Frankl said: "Freedom, however, is not the last word. Freedom is only part of the story and half of the truth. Freedom is but the negative aspect of the whole phenomenon whose positive aspect is responsibleness. In fact, freedom is in danger of degenerating into mere arbitrariness unless it is lived in terms of responsibleness. That is why *I recommend that the Statue of Liberty on the East Coast be supplemented by a Statue of Responsibility on the West Coast.*"[33]

Peace is more than just the absence of war, because it also includes the presence of responsibility and many other ingredients. Peace can be compared to a bowl of soup. The nourishing soup of peace includes

* The word "duties" is mentioned only once in the 1948 declaration. There have been declarations on human rights and responsibilities written since 1948, and the best one I have read so far is the InterAction Council's Universal Declaration of Human Responsibilities, written in 1997.

responsibility, freedom, fairness, environmental sustainability, empathy, and other ingredients that create a healthy society. Justice, which is the force of human conscience acting on the world around us, can be compared to liquid in the nourishing soup of peace. Without the liquid of justice, the nourishing soup of peace is merely dry ingredients that are not interconnected. Without the liquid of justice, peace is a desert. Justice allows the flavors of peace to blend together, transforming peace into more than just the sum of its parts.

Truth is the bowl that holds the nourishing soup of peace. As I mentioned earlier, peace and justice are powerful ideals, but they cannot exist without the ideal of truth. Truth is the container that sustains peace and justice. It is the container that makes all of our other ideals possible. Without truth, the ingredients necessary for peace disperse and slip away.

The ancient Greeks realized peace and justice are related. Today I hear many activists use the phrase "peace and justice" to signify this relationship, but I do not hear them acknowledge that human awareness of this relationship dates at least as far back as ancient Greece. In Greek mythology, *justice* is known as the goddess Dicé (or Diké), *peace* is known as the goddess Eirene, and *good order* is known as the goddess Eunomia. These three goddesses are sisters, and their parents are Zeus, king of the gods, and Themis, the goddess of divine law.

Pindar, an ancient Greek poet, tells us: "Eunomia (Good Order) and that unsullied fountain Diké (Justice), her sister, sure support of cities; and Eirene (Peace) of the same kin, who are the stewards of wealth for mankind—three glorious daughters of wise-counseled Themis (Divine Law)."[34]

When I told my mentor Jo Ann Deck about Greek mythology's depiction of peace, justice, and good order as three sisters, she was pleasantly surprised and said, "The conservatives want good order, and the liberals want peace and justice, but the thing is they're all related. They're the three sisters."[35]

What is a realistic way to define good order? As we discussed in chapter 1, struggle is a part of reality. Hera, as a metaphor for struggle, is an immortal goddess who cannot die, symbolizing that struggle will always be with humanity. Furthermore, as we discussed in chapter 3, life will always be somewhat messy because living is the most difficult art form. The messiness of life includes misunderstanding, conflict, our vulnerability to trauma, our search for trust, our shared human fallibility that causes us to make mistakes, and our shared human craving for purpose, meaning, and self-worth.

A realistic definition of good order is preventing unnecessary messiness as much as humanly possible. For example, racial hatred, child molestation, being violently assaulted, rape, and drug addiction are not necessary forms of struggle that we must experience to be human. Our world may never reduce these unnecessary forms of messiness to absolute zero, but by increasing peace and justice in our world we can reduce how often this unnecessary messiness harms people. The more peace and justice in a society, the less unnecessary messiness and the more good order we will find, because peace and justice heal the root causes of problems rather than dealing merely with symptoms.

Over twenty-five hundred years before Martin Luther King Jr. said, "The arc of the moral universe is long, but it bends toward justice,"[36] the ancient Greek poet Hesiod said something similar when he proclaimed, "Justice beats Outrage when she comes at length to the end of the race."[37] King derived his quote from activist and minister Theodore Parker. Born in 1810, Parker said: "Look at the facts of the world. You see a continual and progressive triumph of the right. I do not pretend to understand the moral universe; the arc is a long one, my eye reaches but little ways; I cannot calculate the curve and complete the figure by the experience of sight; I can divine it by conscience. And from what I see I am sure it bends towards justice."[38]

In the following quote from Hesiod, written nearly three thousand years ago, he describes the immortal goddess Justice, and how Justice in the long term wins the race against Outrage:

> Do not foster violence; for violence is bad for a poor man. Even the prosperous cannot easily bear its burden, but is weighed down under it when he has fallen into delusion. The better path is to go by on the other side towards justice; for Justice beats Outrage when she comes at length to the end of the race. But only when he has suffered does the fool learn this . . .

> There is a noise when Justice is being dragged in the way where those who devour bribes and give sentence with crooked judgments, take her. And she, wrapped in mist, follows to the city and haunts of the people, weeping, and bringing mischief to men, even to such as have driven her forth in that they did not deal straightly with her.
>
> But they who give straight judgments to strangers and to the men of the land, and go not aside from what is just, their city flourishes, and the people prosper in it: Peace, the nurse of children, is abroad in their land, and all-seeing Zeus never decrees cruel war against them . . .
>
> Justice, the daughter of Zeus, who is honored and reverenced among the gods who dwell on Olympus, and whenever anyone hurts her with lying slander, she sits beside her father, Zeus the son of Cronos, and tells him of men's wicked heart, until the people pay for the mad folly of their princes who, evilly minded, pervert judgment and give sentence crookedly. Keep watch against this, you princes, and make straight your judgments, you who devour bribes; put crooked judgments altogether from your thoughts."[39]

Our understanding of justice is still evolving, and will continue to evolve far beyond what Hesiod realized. Hesiod describes Justice as a goddess who seeks help from her father Zeus, but later sculptures depict the concept of justice as a goddess wielding a sword in one hand and a scale in the other while wearing a blindfold (to symbolize impartiality). In other later sculptures, such as the one shown on this book cover, she is not blindfolded but is depicted as a warrior goddess with eyes wide open so that she can see clearly. To take our current understanding of justice to a higher level, we must understand how the proactive force I call "moral fury" (which I discuss in *The End of War* and *Peaceful Revolution*) is the hand of justice transformed into a fist capable of breaking unjust systems.

The Romans called the goddess of justice by the name "Justitia," but I prefer using the traditional name "Lady Justice" to metaphorically describe our evolving understanding of this liquid in the nourishing soup of peace. Our understanding of justice has evolved to a point where most people today recognize that justice is a force that relies on human activity rather than divine intervention, which is why we have courts. However, we must bring justice into our courts and far beyond so that Lady Justice can find a home in every corner of society and throughout our world. Theodore Parker explained how humanity must do the work of justice, rather than relying on divine intervention: "In human affairs the justice of God must work by human means . . . The ideal [of justice] must become actual . . . made real in a reign of righteousness, and a kingdom—no, a Commonwealth—of justice on the earth. You and I can help forward that work."[40]

The next step in our evolving understanding of justice is learning how we can fully serve and raise up justice, how we can become active participants in the bending of the moral universe toward justice. In the rest of this chapter I will describe four methods that allow us to serve peace, justice, and good order. These four methods also allow us to serve Veritas (truth).

These four methods transform Athena from an ally of the deceptive mortal Odysseus into a stronger ally of peace, justice, good order, and truth—goddesses that can be ignored and suppressed, but can never die. In addition, these four methods serve human survival and prosperity while offering us fulfilling ways to attain purpose and meaning in life. These four methods also strengthen our social and ideological infrastructure so that we can wield the weapon of nonviolence with maximum force.

The Transformative Method of Waging Peace

Women's rights and the abolition of state-sanctioned slavery spread around the world because new ideas changed how people thought. If we support women's rights and oppose slavery today, it is because we think differently than most of those who lived before us. All social problems come from how people think, and all progress comes from transforming how people think. In our society people incorrectly assume that facts are the only way to transform how people think, but there are many ways to transform our way of thinking for the better.

When we journey from a viewpoint of fear and cynicism to the proactive perspective of realistic hope, this transforms how we think. When we decrease our hatred, increase our empathy, and heal our trauma, this transforms how we think. When we become skilled in the arts of living, waging peace, and listening, this transforms how we think. When we live courageously by embracing honor in the form of integrity, learn the truth of our shared humanity, strive to fulfill our human potential, elevate our understanding of freedom by strengthening our sense of responsibility, and are guided by the four stars in the constellation of peace, this transforms how we think. By transforming how we think, we transform how we live, and we help transform our world.

In *The Art of Waging Peace* I discuss how waging peace consists of three forms of change: societal change, spiritual change, and ideological change. These three forms of change comprise the *transformative method of waging peace*, which transforms how people think in a way that promotes justice, peace, good order, truth, happiness, and human survival.

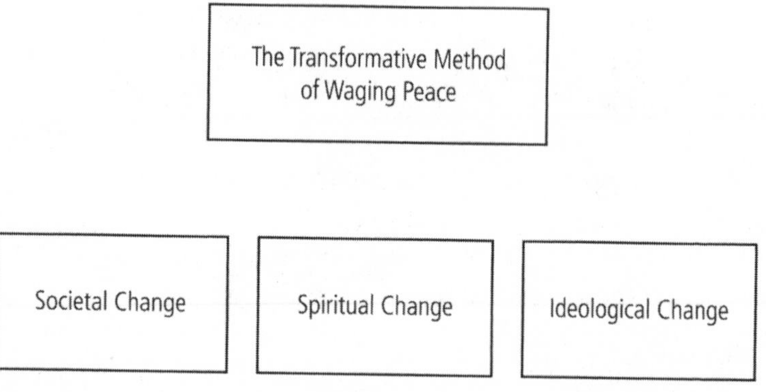

Figure 4.4: The Transformative Method of Waging Peace

In *The Art of Waging Peace* I thoroughly explore the transformative method of waging peace, including a discussion of honest persuasion techniques and how tactics, strategy, and grand strategy apply to this method. Because that book spends a lot of time unlocking the power of the transformative method, I will not repeat that content in this book. However, in this book I must emphasize that we persuade and transform humanity not only with the words that emerge from the muscle of language, but also with the actions that emerge from all the other muscles of our shared humanity (hope, empathy, appreciation, conscience, etc.).

When we listen well with deep empathy and concentration, we become an example that can help others listen better. When we live well, our actions can teach the art of living through the respect, kindness, and attention we give to friends, family members, coworkers, and strangers. And when we skillfully wage peace in our daily lives, we become an example that shows how peace is not merely the absence of war, but a fulfilling way of living that brings more purpose and meaning into our lives while serving the well-being of others.

When we are sincere, honest, and genuinely care about others, we become more persuasive, because we are more likely to gain people's trust. This building of trust makes us more effective at transforming misunderstanding into understanding, because when people trust us, they are more likely to listen to us. To survive during our fragile future, human beings must strive to build trust on a personal, national, and international level. This will benefit us in countless ways, because human beings crave trust in their personal relationships like plants crave sunlight. As I mentioned earlier, nobody in human history has ever seriously said, "I like being around people I can't trust. I like being betrayed."

To wield the weapon of nonviolence with maximum force, soldiers of peace must speak in a way that goes beyond preaching to the choir. We must also lead by example through our actions (in *The Art of Waging Peace* I discuss the power of leading by example). In addition, we must realize that transforming ourselves and our world for the better is not all or nothing. It's a gradual process where every bit helps. But because Lady Justice cannot wait for everyone to transform while injustice is inflicting so much harm around the world, we have another method for waging peace, one that applies pressure.

The Pressure Method of Waging Peace

Nonviolence is often misunderstood as being passive and weak, but there is an important aspect of nonviolence that many peace activists do not want to acknowledge. Nonviolence is coercive. It is a form of arm-twisting. It is like a submission hold in jiu-jitsu, where you apply a chokehold or joint lock to an opponent. If the opponent does not submit, he or she will pass out or suffer from a broken limb. In a similar way, nonviolence can harm people who do not comply with its intent. Contrary to the myth that nonviolence is passive and weak, it is actually coercive and potentially harmful.

To understand how nonviolence is coercive, we must discuss the *pressure method of waging peace*, which consists of three forms of pressure: economic pressure, legal pressure, and political pressure.

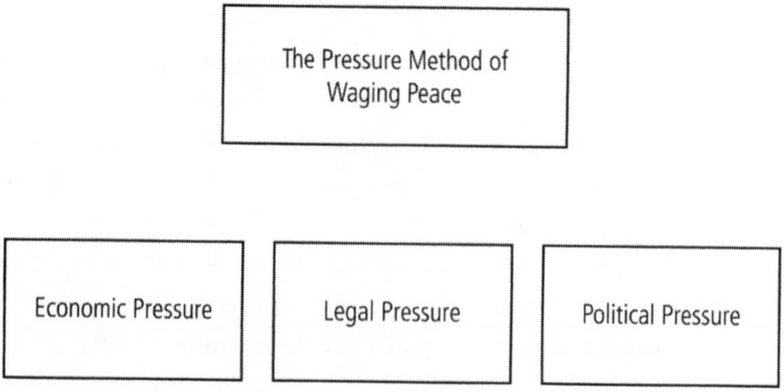

The Pressure Method of Waging Peace

Economic Pressure | Legal Pressure | Political Pressure

Figure 4.5: The Pressure Method of Waging Peace

How is nonviolence coercive? Let's consider boycotts, which are one of the most common forms of economic pressure used in nonviolent movements. When the civil rights movement used boycotts to oppose segregation, Martin Luther King Jr. realized that boycotts are un-Christian. Who else used boycotts? The Nazis against the Jews. Boycotts are coercive, a form of arm-twisting. Boycotts tell people that if they do not comply with what you want, you will do everything in your power to hurt them economically, which may harm their ability to provide for their family and could even put them out of business.

How did King reconcile the coercive nature of boycotts with the ideals of waging peace? He realized that a boycott is most effective when it serves justice. When a boycott serves Lady Justice, it is still coercive, but it is not immoral. In Montgomery, Alabama, King helped lead the struggle to boycott a bus company's racial segregation policies. During a television interview in 1957, he described how he aligned the boycott with peace, justice, and the ethics of Jesus:

> The [Montgomery bus boycott] movement needed some discipline and dignity. A boycott in and of itself would be a very dangerous thing if it didn't have some guidance . . . I like to think of our movement here in Montgomery as more than a boycott, because a boycott is suggestive merely of an economic squeeze, and that can be a very un-Christian thing, it can be immoral . . . If [our movement] stops with the boycott and it doesn't have the element of love and nonviolent resistance, it is opposed to the Christian religion. I faced this problem at a very early stage in the whole struggle. How could this method be reconciled with the Christian faith? . . . Then I reasoned that what we were actually doing was not exactly working on a negative, trying to put a company out of business. That was never our aim. We were not seeking to put the bus company out of business, *but to put justice in business* [emphasis added]. We were dealing with a positive point.[41]

Waging peace uses boycotts not to seek vengeance, but to raise up justice, to *put justice in business*. The forces of injustice, such as the Nazis, also used economic pressure to advance their interests. Because economic pressure can be used immorally and destructively, harming many people at the bottom of the economic ladder, soldiers of peace must counterbalance this risk by embracing an attitude of respect and empathy toward their adversaries.

This creates the kind of pressure that fully serves peace and justice, rather than the forces of injustice.*

Respect and empathy are as essential to the weapon of nonviolence as steel and sharpness are to a medieval sword. Without respect and empathy, nonviolence is soft and dull, and is less effective at defeating the forces of injustice. Respect and empathy strengthen and sharpen the weapon of nonviolence in several ways. First, they create the foundation for the highest level of strategic thinking. When I was in the army a colonel told me, "In order to think strategically, you must be able to see the world from the other person's point of view." This reminded me of a principle from Sun Tzu's *The Art of War*, written nearly twenty-five hundred years ago, where he says, "Know your enemy."[42] If you can put yourself in your opponent's frame of mind during a chess match and see the board from the opposing point of view, then you have a much better chance of making good choices.

Since empathy and its higher expression of unconditional love offer us the deepest insight into another human being, when Sun Tzu said, "Know your enemy" and Jesus said, "Love your enemy" they were essentially saying the same thing. The deepest way to know another human being is through the unconditional love that Jesus, Buddha, Gandhi, Martin Luther King Jr., and many other spiritual teachers taught us to embrace. King realized that the ethics of Jesus were highly strategic. Because empathy and its higher expression of unconditional love give us the deepest way to "know our enemy," this deep way of knowing unlocks the highest level of strategic thinking.

When we know our enemy through empathy, we realize they are not really our enemy. As Elinor "Gene" Hoffman, founder of the Compassionate Listening Project, said, "An enemy is a person whose story we have not heard."[43] Empathy tells us our true enemies are hatred and ignorance, not a particular group of people. The most effective way to fight enemies such as hatred and ignorance is with the techniques of waging peace. By

* Sanctions are an example of economic pressure that can potentially harm a lot of poor people in a country. The national leaders are rarely deprived of basic necessities or even luxuries because of sanctions.

strengthening and sharpening the weapon of nonviolence, respect and empathy allow it to cut deep into the root causes of our problems, unlike other techniques that only cut the surface symptoms.

The second way respect and empathy strengthen and sharpen the weapon of nonviolence is by motivating us to seek a win-win situation that benefits people on both sides of a conflict, rather than the humiliation of our opponent. As Spartan king Ariston said in a quote I shared earlier, instead of doing good to our friends and evil to our enemies, "How much better, my good sir, to do good to our friends, and to make friends of our enemies?"[44] Not everyone in an oppressive system will support a just cause, but nonviolence strategist Gene Sharp's extensive research shows that there are always some people in an oppressive system who will empathize with the oppressed, which creates cracks in the oppressive system. When you approach people in an oppressive system respectfully, persuasively, and with a high level of strategic thinking that looks to create a win-win situation, you increase the amount of people who can be recruited to support a just cause.

Oppressive systems are vulnerable, because they cannot function without the consent of many people. As the European Enlightenment philosophers realized in the seventeenth and eighteenth centuries, it is physically impossible for a single man or small group to control a large population without first controlling the way people think. These Enlightenment philosophers inspired America's Founding Fathers to rebel against the British Empire, but nearly two thousand years before the European Enlightenment, Chinese philosopher Xunzi also understood the timeless truth that oppressive systems require consent. Xunzi said, "The ruler is a boat; commoners are the water. The water can carry the boat; the water can capsize the boat."[45]

In America I have heard a popular myth that Chinese culture has nothing in common with our modern Western values that teach us to resist oppression. But the reality is far more complex, especially when we look at early Chinese history. In his book *The Everlasting Empire*, Yuri Pines calls China the "most rebellious nation"[46] in history and tells us: "The words of Xunzi (ca. 310–230 BCE) cited in the epigraph proved to be prophetic. Prior to his age, China witnessed no popular uprisings that left an imprint in historical texts, but shortly after his death a huge rebellion toppled the first imperial dynasty, Qin (221–207 BCE). Since then mass uprisings have recurred repeatedly in Chinese history, bringing an end to several major dynasties and severely crippling others. The scope, frequency, ferocity, and political impact of these uprisings dwarf any comparable insurrections elsewhere in the premodern world."[47]

Violent rebellions have difficulty confronting the root causes of injustice, whereas the weapon of nonviolence is able to affect these root causes by putting justice in business. When advocates of the civil rights movement boycotted bus companies and stores, they were not trying to put them out of business. Instead, leaders of the civil rights movement sought to create a win-win situation by basically saying, "We want to give you our money, but you have to align yourself with justice first. If you align yourself with justice, we will gladly support you and we will all benefit together."

King realized that white people being racist toward black people (one of the root causes of segregation) actually harmed white people, and that ending segregation would create a win-win situation by benefitting both black and white people. During the 1957 interview I quoted earlier, he said, "And I also reasoned that what we were doing turned out to be a very Christian act because this system of segregation . . . scars the personality of the individuals of both races."[48]

Ending war, abolishing nuclear weapons, and stopping environmental destruction creates a win-win situation by removing these threats to human survival. Solving these global problems will create a more peaceful and prosperous future, protect our survival and the well-being of our planet, and free up resources and brainpower that will allow us to better solve our other global problems.

In chapter 11 of *The Art of Waging Peace*, I cite a study that explains how transforming our society away from war can create more jobs with higher wages. Nevertheless, all who serve Lady Justice must spend more time strategizing about the ways we can alleviate the economic hardship that people experience when societies and industries must adapt to changing times, and how we can reduce the fears of those who have a legitimate concern over economic security and their family's future. At the same time, if we don't work toward ending war, abolishing nuclear weapons, and stopping environmental destruction, these families may not have a future.

When we strive to create a win-win situation, we become more persuasive by genuinely trying to help people, and we decrease bad blood and bitterness by not disrespecting and hating those who initially disagree with us. Coercive actions can have varying degrees of persuasive strength, thereby combining the pressure method and the transformative method. Seeking a win-win situation is one among many ways to make the pressure method more persuasive. As I explain in *The Art of Waging Peace*, we can never convince everyone, but we don't have to. We just have to convince enough people, which creates the critical mass necessary for new social norms and just laws to emerge.

Respect and empathy not only strengthen and sharpen the weapon of nonviolence, but they also transform us in significant ways. Gandhi realized that if people lack respect and empathy for their adversaries, they may use nonviolence when it is tactically advantageous against a militarily superior opponent. But if they gain the upper hand and have an opportunity to use the tactic of violence to their advantage, they will likely use violence against their adversaries.

Gandhi understood that embracing nonviolence only as a tactic, rather than as a way of being, prevents us from wielding the weapon of nonviolence with maximum force. To embrace waging peace as a way of being, we must become literate in our shared humanity and the nature of reality along with the arts of living, waging peace, and listening. Realizing that many Indians used peaceful methods only as a tactic, Gandhi said this prevented the weapon of nonviolence from reaching its full potential during India's struggle for independence: "Had we adopted nonviolence as the weapon of the strong, because we realize that it was more effective than any other weapon, in fact, the mightiest force in the world, we would have made use of its full potency and not have discarded it as soon as the fight against the British was over, or we were in a position to wield conventional weapons . . . If we had the atom bomb, we would have used it against the British."[49]

Gandhi cited the failure of many Indians to internalize the ideals of nonviolence, along with the tension that colonialism creates, as among the reasons why Hindus and Muslims started massacring each other as they gained independence from Britain. This is one of many examples where embracing waging peace only as a tactic and not as a way of being can cause the cycle of violence to repeat itself, keeping people trapped in this deadly pattern. Gandhi blamed himself for these massacres, saying:

> But my eyes have now been opened. What I had taken to be non-violence, I now see, was only passive resistance . . . We were simply obliged to be non-violent while we had violence in our hearts. And now with the British withdrawing from India we are spending that violence in fighting against each other. I am certain that I never had any violence in my heart. But what am I to do about others? They argue that the fact they were non-violent in the fight against the British does not necessarily mean that they should be non-violent now. The fault is mine. My teaching during the last thirty-two years was imperfect.[50]

We must work toward perfecting the teaching of nonviolence, which Gandhi dedicated his life to improving. Since the weapon of nonviolence is the only option the universe gives us for healing the root causes of our global problems, we must make this weapon as strong and sharp as possible. Waging peace skills are life skills that not only empower us to unlock the full potential of a movement, but they also improve our interactions with friends, family members, coworkers, strangers, and even our adversaries. Waging peace brings more joy, purpose, meaning, belonging, and self-worth into our lives, along with the lives of others, creating a win-win situation for everyone.

Peace literacy is the path that allows us to embrace waging peace as a way of being. As I explain in *The Art of Waging Peace*, we cannot truly understand waging peace unless we also understand the anatomy of violence, the ethical use of law enforcement, and the role of personal self-defense. When we are not literate in the nature of reality, it is easy to engage in dualistic thinking that perceives all violence as evil. But just as martial arts taught me that violence is not inherently evil, but is simply a tool with severe limitations, peace literacy also teaches us to deeply understand the limited tool of violence along with the more powerful tool of nonviolence.

So far I have centered this discussion around economic pressure, but what about legal pressure and political pressure? How are those methods coercive? Court cases such as *Brown v. Board of Education* use legal pressure through the act of suing to create just laws. If someone sues you, it is likely you will view it as an act of coercion. In the *Brown v. Board of Education* case, this form of legal pressure was applied after peaceful negotiations failed to work. Harvard Law School professor Charles Ogletree explains: "In *Brown v. Board of Education*, after years of fruitless negotiations with the Topeka school board, black parents sued to desegregate the Topeka school system."[51] However, when we apply legal pressure from an attitude of respect and empathy, we look for a win-win situation that does not seek to take revenge or humiliate our opponents, but to promote justice for everyone involved.*

Where *Brown v. Board of Education* was concerned, legal pressure created laws that caused President Eisenhower to send in the military to desegregate Central High School in Little Rock, Arkansas. Since we cannot convince every single person in the world to reject unjust policies—we cannot even convince every single person in the world that slavery is wrong—we need laws to protect progress.

Political pressure basically tells someone, "If you don't vote the way we would like you to, we will try to get you out of office." Again, this is coercive, but when we apply political pressure from an attitude of respect and empathy, we look for a win-win situation, allowing us to honestly tell a politician: "If you vote on the side of justice, we will support you."

Many other people have written about how to organize a boycott, apply pressure through the legal system, and work effectively with politicians. When discussing the pressure method in this book, I want to instead focus on the *mindset of waging peace*, because I see it being neglected today. Neglecting the mindset of waging peace prevents us from using the pressure

* In *The Art of Waging Peace* I describe just laws as a form of deflection, not as waging peace. However, here I am using the term waging peace to describe the nonviolent legal process that creates just laws.

method to its full potential and wielding the weapon of nonviolence with maximum force.

Where military training is concerned, most of the training is focused on instilling the strong mindset necessary to be an effective warrior. This mindset includes discipline, courage, teamwork, fortitude, determination, leading by example, a sense of duty and service to others, attention to detail, integrity, proactivity, situational awareness, being calm under pressure, commitment to honing one's skills, and a good work ethic, among many other attributes. The military realizes that a strong mindset makes strong warriors. In the army, knowing how to shoot a gun is not nearly as useful if a person lacks the attributes of a strong mindset.

In a similar way, a strong mindset also makes effective soldiers of peace, and knowing how to organize a boycott today is not nearly as useful if we lack the strong mindset of waging peace that views nonviolence not simply as a tactic, but as a way of being. Developing this mindset is not easy, because it requires training in the challenging arts of living, waging peace, and listening, just as military personnel require training in the challenging art of war.

The Assistance Method of Waging Peace

I once heard a radio interview where a person said, "Charity is like painkiller. It helps, but it doesn't solve the problem." To me, this quote does not minimize the importance of charity. Anyone who has ever had a cavity filled can appreciate the importance of painkiller. However, this quote reveals a fascinating truth, which is that charity and violent rebellions actually have something in common, because neither approach effectively confronts the root causes of human problems. Charity and violent rebellions are both reactions to injustice, arising from opposite ends of a spectrum, but neither reaction goes deep enough.

Martin Luther King Jr. also realized that charity does not solve the root causes of human problems. Many people have heard Jesus's parable of the Good Samaritan, a story about a Jew who was robbed and beaten while traveling on the Jericho Road, and was helped by a Samaritan. King used the

Samaritan's kindness as a metaphor for charity, and he used the Jericho Road as a metaphor for the underlying systems that cause many of our human problems. King explained:

> A true revolution of values will soon cause us to question the fairness and justice of many of our past and present policies. On the one hand we are called to play the Good Samaritan on life's roadside, but that will be only an initial act. One day we must come to see that the whole Jericho Road must be transformed so that men and women will not be constantly beaten and robbed as they make their journey on life's highway. True compassion is more than flinging a coin to a beggar. It comes to see that an edifice which produces beggars needs restructuring.[52]

Together we must *transform the Jericho Road*, which is a metaphor for the triumph of justice over unjust systems. I use the term *assistance method* to describe the forms of waging peace that provide vital assistance, but do not transform the Jericho Road. The assistance method consists of charity, humanitarian aid, and disaster relief. Because this assistance is greatly needed and saves lives, we should understand it as a form of waging peace.

Figure 4.6: The Assistance Method of Waging Peace

To transform the Jericho Road, we must transform how people think, and this does not happen overnight. It might take many years to transform the Jericho Road. In the meantime, people around the world are suffering and dying, which is why the assistance method is so necessary. Charity is like painkiller, but it is a form of painkiller that can also save lives.

In *The End of War* and *The Art of Waging Peace*, I describe how the U.S. military could more effectively win hearts and minds around the world (as part of a more economically sustainable security paradigm that better protects our national security) if it focused on humanitarian aid and natural disaster relief, rather than bombing people and maintaining military bases in other people's countries. According to the U.S. military and the vast majority of climate scientists, the impact of climate change during the latter part of this century will be severe, requiring many highly trained people to deal with the serious catastrophes that will result from climate change. However, humanitarian aid and natural disaster relief do not solve the root causes of modern climate change, which include animal agriculture and fossil fuel use.

The transformative method, pressure method, and peace literacy method (which I will discuss next) transform the Jericho Road. The assistance method does not. When we use the transformative, pressure, and peace literacy methods of waging peace to transform the Jericho Road, we will often face opposition because we are challenging the underlying systems and ways of thinking that create injustice. For example, people probably won't criticize you for working to end world hunger. In fact, many people might praise you as a saint. People who talk about ending hunger or helping the survivors of a natural disaster are rarely criticized like someone who questions and challenges the myths that sustain injustice. Catholic archbishop Hélder Pessoa Câmara said, "When I give food to the poor, they call me a saint. When I ask why people are poor, they call me a communist."[53]

Ideologies such as communism, along with modern American political ideologies, have underestimated our human problems, because they see human beings primarily in materialistic terms. They tend to see justice, peace, and good order as goals achieved by shaping our material existence, when the current problems of our material existence are actually symptoms of much deeper problems, which these ideologies do not address.

For example, these ideologies do not have an adequate way of dealing with the root causes of extremism, meaninglessness, depression, and greed—problems that will become worse in the coming years unless more people wage peace. These ideologies do not even seem to comprehend where these problems truly come from, which is why we need a new paradigm that allows us to realistically understand and practically confront the root causes of these problems. This new paradigm is peace literacy.

The Peace Literacy Method of Waging Peace

In the past, more and more people gradually realized that literacy in reading was a necessity when living in a large agricultural civilization. Today, we must help more and more people realize that peace literacy is an *urgent* necessity when living in a global civilization. A global civilization is one where every country is interconnected and our species has the technological capacity to destroy itself, binding all countries to a common fate. As we sail our ship the planet Earth through the dangerous sea of time, we must become peace literate to protect our delicate biosphere and navigate toward survival and prosperity. Peace literacy allows us to use our human abilities to promote peace, justice, good order, truth, human survival, and prosperity rather than war, injustice, illusion, and mass extinction.

Today the international community recognizes literacy in reading as a human right. When people are denied literacy in reading, they are denied one of the most powerful tools for challenging injustice. When people are denied human rights such as freedom of speech and freedom of the press, they are denied other powerful tools for challenging injustice. Just as literacy in reading, freedom of speech, and freedom of the press were not considered human rights for most of human history, today many people don't realize that peace literacy is a human right. When people are denied the human right of peace literacy, they are not only denied the most effective skill set for challenging injustice, but they are also denied the skills that serve the long-term well-being of every community and country, along with our planet as a whole.

Humanity's understanding of human rights has been evolving, and the next critical step in this evolution is understanding that peace literacy is a human right and responsibility. However, peace literacy is not simply a human right and responsibility, because it is the fertile soil that allows our other human rights and responsibilities to fully flourish. Peace literacy is the human right that empowers us to protect all of our other human rights. Peace literacy is the human responsibility that empowers us to fulfill all of our other human responsibilities.

Healthy societies that can withstand the greatest adversity must be built on a strong foundation, and peace literacy is the foundational human right and responsibility that strengthens and sustains every human right and responsibility that makes the healthiest societies possible. Today many people think of "life, liberty, and the pursuit of happiness" as human rights, but a global civilization with the technological capacity to destroy itself needs peace literacy to create the realistic peace that protects life, liberty, and the pursuit of happiness.

Peace literacy gives us the understanding and skills necessary to increase realistic peace, whether it is within a family, friendship, relationship, workplace, community, nation, or our global civilization. There are seven forms of peace literacy that empower us to promote and protect realistic peace. This book focuses on the first five forms of peace literacy (literacy in our shared humanity, literacy in the art of living, literacy in the art of waging peace, literacy in the art of listening, and literacy in the nature of reality), although this book series teaches all seven forms. *The Transcendent Mystery*, the last book in this series, will discuss literacy in our responsibility to animals and literacy in our responsibility to creation. These responsibilities, which are now tied to human survival, are widely misunderstood because of our lack of ethical education and the many myths that romanticize nature and misunderstand the human condition.

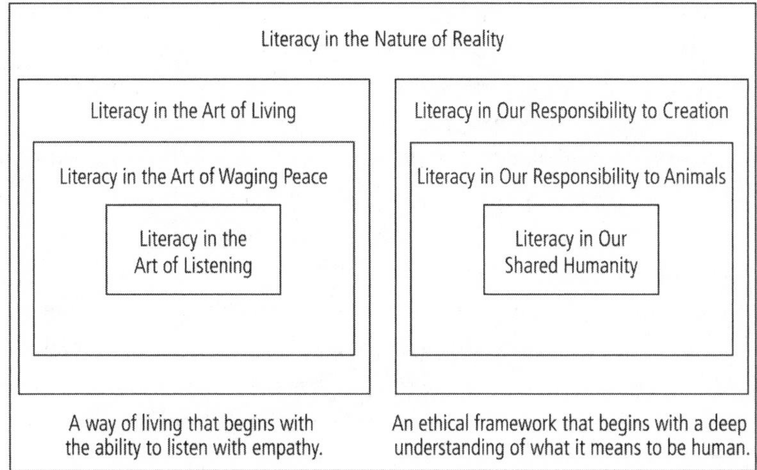

Figure 4.7: The Seven Forms of Peace Literacy

In chapter 2 I discussed how the art of listening is an essential component within the art of waging peace, which are both essential components within the larger art of living. If we cannot listen well, we cannot wage peace well. And if we cannot listen well and wage peace well, we cannot live in ways that empower us to confront the root causes of our problems, become fully human, and increase realistic peace. In a similar way, only by understanding the human condition through literacy in our shared humanity can we develop a realistic understanding of our responsibility to animals, and those two forms of literacy are necessary to develop a realistic understanding of our responsibility to creation. And, of course, literacy in all of these areas depends on us becoming literate in the nature of reality.*

Understanding the seven forms of peace literacy gives me more appreciation for all people. As I said at the beginning of this book, today I would

* "Scientific literacy" is a subcategory under "Literacy in the Nature of Reality." Although a person can make a strong argument that most people in our society are not scientifically literate, our discussion of the nature of reality includes other important topics such as the effects of time, mortality, and other aspects of reality on the human condition.

contend that less than one percent of people currently living in our world are literate in all seven forms of peace literacy. However, I have learned that practically everyone has some literacy in one or more of these seven areas. When I interact with people from any background, I realize that if I listen deeply to their words and example, then I can learn at least one valuable insight that will help me become a little wiser as a human being. In this way, I strive to view everyone I interact with as a potential teacher who can give me at least one valuable insight that will help me become a little more peace literate. Learning depends not only on a teacher's skill at teaching, but also a student's skill at listening. By listening deeply to people from all walks of life, I am able to turn most people I interact with into some kind of teacher who increases or reinforces the understanding that helps me walk the road to peace.

To create a world where people do not possess scattered fragments of peace literacy, but are highly literate in all seven forms of peace literacy, we must integrate peace literacy into our education system. I took over twelve years of math in school, going all the way through Calculus II. However, in my adult life I never use any math that I learned beyond elementary school, while I use the skills found in the arts of living, waging peace, and listening many times a day, whether I am accomplishing daily tasks, striving to make the most of my life, or interacting with coworkers, friends, and strangers.

Math is certainly important, but since peace literacy is necessary for a healthy democracy, human survival, and solving the root causes of our national and global problems, shouldn't we recognize peace literacy as being at least as important as math? In the twenty-first century, peace literacy is a necessary component of our social and ideological infrastructure, a tree of life that is needed to protect the garden of democracy, yet peace literacy is not even acknowledged in the vast majority of school systems today. Together we must change this. As peace educator Colman McCarthy told me, "Our society does not tolerate graduating students who are illiterate in reading or basic math, but every year our society graduates millions of students who are illiterate in peace. Practically everyone, including politicians in all political parties and religious figures in all religions, say that peace is important, so why don't we prioritize peace education in our society?"[54]

There is a practical way to make peace literacy a part of education, and to give people who are no longer in school access to the peace literacy skills that will help them improve their lives and the world around them. This is something that I am working on with a variety of educators, and you can learn how to get involved by visiting the websites www.peacefulrevolution.com and www.peaceliteracy.org. We need your help in spreading peace literacy, because there are two major obstacles to creating a peace literate world. The first major obstacle is that peace literacy does not offer the easy answers and quick fixes that so many people are fond of, which merely address the shallow surface and do not confront the root causes of our problems. Instead, peace literacy is a deep and complex solution to deep and complex problems. The second major obstacle to a peace literate world is that peace literacy threatens the unjust systems that profit from pain. Both of these obstacles can be overcome by committed and skilled soldiers of peace.

Teachers have enormous power to shape a student's life, which I experienced firsthand when my tenth-grade English teacher, Janice Vaughn, told me I should be a writer. Without these few words of encouragement, I do not think I would have found the language of peace literacy that gave me a healthier alternative to my mother tongue of rage. Teachers spend many hours with their students, and a teacher might be the only person who can be a positive influence on a student suffering from trauma, the only example the student has of someone who models skillful listening, deep empathy, genuine respectfulness, and high integrity. Many parents don't know how to model healthy conflict resolution and listening skills for children, and examples of peaceful conflict resolution and respectful dialogue based on deep listening are largely absent in our media. Peace literacy helps teachers, students, and people from all walks of life model the healthy behaviors that bring increased respect, empathy, happiness, and self-worth into our homes, workplaces, communities, and world.

When integrating peace literacy into education, we must be careful to avoid doing what is so often done to history. History is basically a collection of incredible stories, and who doesn't like incredible stories? But by making history about dates and numbers, school can ruin history for many students. I have met many people who say things such as "I hate history" or "History is boring," because school ruined it for them. Just as school can ruin history for people when it is taught badly, we must ensure that peace literacy is not simply taught, but taught *well.*

Stories are as essential to peace literacy as they are to history and other areas of life. Just as our ancestors told stories based on constellations in the night sky, we must tell stories based on the constellation of peace. We must tell stories about the stars of struggle, training, truth, and strategy by sharing stories about the many kinds of struggle, the many forms of the metaphorical goddess Hera. We must share stories that help people learn the arts of living, waging peace, and listening. We must share stories that illuminate timeless truth. And we must share stories that help people learn how to live strategically rather than aimlessly.

However, the constellation of peace is different from every constellation in the night sky, because it involves more than telling stories. By waging peace in our daily lives, we have the power to *create* countless new stories through our actions. This includes creating stories that show how humanity struggled for its survival in the twenty-first century and beyond, and did not fail in its mission. If humanity survives, our distant descendants will cite these stories of waging peace as the reason humanity survived, the reason they are alive to sail and savor the joys of the cosmic ocean.

Whether we realize it or not, we are one human family sailing on the turbulent waters of time through the cosmic ocean. The more people who realize this, the better we can safely navigate our ship, the planet Earth, through the dangerous horizon of our fragile future. It is a long and challenging journey through the cosmic ocean, but we have many reasons to be filled with realistic hope. We have the stars of struggle, training, truth, and strategy to guide us. We have the four methods of waging peace, which are the most effective way to overcome the challenges our species will face during our fragile future. We have our vast human potential that allows us to live with empathy, conscience, integrity, purpose, meaning, and so much more. We have each other.

NOTES

Preface: The Constellation of Peace

1. Frank Newport, "In U.S., 87% Approve of Black-White Marriage, vs. 4% in 1958," http://www.gallup.com/poll/163697/approve-marriage-blacks-whites.aspx.
2. Jeanne Theoharis, *The Rebellious Life of Mrs. Rosa Parks* (Boston: Beacon Press, 2013), 50–51.
3. Frederick Douglass, *The Life and Times of Frederick Douglass* (New York: Dover, 1995), xiii.
4. *Encyclopedia of Race and Ethnic Studies,* ed. Ernest Cashmore (New York: Routledge, 2003), 213, 214.
5. Theodore W. Allen, *The Invention of the White Race: Volume 1* (New York: Verso, 2012), 46–47.
6. Richard Gambino, *Vendetta* (Toronto: Guernica, 2000), ix.
7. Ibid.
8. Ed Falco, "When Italian immigrants were 'the other,'" http://www.cnn.com/2012/07/10/opinion/falco-italian-immigrants/.
9. Judith Wellman, *The Road to Seneca Falls* (Chicago: University of Illinois Press, 2004), 146.
10. Micheline Ishay, *The History of Human Rights* (Berkeley: University of California Press, 2008), 233.
11. Martin Luther King Jr., "Letter from Birmingham Jail," http://kingencyclopedia.stanford.edu/encyclopedia/documentsentry/annotated_letter_from_birmingham.1.html.
12. *The Universe: A Historical Survey of Beliefs, Theories, and Laws*, ed. Erik Gregersen (London: Britannica Educational Publishing), 14.
13. Xenophon, *The Persian Expedition*, trans. Rex Warner (Baltimore: Penguin, 1965), 107.
14. Michael E. Smith, *The Aztecs* (Oxford: Miley-Blackwell, 2012), 155–56.
15. *The Journals and Miscellaneous Notebooks of Ralph Waldo Emerson*, vol. 12,

1835–1862, ed. Linda Allardt (Cambridge: Belknap Press, 1976), 152.
16. Francis Bacon, *Sacred Meditations* (Radford, VA: Wilder, 2012), 22.
17. *Classical Mythology*, Lecture 1, The Teaching Company, 2007, DVD. In the first lecture, professor Elizabeth Vandiver discusses how literacy makes intellectual disciplines possible.
18. Statistics on Literacy, http://www.unesco.org/new/en/education/themes/education-building-blocks/literacy/resources/statistics.
19. Carl Sagan, Pale Blue Dot, https://www.youtube.com/watch?v=wup-Toqz1e2g.
20. Martin Luther King Jr., *Why We Can't Wait* (New York: New American Library, 2000), 16.
21. MK Gandhi's Speech, http://www.youtube.com/watch?v=RlJ00KvsHuQ.
22. *Greek Tragedy*, Lecture 7, The Teaching Company, DVD.

Chapter 1: The Star of Struggle

1. *Dhammapada: The Sayings of the Buddha*, trans. Thomas Byrom (Boston: Shambhala, 1993), 70.
2. The *Iliad* of Homer, Lectures 6–7, The Teaching Company, 1999, DVD.
3. David Zucchino, "Medal of Honor campaign continues for black sergeant who saved troops," http://www.latimes.com/nation/la-na-medal-of-honor-20141207-story.html#page=1.
4. Personal Defense Network: Sheepdog by Lieutenant Colonel Dave Grossman, https:// www.youtube.com/ watch? v = vk2Yx3VdbSo.
5. Homer, the *Iliad*, trans. Robert Fagles (New York: Viking, 1990), 457.
6. *Classical Mythology*, Lecture 4, The Teaching Company, 2007, DVD.
7. General Douglas MacArthur, farewell speech given to the Corps of Cadets at West Point, May 12, 1962, http://www.nationalcenter.org/MacArthur-Farewell.html.
8. Calgary Expo 2015—Peter Cullen on auditioning for Optimus Prime, https://www.youtube.com/watch?v=5Rw7bewf13o.
9. *Edmund Burke: Appraisals and Applications*, ed. Daniel E. Ritchie (New Brunswick: Transaction Publishers, 1990), xiii.

10. Martin Luther King Jr., *Where Do We Go from Here?* (New York: Signet Classics, 2000), 136, 201–2.
11. Erich Neumann, *The Great Mother* (Princeton: Princeton University Press, 2015) 149, 150, 189, 190.
12. *The Oxford Encyclopedia of Ancient Greece and Rome*, ed. Michael Gagarin (Oxford University Press, 2009), 398.
13. Quinton Dixie and Peter Eisenstadt, *Visions of a Better World* (Boston: Beacon Press, 2011), 111.
14. Ibid.
15. Ibid, 112.
16. Frederick Douglass, *Frederick Douglass on Slavery and the Civil War*, ed. Philip Foner (Mineola, NY: Dover Publications, 2003), 42.
17. James H. Dee, "Black Odysseus, White Caesar: When Did 'White People' Become 'White?,'" *Classical Journal* 99, no. 2 (December 2003–January 2004), 163–64.
18. Edith Hall, "Classics for the people—why we should all learn from the ancient Greeks," http://www.theguardian.com/books/2015/jun/20/classics-for-the-people-ancient-greeks.
19. John Steinbeck, *The Grapes of Wrath* (New York, Alfred Knopf, 1993), 192.

Chapter 2: The Star of Training

1. Carl J. Richard, *Greeks and Romans Bearing Gifts* (New York: Rowman and Littlefield, 2009), 17.
2. In his book *Man for Himself*, Erich Fromm discusses living as an art. I first heard this idea from Erich Fromm and Seneca.
3. *Dhammapada*, 70.
4. Homer, the *Iliad*, trans. Richmond Lattimore (Chicago: University of Chicago Press, 2011), 480.
5. Homer, the *Iliad*, trans. Fagles (1990), 155–56.
6. Julius Caesar, *The Conquest of Gaul*, trans. S. A. Handford (New York: Penguin, 1982), 71
7. Ibid.

8. Ibid.
9. Flavius Vegetius Renatus, *The Military Institutions of the Romans*, trans. John Clarke (Mansfield Centre, CT: Martino, 2011), 1.
10. Mahatma Gandhi, *Collected Works of Mahatma Gandhi*, vol. 78, http://www.gandhiserve.org/cwmg/VOL078.PDF.
11. *A Force More Powerful*, A Force More Powerful Films, 2002, DVD.
12. Why Mike Tyson Doesn't Party Anymore: Real Sports with Bryant Gumbel, March 2013, https://www.youtube.com/watch?v=erNYwF9pu6k.
13. Homer, the *Iliad*, trans. Fagles (1990), 574.
14. Homer, the *Iliad*, trans. Lattimore, 485.
15. Homer, the *Iliad*, trans. Fagles (1990), 572, 577.
16. Ibid, 578.
17. Ibid.
18, Thomas J. Fleming, *West Point* (New York: William Morrow, 1969), 308.
19. West Point *Bugle Notes*, http://www.west-point.org/academy/malo-wa/inspirations/buglenotes.html.
20. Peter Vronsky, *Female Serial Killers* (New York: Berkley Books, 2007), 61.
21. Martin Luther King, PBS interview with Kenneth B. Clark, 1963, https://www.youtube.com/watch?v=NjH_zvowJQg.
22. Erich Fromm, *The Art of Loving* (New York: Perennial Classics, 1956), 100–101.
23. James A. Colaiaco, *Socrates Against Athens* (New York: Routledge, 2001), 24.
24. Homer, the *Iliad*, trans. Fagle, 124.
25. *Greek Tragedy*, Lecture 11, The Teaching Company, 2000, DVD.
26. Lawrence A. Tritle, *From Melos to My Lai* (New York: Routledge, 2000), 74.
27. Homer, the *Iliad*, trans. Fagles (1990), 135.
28. The *Odyssey of Homer*, Lecture 3, The Teaching Company, 1999, DVD.
29. Homer, the *Odyssey*, trans. Robert Fagles (New York: Penguin, 1997), 37.
30. 10 Questions for Mike Tyson, https://www.youtube.com/watch?v=ua5XpcCQvuI.
31. "Being Peace in a World of Trauma," On Being interview, http://www.onbeing.org/program/thich-nhat-hanh-mindfulness-suffering-and-engaged-buddhism/74.
32. Fromm, *The Art of Loving*, 95.

Chapter 3: The Star of Truth

1. Mohandas K. Gandhi, *The Mind of Mahatma Gandhi*, ed. R. K. Prabhu and U. R. Rao (Ahmedabad, India: Navajivan, 2010), 44–45.
2. Clive Webb, *Fight Against Fear* (Athens, GA: University of Georgia Press, 2003), 66.
3. *Lives Worth Living*, Storyline Motion Pictures, 2011, DVD.
4. Lisa I. Iezzoni and Bonnie L. O'Day, *More Than Ramps* (Oxford: Oxford University Press, 2006), 165.
5. Ibid.
6. Joseph Shapiro, "How a Law to Protect Disabled Americans Became Imitated Around the World," http://www.npr.org/sections/goatsandsoda/2015/07/24/425607389/how-to-protect-disabled-americans-became-imitated-around-the-world.
7. Hesiod, *Works and Days, Theogony and the Shield of Heracles*, trans. Hugh G. Evelyn-White (Mineola, NY: Dover Publications, 2006), 6.
8. Homer, the *Iliad*, trans. Fagles (1990), 174.
9. Euripides, *The Trojan Women and Other Plays*, trans. James Morwood (Oxford: Oxford University Press, 2008), xxxii.
10. Ibid.
11. Ibid, 46.
12. Ibid, 60.
13. Ibid, 140.
14. *Greek Tragedy*, Lecture 3, The Teaching Company, 2000, DVD.
15. Cynthia Eller, *The Myth of Matriarchal Prehistory* (Boston: Beacon Press, 2000), 19, 41, 56, 58, 59, 109, 113, 180.
16. Frederick Douglass, *Frederick Douglass on Women's Rights*, ed. Philip S. Foner (Cambridge, MA: Da Capo Press, 1992), 40.
17. James Brabazon, *Albert Schweitzer* (Syracuse: Syracuse University Press, 2000), 247.
18. Manning Marable, *Malcolm X* (New York: Viking, 2011), 85, 86.
19. The Pierre Berton Interview, http://www.malcolm-x.org/docs/int_pbert.htm.
20. Colaiaco, *Socrates Against Athens*, 133.

21. I originally wrote this as "promote justice," but Patsy Ferrell recommended that I change it to "raise up justice" so that each characteristic of the peace hero ideal begins with the letter "r."
22. Douglass, *Frederick Douglass on Women's Rights*, 11.
23. Albert Schweitzer, *Out of My Life and Thought*, trans. Antje Bultmann Lemke (Baltimore: John Hopkins University Press, 1998), 90.
24. Wangari Maathai, *Replenishing the Earth* (New York: Doubleday, 2010), 157–59.
25. *The Words of Martin Luther King Jr.*, selected by Coretta Scott King (New York: Newmarket Press, 1987), 21.
26. Homer, the *Iliad*, trans. Fagles (1990), 262
27. Ibid., 498.
28. Ibid., 263.
29. The *Iliad* of Homer, Lecture 5, The Teaching Company, 1999, DVD
30. "The First Duty," *Star Trek: The Next Generation*, season 5 (Paramount, 1992).
31. Plato, *The Last Days of Socrates*, trans. Hugh Tredennick and Harold Tarrant (New York: Penguin, 1993), 64, 65, 67.
32. "Gandhi's Views on Truth," http://www.gandhi-manibhavan.org/gandhiphilosophy/philosophy_truth_truthisgod.htm.
33. *Greek Tragedy*, Lecture 12, The Teaching Company, 2000, DVD.
34. Colaiaco, *Socrates Against Athens*, 187–89.
35. Perhaps the earliest source for this adage is Ecclesiastes 1:9 in the Bible.
36. Friedrich Nietzsche, *Basic Writings of Nietzsche*, trans. Walter Kaufmann (New York: Random House, 2000), 156.
37. Aesop's Fables, trans. Elizabeth Barrial, http://blackphoenixalchemylab.com/product-category/aesops-fables/.
38. *Lives Worth Living*, Storyline Motion Pictures, 2011, DVD.
39. King, *Where Do We Go from Here?* (2000), 76–77.
40. Saul Friedländer, *Nazi Germany and the Jews* (New York: HarperCollins, 1997), 98.
41. Patricia Ann Schechter, *Ida B. Wells-Barnett and American Reform, 1880–1930* (Chapel Hill: University of North Carolina Press, 2001) 89.
42. King, *Where Do We Go from Here?* (2000), 64.

Chapter 4: The Star of Strategy

1. The U.S. Military Academy Coat of Arms and Motto, http://www.usma.edu/news/SitePages/Coat%20of%20Arms%20and%20Motto.aspx.
2. Homer, the *Iliad*, trans. Fagles (1990), 533.
3. Hesiod, *Works and Days,* trans. Evelyn-White, 52.
4. Martin Luther King Jr. (1) Anti-Violent Actions Interview 1957, conducted by Martin Agronsky on *Look Here*, NBC, October 27, 1957, https://www.youtube.com/watch?v=TS8ehUnfJiI.
5. Martin Luther King Jr., *Where Do We Go from Here?* (Boston: Beacon Press, 2010), 57–61.
6. Martin Luther King Jr., *The Autobiography of Martin Luther King Jr.*, ed. Clayborne Carson (New York: Warner, 1998), 268–69.
7. Marjorie Gann and Janet Willen, *Five Thousand Years of Slavery* (Toronto: Tundra Books, 2011), 109–10.
8. Charles E. Cobb, Jr., *This Nonviolent Stuff'll Get You Killed* (New York: Basic Books, 2014), 43.
9. *The Psychology of Black Boys and Adolescents*, ed. Kirkland C. Vaughans and Warren Spieling (Santa Barbara: ABC-CLIO, 2014), 114.
10. King, *Why We Can't Wait*, 16.
11. Ibid, 142.
12. *The Library of Congress World War II Companion*, ed. David M. Kennedy (New York: Simon and Schuster, 2007), 202–4.
13. Bernard E. Harcourt, "On Gun Registration, the NRA, Adolf Hitler, and Nazi Gun Laws: Exploding the Gun Culture Wars (A Call to Historians)," *Fordham Law Review* 73, no. 2: 676, http://ir.lawnet.fordham.edu/cgi/viewcontent.cgi?article=4029&context=flr.
14. German Jews during the Holocaust, 1939–1945, https://www.ushmm.org/wlc/en/article.php?ModuleId=10005469.
15. Jewish Resistance, https://www.ushmm.org/wlc/en/article.php?ModuleId=10005213.
16. Mohandas K. Gandhi, *The Collected Works of Mahatma Gandhi*, vol. 79 (New Delhi: Publications Division Government of India, 1999), 453.

17. Jai Narain Sharma, *Rediscovering Gandhi* (New Delhi: Concept, 2008), 216.
18. Sun Tzu, *The Art of War*, trans. Thomas Cleary (Boston: Shambhala, 1988), 25–27.
19. *A Companion to the American Revolution*, ed. Jack P. Greene, J. R. Pole (Hoboken, NJ: John Wiley and Sons, 2008), 235.
20. King, *Why We Can't Wait*, 16.
21. The Success of Nonviolent Civil Resistance: Erica Chenoweth at TEDxBoulder, https://www.youtube.com/watch?v=YJSehRlU34w.
22. King, *Where Do We Go from Here?* (2010), 61.
23. Sun Tzu, *The Art of War*, trans. Lionel Giles (El Paso: El Paso Norte Press, 2005), 5.
24. Homer, the *Iliad*, trans. Fagles (1990), 583.
25. Sustainability Report, U.S. Army, 2009, http://www.aepi.army.mil/docs/whatsnew/FINALArmySustainabilityReport2010.pdf.
26. Cornelius Tacitus, *The Agricola and The Germania*, trans. Oxford Translation (Stilwell, KS: Digireads, 2008), 40.
27. Ibid. 20.
28. Plutarch, *The Complete Works of Plutarch*, trans. Bernadotte Perrin (Hastings, East Sussex: Delphi Classics, 2013) Kindle version, location 38067.
29. Ishay, *The History of Human Rights*, 107–8.
30. Sue Davis, *The Political Thought of Elizabeth Cady Stanton* (New York: New York University Press, 2008), 68.
31. M.K. Gandhi, "Truth is God," http://www.mkgandhi.org/ebks/truth_is_god.pdf.
32. Gandhi, *Collected Works*, vol. 78, 150.
33. Viktor Frankl, *Man's Search for Meaning* (Boston: Beacon Press, 2006), 132.
34. Dike, http://www.theoi.com/Ouranios/HoraDike.html.
35. Personal conversation with Jo Ann. March 2015.
36. "Our God Is Marching On!," https://kinginstitute.stanford.edu/our-god-marching.
37. Hesiod, *Works and Days,* trans. Evelyn-White, 9.

38. Rufus Burrow, *Martin Luther King, Jr., and the Theology of Resistance* (Jefferson, NC: McFarland, 2015), 261.
39. Hesiod, *Works and Days,* trans. Evelyn-White, 9–10.
40. Theodore Parker, *The Collected Works of Theodore Parker, Vol. II,* ed. Frances Power Cobbe (London: Trübner, 1863), 57.
41. King, (1) Anti-Violent Actions Interview 1957, https://www.youtube.com/watch?v=TS8ehUnfJiI.
42. *Sun Tzu on the Art of War: The Oldest Military Treatise in the World*, trans. Lionel Giles (El Paso: El Paso Norte Press, 2005), 13.
43. Gene Knudsen Hoffman, interview, January 2002, http://www.peaceheroes.com/PeaceHeroes/ jeanknudsenhoffman.htm.
44. Plutarch, *Complete Works*, trans. Perrin, location 38067.
45. Yuri Pines, *The Everlasting Empire* (Princeton: Princeton University Press, 2012), 134.
46. Ibid, 136.
47. Ibid, 134–35.
48. King (1) Anti-Violent Actions Interview 1957, https://www.youtube.com/watch?v=TS8ehUnfJiI.
49. Mahatma Gandhi, *The Essential Gandhi*, ed. Louis Fischer (New York: Random House, 2002), 311–12.
50. Gandhi, *Collected Works*, vol. 96, 112.
51. Charles J. Ogletree, Jr., *All Deliberate Speed* (New York: W. W. Norton, 2004), 5.
52. *A Call to Conscience: The Landmark Speeches of Dr. Martin Luther King Jr.*, eds. Clayborne Carson and Kris Shepard (New York: Grand Central Publishing, 2002), 158–59.
53. Laura Smith, *Psychology, Poverty, and the End of Social Exclusion* (New York: Teachers College Press, 2010), 127.
54. Paraphrase of a conversation with Colman McCarthy in 2015.

Index

I